JAGUAR
THE ENGINEERING STORY

JAGUAR
THE ENGINEERING STORY

JEFF DANIELS

First published in August 2004

A catalogue record for this book is available from the British Library

ISBN 1 84425 030 X

Library of Congress catalog card no. 2004104450

Published by Haynes Publishing, Sparkford,
Yeovil, Somerset, BA22 7JJ, UK

Tel: 01963 442030 Fax: 01963 440001
Int. tel: +44 1963 442030 Int. fax: +44 1963 440001
E-mail: sales@haynes.co.uk
Web site: www.haynes.co.uk

Haynes North America, Inc.,
861 Lawrence Drive, Newbury Park,
California 91320, USA

Printed and bound in England by J. H. Haynes & Co. Ltd, Sparkford

Contents

Introduction and Acknowledgements

Many books have been written about Jaguar. When first contemplating the writing of this one, I was able at once to pull half a dozen volumes from my own bookshelves, among them the late Andrew Whyte's definitive history of the marque to 1985, a late edition of Lord Montagu's history (presented, I am reminded, on Jaguar's 75th anniversary in 1997, counting from the foundation of Swallow Sidecars in Blackpool in 1922), and the excellent biography of Sir William Lyons by Philip Porter and Paul Skilleter. Along with this apparent wealth of information came a full supporting cast of Jaguar new-model press kits, and magazine and review articles, including some I had written myself well over 30 years ago. Then again, there is the mass of information now available on the Internet.

Why, then, yet another book? Because for their various reasons, none of the books so far published go deep into Jaguar's overall engineering story. Here and there are tales from the drawing board and the workshop, but there is an understandable fascination with the human story of the company, rather than the nuts and bolts. As Andrew Whyte brilliantly shows, it is an amazing story; but where is the attempt to get inside the collective engineering mind of that formidable quartet of Bill Heynes, Walter Hassan, Claude Baily and Bob Knight, later aided and abetted by Harry Mundy and the then-young Jim Randle and Trevor Crisp? What were their options, and why did they take particular decisions? That was what I wanted to do, encouraged by the fact that during the 1960s and 1970s I had talked engineering at reasonable length with both Heynes and Knight, and during the 1980s and 1990s with Randle and Crisp. As for Harry Mundy, we had a special link in that Harry was my predecessor-but-one as Technical Editor of *Autocar*, which at times put me into a privileged

position that I was then careful not to abuse. I hope the shadow of Harry, now too many years dead, will forgive me if, in this book, I am at last a little less circumspect. Equally, of course, I cherish the ongoing friendship – or the memory – of other Jaguar figures: Sir William himself, to be sure, Sir John Egan, Sir Nick Scheele, and on the Public Relations front, Andrew Whyte, Bob Berry, David Boole, Joe Greenwell and Martin Broomer among others.

Some I missed. As an aero engineer by training and for the first four years of my working life, I wish I had had the chance to talk aerodynamics with the outstandingly gifted Malcolm Sayer, but it was not to be. Somehow I never managed to exchange much more than a nod with Walter Hassan or with 'Lofty' England, and I never set eyes on Claude Baily; but you would have needed astounding luck to have personal access to the entire process. That is where the archives come in.

For many years, Jaguar kept a small number of special cars in a museum environment but had little in the way of properly organised historical material to support them. Only in the last few years has Anders Clausager, with the support of a handful of retired volunteers, begun to sort through what has become available. Even then, understandable emphasis has been given to what the owners of classic Jaguars most want – the original specification, the production and sales history of their individual vehicles. A team can only do so much, and the surviving 'pure' engineering background is patchy. In many cases it was beyond saving. 'Engineering departments used to have a clear-out, and throw everything in a skip', Clausager laments. 'Now, we have persuaded them to throw their old stuff at us instead, but a lot must have gone for ever.' It means there are some apparently irretrievable gaps in the technical history, even though

Bob Knight kept much of his own voluminous paperwork – to which his family generously gave the archive access after his death – and there are other cabinets full of documents originating from Walter Hassan and later from Trevor Crisp. In four solid days of sifting through some of this paper I discovered a wealth of facts that were new to me. In four weeks, no doubt, I would have lain bare even more, but I didn't have that kind of time. I emerged, however, with enough material to put some flesh on the engineering bones. One spectacular seam of information was Bob Knight's collection of minutes of the monthly Model Progress Meetings (MPMs) through the late 1960s and early 1970s in particular – a key period surrounding the launch of the XJ6 and the V12 engine. If you are a prospective auto-motive historian, be assured that in those dye-line duplicated pages there is still plenty of material which, in my skimming haste, I must have missed – not only for shortage of time, but in acknowledge-ment of the fact that I had only 80,000 words for the entire story.

All this background apart, where to start? When first planning the book, I proposed a tidy chron-ological layout, with a first chapter beginning when the original company did, in Blackpool in 1922. It was Andrew Whyte's history which convinced me to change my approach. Almost halfway through his story – indeed, on page 92 out of 184 in my library edition – Andrew notes that in 1935, given the company's expanding plans and its realisation that it had to transform itself from a body-building adapter of other people's chassis into a car manufacturer in its own right, 'the first priority was to create an engin-eering department'. The man who, in effect, was hired to create it was Bill Heynes.

It wasn't that Jaguar – or rather, SS Cars – had never previously had any engineering expertise. But since it had simply adapted its bodies to a variety of chassis from different manufacturers, and used mainly standard (and indeed, Standard) engines with some tuning input from Harry Weslake, that skill had been largely confined to what was needed to make sound and elegant bodies. Now the need arose to create bespoke, or at least heavily adapted chassis – and even more important, to develop a new series of engines sufficiently powerful to make the SS series go as fast as it looked.

So my engineering story takes April 1935 as its starting point, that being the moment at which Bill Heynes arrived to assume the responsibilities of Chief Engineer of SS Cars Ltd. It works through the post-war renaissance built around the XK engine, the glory days of the Le Mans victories and the launch of the original XJ6, the dark days of the merger with BMC which led in turn to the company almost drowning in the cess-pit that was British Leyland, the struggle to survive, the astonishing single-handed rescue act performed by Sir John Egan, the 'second coming' bankrolled by Ford, and its eventual expansion in terms both of numbers and of model range – even into diesels, reflecting a train of thought which can be traced back further than most people (and especially Jaguar traditionalists) would believe.

My concern has been to approach the story not from the point of view of personalities and politics but rather that of product engineering. As the fate of the volume-production side of British Leyland showed, you can exert yourself in management, in industrial and public relations, but unless you have products that command respect and demand, you remain nothing. It was Jaguar's fortune that even in the darkest days it had such products, even if (be it now admitted) the quality of these was sometimes dreadful. That strength of product was very much down to Sir William Lyons and a small team of gifted engineers. Indeed, Jaguar was doubly fortunate in that as the 'old guard' retired, a new generation arose to continue and build on the tradition. The aim of this book is to explain not only what they did, but as far as possible why they did it. I have concentrated almost entirely on the production cars, because so many of the existing books deal partly or exclusively with Jaguar's racing successes. In that way, I hope, I can plug some more gaps in the history of one of Britain's most worthy manufacturing names.

I have a good many people to thank for their help and patience while I pulled the story together. To Jaguar archivist Anders Clausager, of course, to Kerem his photo archivist, and his willing and knowledgeable team of volunteers; to the present-day Jaguar PR staff and especially to Martin Broomer with his treasure-trove memory founded on long Jaguar experience; to old Jaguar engineering friends and especially to Trevor Crisp who was astonishingly amiable when disturbed in his well-earned retire-ment; to all those who authored earlier books and articles from which I have drawn and learned; and most of all, to old friend and renowned Jaguar historian Paul Skilleter, who had first sight of the draft manuscript and devoted much time and effort to suggesting invaluable amendments and additions.

1 A proper manufacturer

Bill Heynes, by 1935, was already an engineer of many parts. He had designed engines, gearboxes and chassis systems, including some independent front suspensions for Hillman, during the course of several years spent with Rootes. He was also an engineer with his feet firmly on the ground. In 1960, when I was an undergraduate at Bristol, Heynes delivered the second best-attended of all evening lectures to the Engineering Society (he had to yield pride of place to Barnes Wallis, for whom there was barely even standing room in the big main lecture theatre). Responding to a question about when he thought fuel injection would become commonplace on mass-produced cars, he said with complete sincerity that if he had been designing fuel-injected engines for years, and some inventor came to him with a simple stand-alone hydro-mechanical device (called a carburettor) guaranteed to deliver something very close to the right mixture strength for the vast majority of the time, he would have jumped at the saving in cost and complication! In other words, Bill Heynes could see both sides of any engineering argument and was not readily led astray by the siren-song of high technology regardless of expense. Since even in those days, SS Cars was acquiring the reputation, which grew large in the post-war Jaguar years, of delivering astonishing value for money, this mind-set was vital.

There were two engineering priorities for Heynes when he joined what was then SS Cars (Jaguar Cars Ltd was not registered until 1937). The first was to develop an engine (or engines) with substantially more power than could be delivered by the side-valve Standard engines, even in tuned form. The second was to develop a more advanced chassis than the ones supplied by Standard, even though – as often quoted – Standard's John Black had promised that 'We agree to supply you with special 6-cylinder chassis to suit special body requirements [which will] be reserved exclusively for you.' But the Standard chassis, even in its evolved form, dramatically lowered and eventually 'underslung' (the main side rails passing beneath the live axle) at the rear, was scarcely advanced. In the manner of all ladder-frame chassis, unless the side members and in particular the cross-beams are deep, it is very difficult to achieve anything in the way of satisfactory torsional stiffness, or even beam-stiffness, in modern terms. In fact, the main anxiety in those days was to stop the whole frame from deforming lozenge-fashion in plan, and so the SS Cars chassis had additional cruciform bracing between the

'steps' of the ladder to minimise this danger. Beyond that, the use of beam axles (production Standard components, on semi-elliptic springs) front and rear meant a horizontal roll axis, imposing severe limits on the extent to which the handling could be 'tuned' – not that many people, even Bill Heynes, appreciated such niceties at the time. However, more serious drawbacks lay in the continued use of components from Standard's suppliers, not least the cable-operated Bendix-Perrot brakes, which evidently had a hard time coping with the larger-diameter drums fitted to the more powerful SS Jaguar cars (no Jaguar had hydraulic brakes, or independent front suspension, until after the Second World War).

The limitations of the chassis were thrown into ever sharper focus as engine power and vehicle performance increased. The SS range of the mid-1930s consisted of three basic models, one 4-cylinder and two 6-cylinder, simply designated 1½-litre, 2-litre and 2½-litre (rated, according to the idiotic 'RAC horsepower formula', at 9hp, 16hp and 20hp respectively), and all used side-valve Standard engines to begin with. None of these units, even the largest, could have been called a brilliant performer. On the other hand, the 6-cylinder engines had the benefit of a strong bottom end, with a stiff (by the standards of the time) 7-bearing crankshaft. In other words, if the engine could be made to breathe better, there should be few problems in coping with a higher power output. Well before Heynes's arrival, in fact with the appearance of the SS Series 2 for the 1933 model year, the Standard engines – with the manufacturer's blessing – were given aluminium cylinder heads to replace the original cast-iron. It was already well appreciated that the ability of aluminium to conduct heat away from the combustion chamber could allow more power to be developed without overheating. Unfortunately, aluminium is also far less stiff than cast-iron, and the relatively shallow heads made for the side-valve engine suffered distortion when the cars were used in real anger, as in the Alpine Trial of 1933. The silver lining to this particular cloud was that it brought William Lyons into contact with Harry Weslake, already established as an engine developer of genius. Weslake began to make suggestions to improve the reliability and the breathing of the Standard engines, but even when the nominal 2½-litre was bored out to

The SS100 sports car was the first serious fruit of Bill Heynes's design efforts – although the saloon cars were always built in far larger numbers. (Jaguar)

2.7 litres (73 x 106mm, 2,664cc) the output was still only 70bhp when developed as far as SS Cars and Harry Weslake could take it.

Some fairly desperate short-term measures were considered in an attempt to increase the performance of the SS to match its looks. A scheme was drawn up to insert the straight-8 Studebaker Commander engine, and although one such car was imported and delivered to the SS works, the idea was abandoned on the drawing board. Not so the project to add a Zoller supercharger, one of which was fitted to a development SS. A contemporary photograph shows the massive supercharger installed alongside the crankcase, and shaft-driven from a transfer drive

Above: Bill Heynes – founder of Jaguar's engineering department – was equally at home working with engines or chassis, and one of the four 'fathers' of the XK engine. (Jaguar)

Right: The 2½-litre Standard engine was converted to OHV configuration which, along with the 3½-litre version shown here, used a Weslake-developed combustion chamber. Note that this was a cross-flow design – also the need to reposition the distributor. Torque output was excellent and the bottom end was strong enough to form the benchmark for the XK. (JDHT/Paul Skilleter)

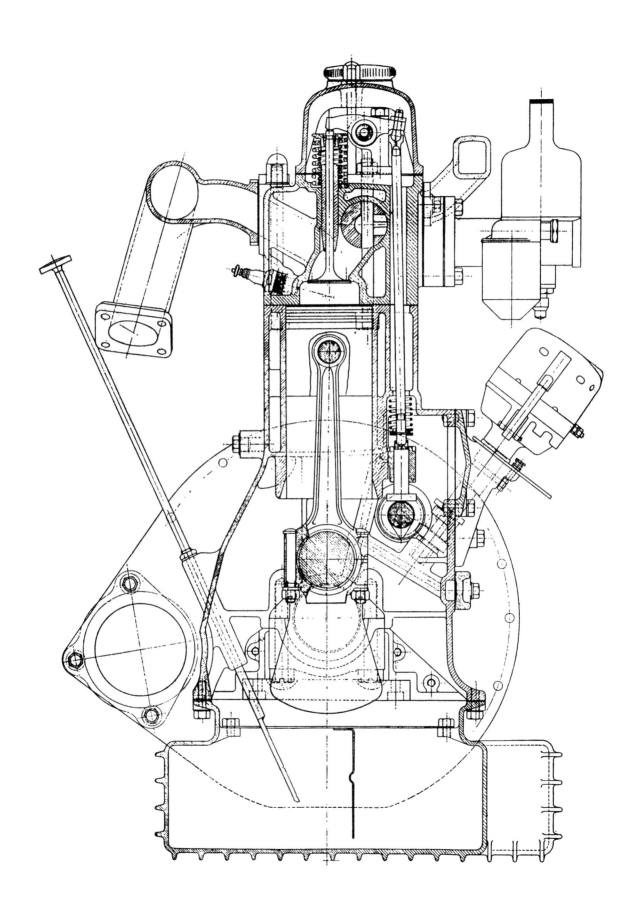

from the crankshaft nose. There appears to be no record of the performance improvement which must have resulted, but the higher brake mean effective pressure would have placed a considerable additional strain on the already fragile cylinder head. It seems also to have suffered lubrication problems, and one of the first things to happen to Heynes in his SS Cars career was to have the unit seize up on him while driving back to Coventry from a Shelsley Walsh hill-climb meeting. That was the end of the project, and it was to be many years before Jaguar returned to the idea of supercharging in any form.

For the pragmatic Heynes, there were two ways to increase power output significantly. The first was to increase engine size, while the second was to convert the strangled side-valve configuration to overhead-valve, retaining the existing side camshaft but replacing the existing tappets and valves with push-rods to operate the valves in a deeper, narrower head via rockers. The overhead valve arrangement meant that as the quality of petrol and materials improved, the compression ratio could be increased; but far more importantly, the OHV layout meant the gas flow through the engine could be greatly improved – something at which Weslake, already firmly estab-lished as a company consultant, was a master. Of course, more power called for more air which required higher operating speeds, but as already noted, the Standard bottom end was strong and stiff enough to take it.

The OHV conversion came first, therefore, and extremely quickly. Interestingly, Weslake and Heynes chose to revert to cast iron for the OHV head, not only because it needed far more machining but also because its stiffness would avoid the warping and distortion with which SS was already distressingly familiar – and this was to be an engine developing much higher output. Comparisons are certainly interesting. The 2.7-litre alloy-headed side-valve engine in the SS90 of 1935 developed 70bhp at 4,000rpm, or so it was claimed. Essentially the same engine, but bearing Weslake's OHV head and breathing through two SU carburettors, in the SS Jaguar 100 of 1936 developed 102bhp at 4,600rpm (and still with a compression ratio of 7:1, in deference to available petrol quality). Now, at last, the SS Jaguar not only looked fast, but could actually achieve a speed comfortably in excess of 90mph. The peak power speed of 4,600rpm may not seem fast by today's standards, but bear in mind it represented a 15 per cent increase on the SS90 engine and was

therefore in itself responsible for a large chunk of the power increase – the rest coming mainly from the considerably lower pumping losses associated with the OHV layout.

It would be wrong to think of the OHV reworking as a simple conversion. There was, for example, the need to reposition the distributor and redesign its drive; in the side-valve unit the distributor had been the highest point of the long but remarkably shallow engine. The OHV distributor with its canted drive emerged from one side of the cylinder block, no doubt to grumbles that it was far more difficult to access for service. As for the induction and exhaust systems, they were of necessity completely different. Remarkably for its day, the engine was crossflow, in other words with the inlet manifold and SU carbur-ettors on one side and the six-into-two-into-one exhaust manifold on the other.

Where transmission was concerned, there was by the standards of the day little wrong with the 4-speed Standard gearbox with synchromesh on second, third and fourth, and its use avoided the need to adapt a different unit to mate with the Standard engine bell-housing. Standard itself in the 1930s offered the option of a Wilson pre-selector gearbox and fluid flywheel – the great speciality of Coventry neighbours Daimler – and although some correspondence exists to suggest SS Cars contemplated using it, there is equally no evidence to suggest it ever actually happened. Overall gearing was adjusted to suit vehicle characteristics, or even individual customer needs, by changing the final drive ratio. This was something which was far more readily contemplated in the 1930s and, indeed, up to the late 1950s. Today, by contrast, any such change would involve a nightmare of emissions re-certification at the very least, and optimum gearing is decided at a relatively early stage.

While Weslake had been performing wonders with the 2.7-litre engine, Heynes had been at work on the SS chassis, not so much for the sports cars as for the new steel-bodied saloon series then in an advanced stage of preparation. In fact, the SS100 continued to use the SS90 chassis but adapted to use many of the better components adopted for the saloon. There were Luvax hydraulic rear dampers on Silentbloc mountings – with Hartford friction dampers retained at the front. The steering was the much nicer Burman Douglas worm-and-nut system, and Girling now supplied the brake system which was still mechanical rather than hydraulic, but again more satisfactory. One of the reasons why so few SS100s were made was that carrying out these adaptations was both expensive and disruptive in a factory which was increasingly dedicated to production of the new saloon series, the real money-makers.

Until 1936, SS Cars had concentrated entirely on traditional 'coachbuilt' bodies – which was how the company had established itself, after all. But coach-building is an expensive business once production volume builds. It has the advantage that 'up front' tooling costs are small (and among his close colleagues, William Lyons was notorious for his lifelong aversion to committing large investments very far ahead of any payback). The coachbuilding approach had, up to the mid-1930s, helped to establish SS Cars as a producer of products offering remarkable value for money, a reputation which it maintained at least into the 1960s and arguably later still. The problem with coachbuild-ing is that the only way substantially to increase vol-ume is to increase factory floor space and the work-force, and this too is expensive – and in ongoing terms, not as a one-off tooling investment. Consequently it was decided that a new range of SS saloon cars would be created with standardised welded steel bodies.

These would not be fully-stressed 'unitary' bodies – that would have been a step too far. The main loads would continue to be carried through the separate chassis. The idea behind the change was simply to achieve much higher productivity. The bespoke coachbuilding shop – although it survived until after the Second World War – was to give way to a body assembly facility which would mainly involve the welding of sheet steel.

Even so, the styling, naturally overseen by William Lyons himself, remained of crucial importance. There was particular agonising over the housing of the spare wheel, which it was first proposed to inset into the long front wing, but which ended up under the floor (with a hinge-down rear bumper section to allow access!). Much more important to the learning process was the realisation that the panels would have to fit together with the minimum of adjustment, and prefer-ably none at all. SS Cars had no press facilities of its own, then or for decades afterwards, and the initial approach, according to Andrew Whyte, was that '… the all-steel 'trial' body was cut up into separate com-ponents, which were to be contracted out to several different body-pressing specialists … when it came to assembly, the new bodies would not fit together.'[1]

The learning curve through the winter of 1937–38

was very steep indeed, and some of the methods used to create decent-looking bodies, not least the use of pounds of lead loading, were questionable, if unavoid-able. Fortunately the problems did not affect the way the cars behaved, since the bodies sat on the firm foundation of Bill Heynes's stiffened chassis, now with deeper, box-section side members to provide a greater degree of torsional stiffness. Although the problems of body component quality control were hardly Bill Heynes's real area of responsibility, the challenges of the steel body, the new chassis, and power unit development meant he needed the backing of at least one powerful and capable engineer, and had the good fortune to be pointed towards Walter (Wally) Hassan, ex-Bentley, ex-ERA, ex-Thompson & Taylor. Hassan's pre-war responsibilities included competition-related work, on both the company's own cars and on the cars operated by a number of distinguished 'privateer' customers, leaving Heynes free to get on with the fundamental engineering of the product.

The other great step forward pre-war was to fulfil the other part of Heynes' wish-list and enlarge the engine. Strictly speaking it was Standard who did so, since the company had, some time before, created a nominal 3½-litre (82 x 110mm, 3,485cc) engine to complement the 2½-litre. This was by no means a simple 'stretch' but an essentially larger unit, again with a 7-bearing crankshaft of very strong design. When subjected to the Weslake OHV treatment, it produced 125bhp at 4,250rpm, breathing through a pair of 1½in SU carburettors (the 2½-litre had 1¼in SUs). This new engine, still manufactured by Standard, was installed both in the top-end saloon and in the final series of SS100s, of which an extremely modest 118 were built before the outbreak of war. By contrast, the 1938-39 financial year saw the company make comfortably over 5,000 of the steel saloons in the three engine sizes, nominally 1½-litre, 2½-litre and 3½-litre (actually 1.8-litre, 2.7-litre and 3.5-litre). Of these, the consider-able majority were the relatively humdrum 4-cylinder 1½-litre, but despite the iniquities of the horsepower taxation scale, over 1,000 3½-litres also emerged. By this time, SS Cars had become very much a manufacturer in its own right and not merely a coachbuilder – even though its chassis, basic engine and transmission were supplied by Standard, and most of its body components were bought-in for assembly. Things were to change, however, during and after the war.

1   Andrew Whyte, *Jaguar*, p.105

2 War and post-war

As the proprietors of a considerable factory and a large skilled workforce, SS Cars quickly became a major supplier of aircraft components and military vehicles – vehicles in the widest sense, since most of them were trailers and special sidecars. In the early 1940s the engineering department was at least nominally occupied in the design and development of an ultra lightweight vehicle which could be air-dropped, landing by parachute.

It had been anticipated that the SS Cars engineering department would be needed to undertake various design and development tasks in support of the war effort, and to this end Claude Baily, a highly competent engineer who had spent time with Morris Motors, was recruited to SS Cars in 1940. As things turned out, however, the 'airdrop special' was not only the first, but as it turned out almost the only such requirement, although it was sufficient to lead to the recall of Walter Hassan who had been seconded to Bristol to work on aero engine carburation. Thus the core engineering team of Heynes, Hassan and Baily, overseen by William Lyons and with outside support from Harry Weslake, came into being.

The airdrop requirement led first to the VA, and then to the VB, two tiny vehicles with little in common beyond fairly crude folded-and-welded steel bodies (but unitary, for the sake of light weight) and all independent suspension with double wishbones at the front and swing axles to the driven rear wheels – again good for weight saving, but posing ground clearance problems on rough going. To fulfil the specification, both vehicles were extremely small, the VA practically 'square' with near-equal track and wheelbase. The VA was powered by a rear-mounted, air-cooled 1,096cc vee-twin engine, with chain drive to a lockable differential, but the VB used a mundane Ford Ten side-valve engine, a three-speed main gearbox and a two-speed auxiliary gearbox to provide six forward speeds in all. The VB in particular was well received by the military but was overtaken by events: with American transport aircraft like the C47 (Dakota) becoming available, it proved possible to air-drop the Jeep, and the two tiny 'specials' were consigned to history. They may have provided an amusing and instructive aside for the engineering staff, but the minds of Heynes and the other engineers were mainly occupied in other ways.

William Lyons was occupied too, since the war saw him conduct a surprising amount of corporate business. First of all he bought Motor Panels

Left: Like many manufacturers, Jaguar carried on building in 1945 what it had been making in 1939. Its biggest seller before and after the war was the relatively modest 1½-litre saloon, although it would not be long before Jaguar lost its 'small' saloon, leaving the concept to be revived in the 1950s with the 2.4 and its successors. (JDHT)

Above: Engine wizard Walter Hassan played a major role in the evolution of the XK engine by way of the XF and XG, then left Jaguar for Coventry Climax in the 1950s, but returned to the fold when Jaguar took over Climax in 1963, and then played a major role in bringing the V12 to production. (Jaguar)

(Coventry) Ltd, perhaps feeling that if body pressing was brought 'in house' the fit-and-finish challenge would be more easily overcome. But SS Cars was not then (or, as Jaguar, for many years afterwards) ready to run its own major press-shop operation. Possibly the sheer scale of the up-front investment needed for press tools appalled Lyons when he took a proper look at the figures. In any event, he fairly quickly re-sold Motor Panels to Rubery Owen, for a sum which put his company on a sounder financial footing.

Engine manufacture was another matter. Jaguar had been buying its engines from Standard for many years; but when Standard's John Black told William Lyons he had decided that after the war, his company would concentrate on the large-scale production of a single model (the Vanguard) with a new 4-cylinder, 2-litre engine, Lyons at once offered to buy the tooling for the existing 2½-litre and 3½-litre units. As Andrew Whyte puts it[1], 'Hardly had Black had time to say 'yes' when Lyons's cheque was there on his desk and the equipment on its way from Canley to Foleshill.' The importance of this investment was not simply that Lyons had secured supplies of the existing OHV engines for the post-war period. That alone might not have compensated for the effect of the move in creating a major rift with John Black, which meant that Jaguar (as SS Cars become towards the end of the war) would need to source its chassis elsewhere. The underlying importance lay in the fact that Lyons had conceived a new post-war strategy built around a new 6-cylinder engine of advanced design. Most of the engine tooling 'liberated' from Standard, such as the massive crankshaft lathes, could also be adapted to make the new unit, and Lyons quickly had people scouring the war-surplus market for the other machines he needed.

New **engines:** the first **glimmerings**

But what kind of engine did they have in mind? Lyons, Heynes, Hassan and Baily had been considering their options since the very early 1940s. There were many factors to weigh in the balance. Their basic specification consisted of two clauses only. The first, as Heynes put it, was 'to produce a series of engines with a higher output than is normally obtainable, which would not call for constant revision of design to keep ahead of competition.' The second requirement was very simple and entirely down to William Lyons: the engine had to look good.

Note that the need was for a 'series of engines' rather than just 'an engine'. As we have already seen, when the war began Jaguar had been making cars with three different engine sizes. The 6-cylinder 3½-litre was top of the performance tree but the 4-cylinder 1½-litre sold in the largest numbers, and Lyons rightly foresaw a period of post-war austerity

1   Andrew Whyte, *Jaguar*, p.115

in which the greater demand would be for smaller, more economical models. At the time, therefore, the new engine series would include both 4-cylinder and 6-cylinder versions, if possible with common principal dimensions – especially cylinder bore spacing – and therefore capable of being produced on a common line. That being so, it is hardly surprising that much of the early research and development work was carried out on 4-cylinder engines.

The need for high specific output and 'future-proofing' pointed the team fairly clearly in the direction of opposed valves in a hemispherical combustion chamber, something which gas-flow wizard Harry Weslake could exploit to the full. It is easy, with the benefit of 21st century hindsight, to say that the DOHC layout was thus the obvious choice but from the perspective of the 1940s there were a number of valvetrain arrangements to be considered. For example, one much admired British engine of the time was the Riley RM which had a low-set camshaft on either side of the cylinder block, operating the valves in a cross-flow hemispherical head via pushrods and rockers. A possible alternative was to use a single overhead camshaft operating one set of valves directly and the opposed set by means of rockers. After kicking the possibilities around for a while the team narrowed the choice of layout to just two, a 'proper' DOHC and an alternative, which was exploited brilliantly by BMW in the pre-war 328, in which the opposed valves were operated by a complex pushrod arrangement driven from a single camshaft mounted conventionally low in the block.

The DOHC layout most obviously met Lyons's requirement for tidy and impressive appearance. On the other hand, everyone was wary of the valvetrain noise it was believed the DOHC layout would create, unless great care were taken with the detail design of the long chain drive to the camshafts, and the high-mounted tappets. It seemed also that the 'BMW' layout might prove substantially cheaper to manufacture, especially if the existing Standard bottom end could be mated to the new head. In the end, a

Right: As described, the XG engine with its BMW-inspired pushrod valve gear to a hemispherical head, was first run in 1943 and was in effect a converted Standard 1½-litre unit. Initial noise

problems were quickly overcome, but the development path followed the rival XF. Downdraught induction did not favour efficiency, according to Hassan. (JDHT/Paul Skilleter)

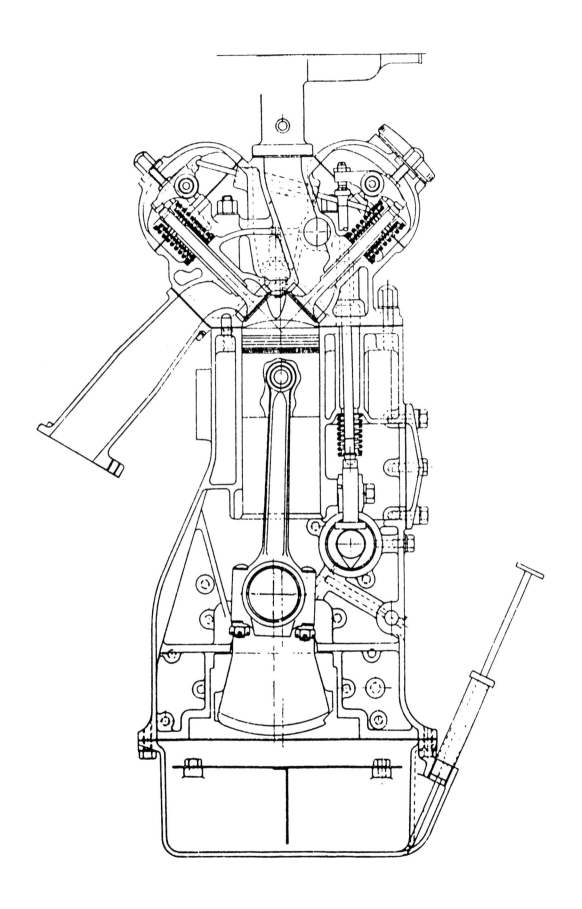

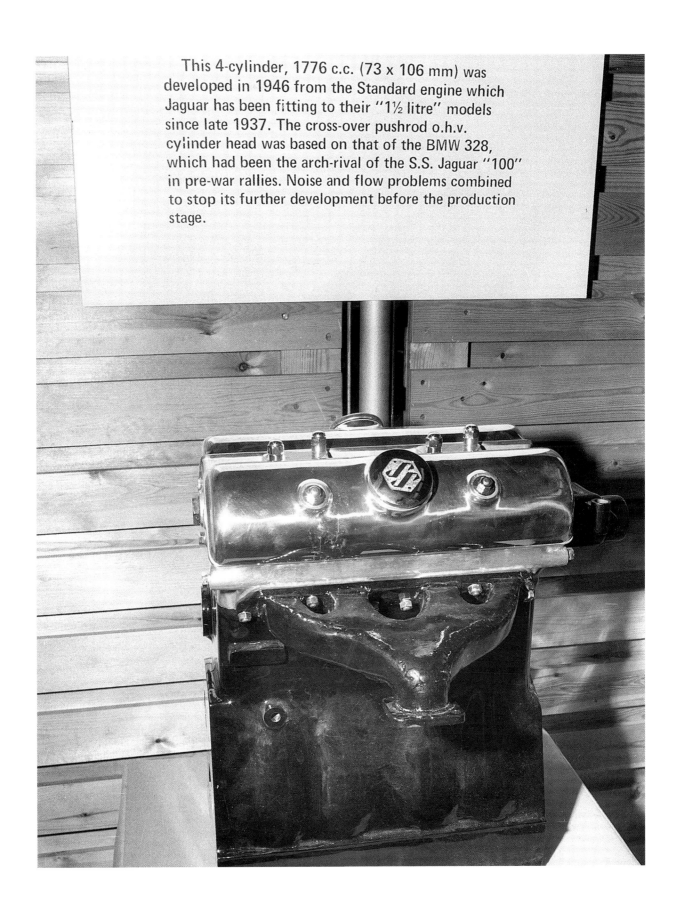

This 4-cylinder, 1776 c.c. (73 x 106 mm) was developed in 1946 from the Standard engine which Jaguar has been fitting to their "1½ litre" models since late 1937. The cross-over pushrod o.h.v. cylinder head was based on that of the BMW 328, which had been the arch-rival of the S.S. Jaguar "100" in pre-war rallies. Noise and flow problems combined to stop its further development before the production stage.

serious look was taken at both layouts to the extent of building prototype engines of both configurations.

Now there comes the vexed question of timescale. For many years the accepted wisdom was that the entire programme was carried through post-war, on the basis of discussion and design-sketching which took place on Sunday nights when the senior engineering team took on fire-watching duties at the factory. The trouble is that this scenario, consistently supported through a long series of post-war publications, implies that a whole series of prototypes of two distinct configurations was built, tested and compared, the necessary conclusions drawn, and the XK design finalised and made ready for production, in the three years 1945–48. Lord Montagu's history for example cheerfully accepts this notion, saying that 'In the immediate post-war years, a series of engines with 'X' (Experimental) designations were evolved …'[2] Andrew Whyte, in the best position of all actually to know, carefully skirts around the whole question by saying: 'From William Heynes's published engineering papers, and many subsequent writings on the subject, the story of the first 'all-Jaguar' engine's birth and early life is well known'[3] and leaves it at that. However, in 1975 Paul Skilleter was far more specific in his book on Jaguar sports cars[4], pointing out that '… before the war was out, several experimental engines had been built to test various forms of valve gear, and to evaluate cylinder head design.' By 1980 Skilleter – who recalls Walter Hassan still being reticent on this subject in the early 1970s – could be even more specific, stating that '… the company's (engine) experiments … began in 1943 with the tacit approval of the authorities.'[5] Eric Dymock in his much more recently written book[6] points out that 'the engine was a secret project of the engineering staff in the later stages of the war. But diverting resources from war-work might have been

thought unpatriotic, so the inspiration for the engine was attributed to those fire-watching sessions.'

Dymock makes a valid point. So long as there was a war on, the company was supposed to do only what was sanctioned by the Ministries. Company executives could not be prevented from planning for the peace; but any cutting of metal, or expenditure of fuel on bench-running in connection with programmes not directly related to the war effort would have contravened any number of regulations and been severely frowned upon. (Despite which, any number of British engineering companies discreetly did just that, and indeed with 'the tacit approval of the authorities' as Paul Skilleter points out.) Thus there was every justification, for many years after the end of the conflict, for encouraging the idea that prototyping and testing did not begin until after VE-Day in May 1945.

Any lingering notion that this might have been so is blown apart by the existence in the archive of a two-page report plus performance curves, signed by Walter Hassan, entitled 'Preliminary Report on X.G. Engine'. The report is dated 22 October 1943 although the hand-drawn curves, presumably by Hassan himself, show the date 16-10-43. It is interesting that this report makes no mention of the XF engine, the performance curves comparing the XG with the standard single-carburettor 1½-litre engine, plus the same engine with twin carburettors as a fairer comparison. This implies that the while the XF and XG were designed side-by-side, the XG was built first – which is entirely logical since it involved no more than fitting a new head to an existing, although modified block. The report does however show that metal had been cut, and running commenced, as early as mid-1943. Had this emerged at the time it might have led to trouble or at least to recriminations, but now it is far too late to send any of those involved to the Tower. What it does prove is that the whole programme was not carried through in the highly improbable three years, but much more credibly in a five-year period during 1943-48.

XF versus XG

As already suggested, the XG consisted of a brand-new cylinder head mated to the standard (Standard) 1½-litre block, which had some time since been stretched to 73 x 106mm for a capacity of 1,776cc. The test programme conducted through 1943 and 1944 established that although the XG configuration would probably deliver the required power, the

2   Lord Montague, *Jaguar*, p.67
3   Andrew Whyte, *Jaguar*, p.121
4   Paul Skilleter, *Jaguar Sports Cars*, p.48
5   Paul Skilleter, *Jaguar Saloons*
6   Eric Dymock, *The Jaguar File*, p.114

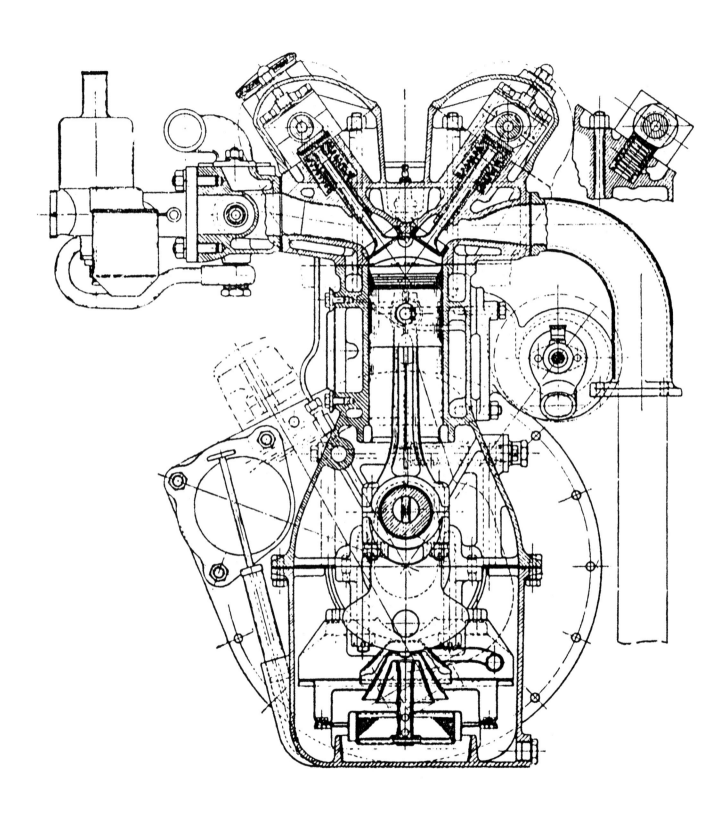

Even in its earliest form the XF engine exhibited many XK features including the principle of valve operation, the cams working directly

through 'bucket' tappets. In this engine the valve inclination is 36° each side, narrowed in the XK to 35°. (JDHT/Paul Skilleter)

DOHC alternative was beyond doubt preferable. The team proceeded first to a larger and more definitive 4-cylinder XK (or possibly XJ, see below) engine with dimensions 80.5 x 98mm (1,995cc) and thus to the 6-cylinder XK which ended up, via a small increase in bore (to 83mm) and a much larger increase in stroke (to 106mm) in order to fatten the mid-range torque curve, resulting with the famous capacity of 3,442cc.

Before moving on to the post-war story of how that engine was perfected and put into production, it is worth looking especially at the XG, the engine which failed to make it. In that first test-run report of 1943 Walter Hassan describes the XG as 'the Standard 1½-litre cylinder block and lower half, to which the conversion head has been fitted … the head is an aluminium alloy casting with hemispherical combustion chambers and valves set at 45°.' As already described, in the XG all the valves were operated from the existing single camshaft, tappets and modified pushrods, up to rockers situated in the near-side rocker box. The usual type of rocker was used for the inlet valves, but for the exhaust valves the motion was taken across the head by means of a bell-crank rocker, horizontal pushrod, and second rocker operating the valve, more or less exactly, in principle if not in detail, as in the BMW 328. Hassan describes the inlet ports as being 'practically vertical, and formed in pairs, connected by a large balance passage and fed by two 1¼-inch bore SU downdraught carburettors.'

The problems of prototyping in those difficult days were emphasised by Hassan's admission that 'the design of the new cylinder head calls for a re-arrangement of the holding-down studs, and as a standard cylinder block was adapted, the studs are not screwed into cast bosses but into the relatively thin section of the cylinder block roof.' Worse still, 'difficulty in obtaining valve seat inserts led to the decision to run the first head with the valves seating direct upon the aluminium. The casting did not permit the valve seats being machined to the dimensions of the proposed valve seating inserts, and as a result, the seatings are set further back in the head and the valves required to be shortened correspondingly.' As a result, the compression ratio fell from the designed 7.5:1 to an even more modest 7:1.

In that first test the XG engine suffered a number of teething problems, some of them entirely predictable – such as water leaks as the cylinder head (and, one suspects, the cylinder block face) flexed around the inadequately stiff studs, while the strange valve gear proved extremely noisy until additional return springs were fitted to the exhaust valve rockers. However, Hassan was moved to describe the test results as 'quite promising … the power compares favourably with that obtained from the standard engine of 7.5:1 compression ratio, and when the compression is raised, power in excess of the special twin-carburettor set-up may confidently be expected.' It is worth noting that 'compares favourably with' meant 'roughly the same as' although little more could be expected on that first run. Hassan's curves show the XG power output as being inferior to the standard 1½-litre engine up to almost 4,000rpm, beyond which it showed a small superiority as its power curve peaked, rather sharply, to some 68bhp at 4,500rpm. It was inferior to the standard engine with twin carburettors, which peaked at 74bhp at 4,750rpm, at all speeds. This is not surprising because its brake mean effective pressure (BMEP) was inferior at all speeds above 1,500rpm, inevitably so given its lower compression ratio. Where the XG was concerned, the developers had a lot to work on.

Meanwhile, the archive indicates that the XF twin-cam engine was first run on 30 November 1944, achieving 54bhp at 4,500rpm on part-load in that initial run. Contemporary notes say that it had a 'cylinder head with ports modified by Mr Weslake.' A full-load run followed, bringing the comment that 'as erected the engine gave 89bhp at 5,000rpm.' In a second test, conducted on 2 December 1944, it produced 88.25bhp at 4,750rpm, with a compression ratio of 7.45:1 and running on 'pool' petrol rated at 80RON. A set of hand-drawn curves in the archive, dated 18-12-44, show power, BMEP and specific fuel consumption curves for both the XF and XG prototypes tested against the 1½-litre Standard engine. The latter continues to achieve its reliable 65bhp at 4,750rpm, but now the XG power curve rises in a notably sharp peak to 80bhp at only 4,000rpm, while the XF runs to no less than 93bhp at 5,000rpm (so even more tests must have been run very soon after 2 December). At that point the XF power curve is still rising, so the tests must have been limited to 5,000rpm either to ensure mechanical integrity or (quite possibly) because that was as fast as the test bed machinery would run. As might be expected the

XG, cured of all the problems discovered during that initial firing-up in 1943, now achieved much better BMEP than the Standard engine, peaking at around 3,300rpm, but its curve fell off extremely sharply towards 5,000rpm, explaining why the power peak looked so sharp. The XF on the other hand maintained strong BMEP across the speed range, with 140lb/in^2 or better all the way from 1,850rpm to 5,000rpm.

With results like this coming off the bench, it was beginning to look like no contest unless the XF showed some fundamental flaw – such as impossible noise levels – and it didn't. They were going to choose the beautiful-looking engine William Lyons wanted. When one considers that the XG with its downdraught inlet ports with the SU carburettors sitting above them was inordinately tall, it is even less surprising that the decision was taken, certainly well before the war's end, to proceed with the DOHC engine. Yet the record also shows that the XG continued running as a handy tool to investigate various ideas, especially relating to inlet and exhaust manifolding. At a test run in February 1947 with open air intakes the test house silencer produced a power output of 80bhp at 5,100rpm, but with 'excessive running-on'. Use of the XG as a component-testing workhorse continued even into 1948, when a series of tests were conducted with plated bores.

As for the XF, the archive material intriguingly but consistently refers to this engine as having dimensions of 75mm bore by 98mm stroke for a capacity of 1,732cc. This conflicts with the conventional wisdom (with Heynes as the reference) that its dimensions were 66.5mm bore by 98mm stroke for a capacity of just 1,360cc. It seems clear that at some quite early stage the XF was bored-out in order to make it as nearly as possible the same size as the XG, most likely to avoid any scale-effect arguments during comparative testing (even though boring-out from 66.5mm to 75mm is quite a jump). The annoying thing is that there is no surviving indication of when this was done, despite one strip-down report referring to '75mm diameter Aeroflex pistons' and a more specific reference in one engineering report that 'the entry point of the water pump into the cylinder block with 75mm bores was too restricted and caused poor distribution of coolant.'

Left: The 4-cylinder XK appeared in a number of experimental guises but never entered production even though it was catalogued (in the 'XK100') for a year. This unit has an interesting-looking exhaust manifold, early twin SU carburettors and the cast alloy cooling fan also seen in early 6-cylinder units. (JDHT/Paul Skilleter)

Right: The cross-section through a 4-cylinder engine shows three main bearings, a much wider water passage between Nos 2 and 3 cylinders, and duplex chain drive to camshafts, apparently identical with 6-cylinder. (JDHT)

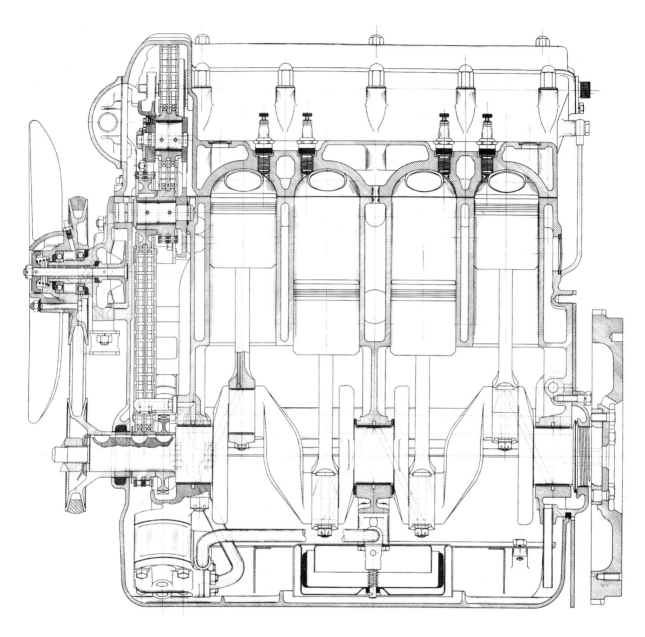

Developing the XK

In any event, development was moving on. In another intriguing break with accepted history, the archive section devoted to engine testing in the immediate post-war period makes no reference to an XJ engine. Following the folders devoted to the XF and XG there comes the first test report on 'XK No. 1' in October 1945 – a 4-cylinder engine with dimensions 76.25mm by 98mm for a capacity of 1,790cc. Yet again, in other words, we have a 4-cylinder engine with a capacity of just under 1.8-litres, just like the

XG, the bored-out XF and, of course, the standard (Standard) OHV '1½-litre'. For some considerable time, therefore, this size and configuration was the baseline for the new DOHC series, with the 6-cylinder derivatives to come later.

A series of tests, recorded in Walter Hassan's 'abbreviated log' was carried out on XK No. 1, erected (as they always put it in those days) with two 1⅜in SU carburettors. The first reliable power output was 76bhp at 4,500rpm on 19 November; this progressed to 84.3bhp at 5,000rpm on 9 January 1946. A subsequent log covers testing of 'XK

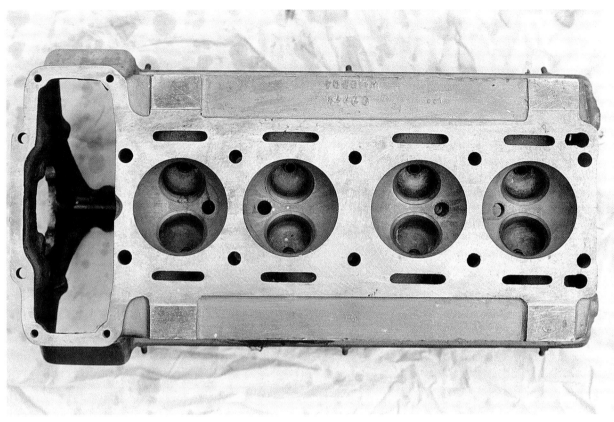

The underside of a 4-cylinder head shows a few interesting details. As the engine had no 'squish', so the combustion chambers are full cylinder-width; also the axes of the valves do not pass through the cylinder centre line but are offset away from the sparking plugs. The wide gap between the cylinders is very evident. (JDHT/Paul Skilleter)

4-cylinder MkII – originally XK4' but the whole 4-cylinder line of development appears to have petered out as the 6-cylinder began to show its promise, despite the fitting of a highly developed – effectively race-prepared – 4-cylinder, 2-litre (80.5 x 98mm, 1,995cc) unit to 'Goldie' Gardner's MG Special for its class record-breaking 176mph runs at Jabbeke in September 1948. This engine, running a compression ratio of 10:1, had a 5-bearing crankshaft and yet the majority of experimental 4-cylinder engines retained a 3-bearing crank as in the 1½-litre Standard. Paul Skilleter, quoting retired Jaguar engineer Tom Jones, suggests that in any case, Gardner's engine was specially developed, with the 1½-litre (actually 1.75-litre) block bored-out to provide a 2-litre capacity.

Certainly the 'MkIII' engine which first ran on 15 December 1947, and which had the same dimensions as Gardner's record-breaking power unit, had only three main bearings and produced a relatively modest 96bhp at 5,400rpm, rather than the latter's 146bhp at 6,000rpm. As noted in Chapter 3, a 4-cylinder engine of similar dimensions was officially listed for a whole year as the power unit of the XK100 sports car, but none was ever made.

It seems as though it was a long time before the notion of a 4-cylinder XK for a smaller Jaguar was entirely given up, however. An alternative layout with the classic 83mm Jaguar bore but 91mm stroke, for a capacity of 1,970cc, was run from 1949 all the way through to 1953. A series of at least three engines were run, the first two having 3-bearing crankshafts and the last one a 5-bearing crank. The first engine was initially run with a remarkable 12:1 compression ratio and produced 105bhp at 6,000rpm, usefully more than the stillborn XK100 unit. In support of these tests, the archive contains a 1951 memorandum which says that 'a series of preliminary tests … indicate this bore/stroke to show promise worthy of further development' but in the end, the whole idea of a 4-cylinder engine was clearly abandoned.

As to the classic 6-cylinder XK, the earliest surviving test report on an engine with dimensions 83mm bore by 98mm stroke for a capacity of

3,181cc is dated 15 September 1947. The peak power output was 145.2bhp at 5,000rpm, a generally satisfactory result, although as related in Chapter 3, it was felt that this 3.2-litre engine lacked sufficient torque – it failed to match the old OHV 3½-litre in this respect – and this led to the stroke being lengthened to 106mm to create the production engine with 3.4-litre capacity. Apart from this change, it appears very much to have been a case of 'right first time' and the 6-cylinder was always notable for being far more refined than the 4-cylinder engines with which the whole development process began.

Consequently, and still very early in the life of the XK, thought was given to creating a smaller capacity engine by shrinking the dimensions of the 'six' rather than by taking two-thirds of it to make a companion 4-cylinder. In 1951, tests were run on a 6-cylinder engine with dimensions 80mm bore by 66mm stroke for a capacity of 1,986cc; as run on 9 July of that year, this unit delivered 113bhp at 6,000rpm, and a disappointing best BMEP of 133lb/in² at 5,000rpm. It was noted that 'the combustion space was machined to match the 80mm bore' but obviously it needed a good deal of work on porting and cam profiling, not least because 'in order to obtain readings at 750, 1,000 and 1,500rpm it was necessary to use an ignition timing which caused heavy pinking to achieve stable running.' In December 1952 it was noted that 'nothing has been done to the engine since it was removed from the test bed on 8 May', and its total running time was only 27 hours. The idea of reducing the 6-cylinder to this extent was abandoned, and the next report on test results for a smaller engine cover the running of 'EXP3' which, in January 1954, produced 155bhp at 6,000rpm. This engine had dimensions of 83mm bore by 76.5mm stroke for a capacity of 2,483cc; in other words it was physically the engine that appeared a year later in the Jaguar 2.4, even though that officially offered only 112bhp.

The evolution of the 6-cylinder XK engine may appear complex, but the bare bones of the story are simple enough. A range of configurations was considered (1942–43), two were selected for prototype comparison (1943), the comparisons were made and the DOHC layout was selected (1944–45), the decision was taken to develop it primarily as a 6-cylinder (1947), and the 3.4-litre initial production capacity was decided upon (1947-48) and this went on to power the XK120 (Chapter 3) and the Mark VII (Chapter 4). Eventually, a shorter-stroke derivative was developed to power the 240 (1954–55). The rest of the story forms the remainder of this book.

Although Jaguar's history in the later years of the war and immediately afterwards is bound up in the evolution of the XK engine, life and the business of building cars had to go on once the war was over. Like almost all the car manufacturers who survived the conflict, Jaguar put its pre-war range back into production with very few changes. It had prepared a change to hypoid bevel final drive units, allowing the transmission tunnel in the rear of the saloons to be made smaller, for 1940, and this feature was now adopted. Some changes were also made in an attempt to improve braking performance, although mechanical rather than hydraulic brakes were retained. Because, as previously explained, Jaguar could now manufacture the 6-cylinder 2½-litre and 3½-litre OHV engines for itself, production concentrated more on these engine sizes. The 1½-litre cars continued to be offered but still with engines supplied by Standard.

The first post-war car was something of a hybrid. The Mark V was built on a new, much improved and substantially stiffer chassis developed by William Heynes, incorporating two vitally needed features, independent front suspension and hydraulic brakes. The front suspension used double wishbones and longitudinal torsion-bar springs, like the Citroën *Traction Avant* which Heynes is known to have admired, the RM Rileys, and indeed the post-war Morris Minor which appeared at about the same time as the Mark V. On this new chassis was mounted a body whose styling seemed no more than halfway into the post-war era and which was still built using the same method as its predecessors, from a collection of pressings sourced from various West Midlands specialists. But the Mark V was in this sense a hybrid, for Jaguar – having sacrificed its original option of using Motor Panels (Coventry) Ltd as its in-house body shop – now sought to evolve a new approach to body building which would involve sourcing the complete shell from a single external supplier. This was the principle on which the next new Jaguar saloon would be designed, for mounting on the new chassis, but to be powered by the 6-cylinder XK engine. The result would be impressive, but for various reasons it took longer than expected to arrive, and in the meantime Jaguar evolved a stop-gap model which turned into one of the motoring sensations of its era.

3 The **birth** of the **XK engine** and **XK sports cars**

Few cars have been so extensively written about as the XK sports series and it is certainly not the author's wish to add much more in terms of admiration or to the record of their achievements. Analysing the cars from a purely engineering point of view, it may in fact seem astonishing that so much was achieved by such a fundamentally simple design, and indeed, by a car of which relatively few were built – just over 30,000 examples in 11 years of 'real' production. The 'big saloons' may not have had the glamour but were actually built at a higher annual rate, as were the small saloons (see Chapter 6) whose early years overlapped the XK's later ones. For all its appeal, if you were a hard-headed engineering administrator, the XK120 and its successors were always a minority interest.

It was also a car which emerged almost by accident. Before the war and afterwards, William Lyons centred his programme on a saloon car range which, while providing above-average performance, handsome looks and excellent value for money, would sell in reasonable quantity. Sports cars might have been good for the company image but they were a distraction, and a potentially expensive one, from the mainstream business. That had been his attitude to the SS100 prior to 1939, and the post-war programme did not, at first, contain anything more sporting than drophead versions of the saloons, built in a special section of the Foleshill works. The focus of post-war business was to be a new saloon powered by the XK engine, which eventually emerged as the Mark VII (Chapter 4). Unfortunately, a key feature of the Mark VII programme was that its body was to be pressed and welded complete by Pressed Steel, and delivered to Jaguar for painting and final assembly. The company had had enough of assembling its own bodies-in-white from a jigsaw of panels sourced from several suppliers. But organising this process took far longer than anticipated, eventually leading to two decisions. The first, detailed in the previous chapter, was to evolve the Mark V saloon as an interim measure, using the new chassis but with the old 2½-litre and 3½-litre engines, and with a body which was intended to be the last to be made using the pre-war system.

Paul Skilleter[1] best describes the process via which the XK120 then came to pass. 'The rolling chassis intended for (the Mark VII) was all ready and so was the twin-cam power unit, a very frustrating situation for Jaguar's engineering staff. Then came an idea – why not take this chassis, shorten it, place a two-seater body on top and turn it into a sports car?' The idea was very quickly taken up (there were only months to go before the 1948 London Motor Show at which it would be displayed) and the work was carried through with amazing speed. Most amazing of all was the fact that William Lyons and his small team of prototyping craftsmen finalised the body design, from scratch, in two weeks!

Once one has accepted this almost alarming story of lightning creation, there were three overwhelmingly important aspects to the XK120. First and most important of all, it was the first model to become available with the XK twin-cam engine. Second, it was clothed in its Lyons-styled body of outstanding beauty. Third and least admirable, therefore least commented upon, it chassis design was derived from that of the big Mark V saloon, for the good and simple reason that the Mark V had Bill Heynes's carefully developed independent front suspension, and hydraulic brakes, clearly essential ingredients for a 1950s sports car. These three things, the engine, the styling and the advanced (or at least, up-to-date) features of the chassis, were the difference between the XK120 and the pre-war SS100.

The XK120 came about almost by accident, using a shortened and adapted chassis from the big Mark V saloon and a body designed at lightning speed by a small team led by William Lyons himself. Its success caught the company on the hop and more than a year was spent ramping-up production and tooling for a steel rather than an aluminium body. (JDHT)

It is interesting to compare the XK120 in its first production form with the 3½-litre SS100. The engines one might assume to be completely different, since one is the 'completely new' DOHC XK while the other is a pushrod OHV derivative of a side-valve Standard power unit. Yet in dimensions they are astonishingly close, those of the SS100 engine being 82mm bore by 110mm stroke for 3,485cc, and the XK being 83mm bore by 106mm stroke, for 3,442cc. In a preamble to his famous paper[2] on the V12 engine, Walter Hassan pointed out that 'the Jaguar 6-cylinder 3½-litre pushrod engine used in cars in the pre- and immediate post-war periods was considered to be an excellent engine of its type and its crankshaft, proven to have been a very satisfactory com-

---

1 Paul Skilleter, *The Jaguar XK – a Collector's Guide*

2 Walter T. Hassan, Jaguar V12 Engine – Its Design and Background

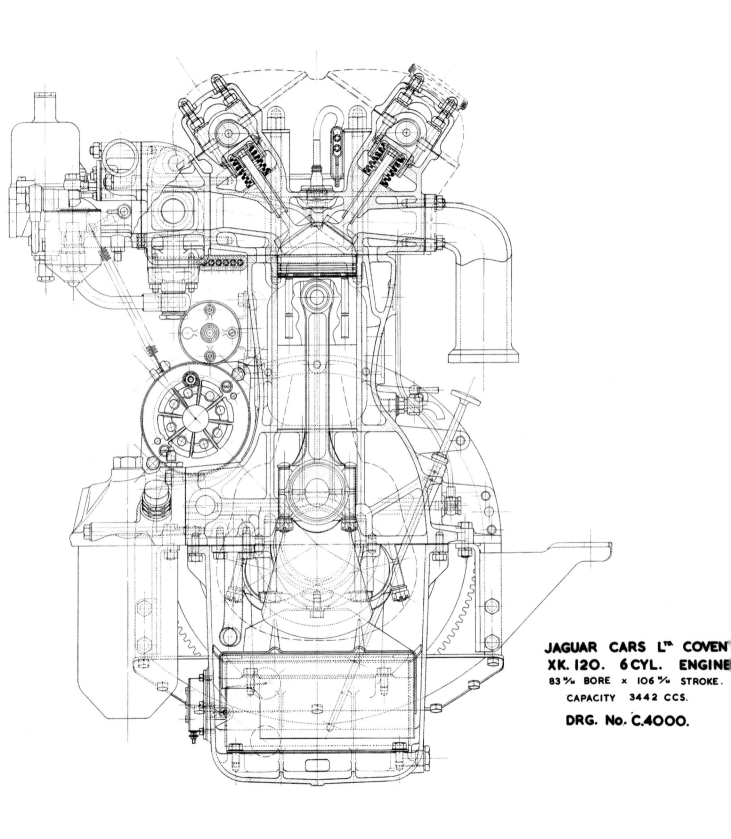

JAGUAR CARS L^{TD} COVEN
XK. 120. 6 CYL. ENGINE
83 ¹⁶/₆₄ BORE × 106 ¹⁶/₆₄ STROKE.
CAPACITY 3442 CCS.

DRG. No. C.4000.

ponent, provided a sound basis on which to design the XK twin cam engine.' Thus there is a clear link between the two, and you might well argue that the essential difference lies in that cylinder head, in which the vee-opposed valves (with 70° included angle) allowed the fitting of larger valves and the improvement of gas flow, hence the power output of 160bhp, on 8:1 compression, compared with the respectable 125bhp, on 7.3:1, of its pushrod predecessor. There was of course even less difference in maximum torque, the XK initially achieving 261Nm compared with the 247Nm of the 3½-litre. Both engines were effectively hamstrung by the old RAC horsepower taxation system, the XK design having been frozen too soon to take advantage of the system's abolition and its replacement first, in 1947, by one based on capacity and then, in 1948, by a flat rate. All through its life, therefore, the XK had to live with the consequences of being far more 'under-square' than its designers would really have wished.

We have already seen how the XK engine design evolved, through a long development process which at first concentrated on a 4-cylinder DOHC configuration from which the 6-cylinder was to be 'spun off'. The first foray into 6-cylinder territory was, as related in Chapter 2, an engine with dimensions 83mm bore by 98mm for a capacity of 3,181cc (nominally 3.2 litres). This engine was found to have no more torque than the 3½-litre OHV unit, with the result that it felt 'flat' on the road, and consequently the stroke was lengthened to the familiar 106mm to establish a positive differential. Even then, because the torque difference was not that great and the XK120 was substantially heavier than the SS100, its acceleration was not, therefore, its most startling aspect. *The Motor* road test of 1949 credited it with a 0–60mph time of exactly 10sec, excellent in its day, but that was an aluminium-bodied car running in test

conditions that were somewhat 'special'. The first test carried out by *The Autocar* the following year, on one of the first steel-bodied cars which was around 50lb heavier, yielded a 0–60mph time of 12sec which is much more credible. But maximum speed was the XK's forte, partly thanks to its superior aerodynamics but also and largely due to the far better breathing of the DOHC engine with its peak power coming at 5,000rpm compared with the 4,250rpm of the pushrod unit. *The Motor* achieved a mean maximum speed of 124.6mph 'with the hood raised and the side screens in position', and that was truly startling. Indeed it was probably a little too startling, and it seems likely that representative production cars might just have scraped the 120mph true maximum which lay behind the choice of the car's name.

It has also often been noted that there was a companion 4-cylinder engine, XJ or XK, which retained the 98mm stroke and with a bore of 80.5mm, had in consequence a capacity of 1,995cc. It is often asserted that this engine 'broke cover' in the early days when it was used to power 'Goldie' Gardner's MG Special to a class record-breaking 176mph at Jabbeke in 1948. Recent evidence suggests this was not a true 4-cylinder XK but a one-off exercise in which a '1½-litre' engine was bored-out to 2-litre capacity and tuned to deliver no less than 146bhp at 6,000rpm, with the aid of a 10:1 compression ratio. The might-have-been definitive 4-cylinder XK developed 95bhp at 5,000rpm, in other words just about what one would expect from the ratio of capacities: 160 multiplied by 1.995 and divided by 3.442 yields 92.7bhp, and you can add a little for the lower frictional losses in a 4-cylinder. At one time it was intended that this engine should also be fitted to the new sports car to create the XK100, and indeed it is so listed in, among other authorities, the World Specification Tables section of *The Motor Yearbook* for 1950. The trouble was that with only 95bhp and similarly reduced torque, the XK100 would have been pushed actually to achieve 100mph, and its 0–60mph acceleration time, even allowing for revised gearing and slightly reduced weight, would have been of the order of 16 seconds. This would still have been faster than any other car road tested by *The Motor* in 1949, but it would not have been fast enough. In the end, the decision to shelve the 4-cylinder and standardise on the 3.4-litre 6-cylinder was the right one. It would be all too easy to see the XK100 being damned as 'all show and no go'. It may well be, as has been suggested, that the 4-cylinder felt pretty rough compared with the

Left: The cross-section through the initial 3.4-litre production version of XK engine makes an interesting comparison with the XF prototype shown earlier. In many ways there are more similarities than differences, suggesting the XF was a 'right first time' concept. It is not clear why the outer walls of the block had to be so elegantly curved – it would have done little for the stiffness of the unit and probably cost weight. The block ends abruptly at the crankshaft centre-line, with only a massive sump below. Crankshaft oil sealing would eventually become an issue with the XK along with lack of beam-stiffness. (JDHT/Paul Skilleter)

remarkably refined 3.4-litre, but that was not the reason why the engine was shelved. All else apart, there is evidence that during the 1950s, Jaguar contemplated reviving it to power a small saloon series. One factor which heavily influenced the decision to abort the XK100 was that the US market became even more important than Lyons had envisaged, and took all the XK120s the factory could produce – and the Americans always wanted cubic inches.

As it was, XK engine development throughout the life of the sports car (and indeed throughout the engine's life) was dominated by the need to eke out more power without making it run too fast. Because of that long stroke and consequently high piston speed, taking any XK beyond 6,000rpm – and it was

Above: A very early 3.4-litre XK engine, identifiable, among other things by the tall-dashpot SU carburettors and the cast-alloy cooling fan. The sump looks especially massive in this view, and also rather rough-cast. (JDHT/Paul Skilleter)

Top right: The underside view of 6-cylinder head makes an interesting comparison with the 4-cylinder component shown earlier. There is now a

wider gap between cylinders 3 and 4, and this remained until the cylinder centre re-spacing which created the 4.2-litre. (JDHT/Paul Skilleter)

Bottom right: Not often seen this way: a section through the cylinder head on a cylinder centre-line shows sleeves in which bucket tappets operated, the valve guides, valve seats and coolant passages. (JDHT/Paul Skilleter)

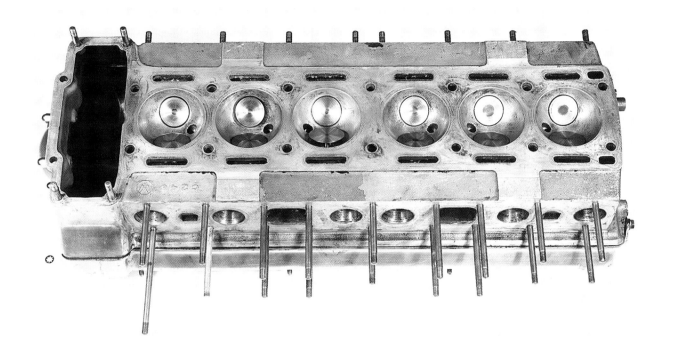

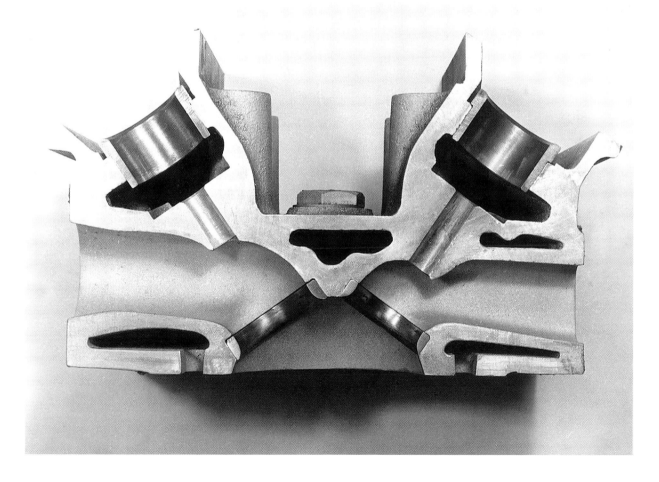

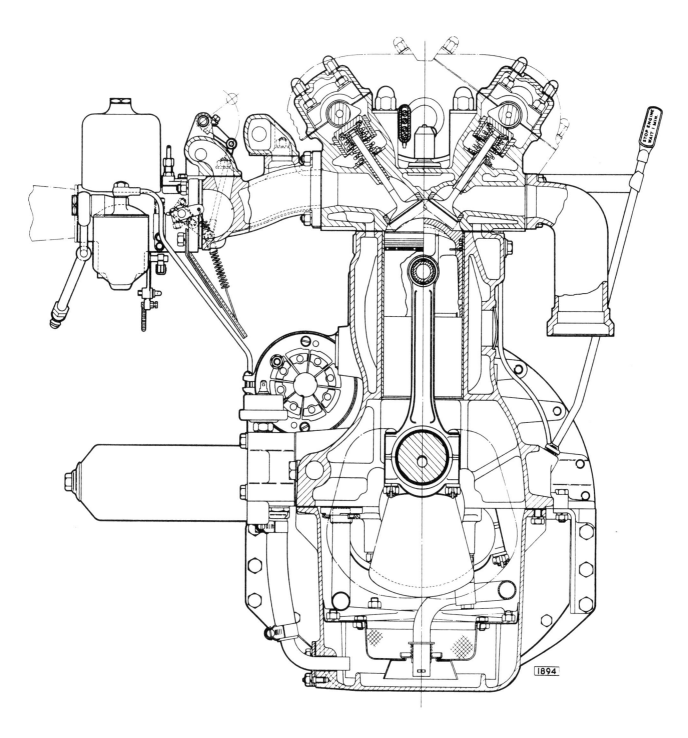

Left: The XK chain-drive arrangement to the camshafts (with the engine upside-down on a bench!). Note the use of duplex chain throughout, the 'splitting' of the drive through an intermediate sprocket and the details of main chain tensioning with the angled drive to the distributor also visible. (JDHT/Paul Skilleter)

Above: The XK 3.4 was enlarged to 3.8-litre capacity by boring-out and retaining the original bore centres. Intercylinder clearances became small enough that liners were thought to be essential. There are many minor detail differences between this unit and the 3.4 – in the valve gear and the carburetion for example. (JDHT/Paul Skilleter)

usually red-lined below that – was a recipe for a shortened life. As an indication of what was needed to achieve race-long reliability at 6,000rpm, a surviving 1954 note from Bill Heynes and relating to 'XK120D Le Mans Cars – Engine Development' spells out the measures needed for bottom-end survival: 'New steel crank, EN40 nitriding steel, reinforced webs (shorter rear bearings), smaller oil feed holes. Standard connecting rods but 100-ton steel bolts.' It is worth noting that even the connecting rods were all crack-tested after an early and spectacular racing failure; but it underlines the fact that the bottom end of the XK was barely capable of handling what the top end could throw at it, and it is still worth latter-day XK owners noting that for long engine life, it is better to paint a mental red line 500rpm short of the real one.

Yet the XK120 was an admired sports car and from the beginning, people expected an ongoing process of performance improvement. In order to achieve this without running the engine any faster, the BMEP (brake mean effective pressure) had to be improved, and as far as possible, internal losses due to friction and windage reduced. Increasing BMEP has the welcome effect of also improving torque, to the benefit of mid-range acceleration, while the higher efficiency also improves fuel consumption, unless all the extra performance is exploited. The easiest way to increase BMEP is to increase compression ratio but in the early days of the XK the British market at least was still subject to the poor (and even worse, variable) quality of 'pool' petrol. As a result, for a long time it was felt unwise to raise the compression ratio from the 8:1 at which it was set for the production XK120. Any power increases had to be eked out by 'tweaking' the gas flow to improve mid-range BMEP, torque and engine response without tempting owners to court disaster at the red line. Eventually, in short-stroke 3-litre (85 x 88mm) racing form the XK managed the remarkable BMEP figure, for a naturally aspirated engine, of 205lb/in^2, at which point it was delivering 312bhp at 6,750rpm – figures a standard XK could only dream about, but an indication of the quality of the design.

In the road-going cars, the XK power output rose by gentle stages – detailed in a number of existing publications – from the initial 160bhp, through 180bhp (XK120SE 'Special Equipment') to 190bhp (standard) and 210bhp (SE) in the later XK140 and XK150, to as much as 250bhp in the XK150SE with a 'straight port' head and the compression ratio raised to 9:1. The challenge was to find the optimum combination of port shape and size (throat diameter) and

exhaust valve diameter (inlet valves in production engines were always 1¾in diameter) for the strongest BMEP over as wide a range as possible. One notable stage in this evolution, prior to the straight-port cylinder head, was the so-called C-type cylinder head which, confusingly, was not the head from the C-type but which combined the narrower standard inlet ports – for a higher gas speed at moderate revs – with larger exhaust valves for better top-end breathing.

Ultimately, in 1958, the XK block was opened right out and dry-sleeved for sufficient cylinder wall strength, allowing the bore to be increased from 83mm to 87mm, and thus the capacity to 3,781cc (nominal 3.8-litre). Because there was no alteration of the stroke, the bottom-end limitations were unchanged but the greater piston area brought increases in both torque and power, the latter to 220bhp (standard) and no less than 265bhp (SE, with straight-port head). These, it should be noted, were power outputs measured according to the then-SAE standard, which produced significantly inflated figures when compared with 'honest' output measured at the flywheel of a fully equipped engine running with a standard exhaust system; but it was the system the Americans themselves were using, and Jaguar had to appear competitive in its key market.

One advantage of the steady improvement in mid-range BMEP was that the acceleration performance became consistently better, which is more than can be said for the maximum speed. The adoption of over-drive helped too, allowing the overall gearing to be lowered. Thus in 1958, *The Autocar* tested VDU 882, an XK150 Fixed Head Coupé, taking it to a mean maximum speed of 123.7mph in overdrive (114mph, effectively rev-limited, in direct top) with a 0–60mph time of 8.5sec, going on to 100mph in 25.1sec. A less desirable effect of the higher torque in the later cars was that the very simply-located back axle could be made to tramp during a standing start, but the magazine road testers were mostly too polite to say so.

For a long time, through most of the life of the XK sports car certainly, there was a tradition that XK

Right: A sadly familiar part of the Jaguar character until the later 1960s was the 4-speed Moss gearbox, with no synchromesh on first and, according to many, precious little on the higher gears either – but it was extremely durable and provided high torque capacity. As shown here, it was made either with a long or a short output shaft to suit installation, the latter making it suitable for use with overdrive. (JDHT/Paul Skilleter)

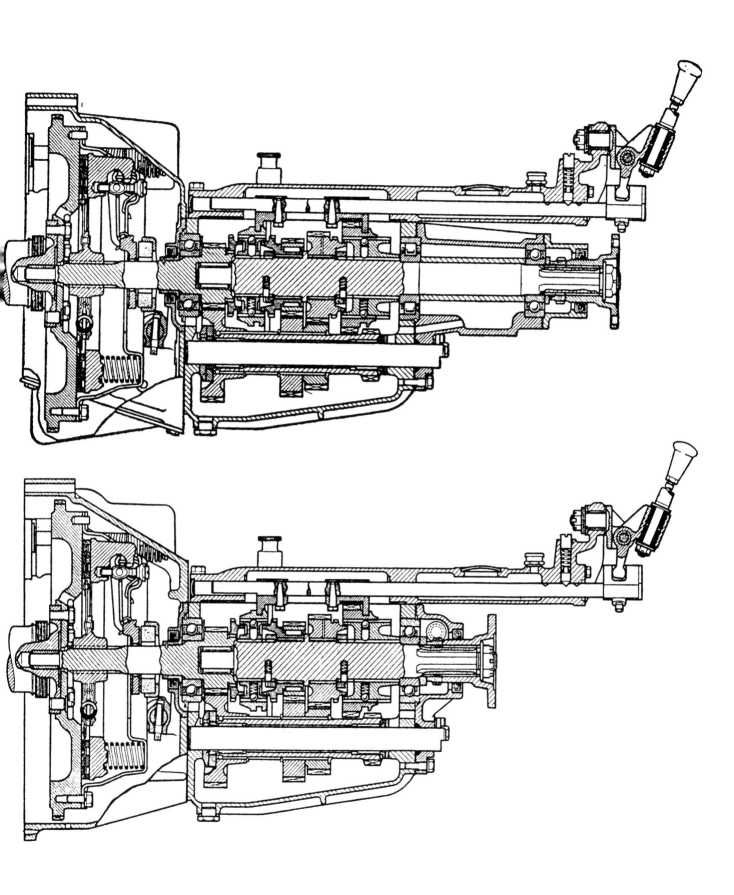

cylinder heads should be painted different colours – beneath the polished alloy cam covers – to indicate their construction standard. These culminated in the 'gold' straight-port heads for the XK150S, E-type and S-type. In 1967 however, admittedly long after the XK series had given way to the E-type, a stern little note appears in the minutes of one Model Progress Meeting (MPM) that 'Cylinder heads are no longer to be coloured.' There is no elaboration to indicate why not, but could there possibly have been fears about unscrupulous renovators painting heads different colours? The notion may appeal to the conspiracy theorists, but more likely it was done to expedite production.

Throughout its career, the XK depended on the faithful Moss 4-speed gearbox, admired for its strength rather than its subtlety and devoid of synchromesh on first gear. But the 1950s were when the Laycock-de Normanville was in vogue, built into the driveline downstream of the gearbox, so to speak, and offering – depending on torque demands, the way it was wired-up, and the vehicle's basic gearing – a number of additional gear ratios. As already mentioned, overdrive was an option on the later XK sports cars, but the high torque of the 3.4 (let alone the 3.8) XK engine meant that the installation took its simplest form, adding a single 'fifth' gear, engaged after selection of top gear to reduce engine speed, noise and fuel consumption. Changing down automatically de-selected overdrive, which occasionally had engine overspeeding implications if you forgot it was engaged in the first place. The overdrive unit was quite bulky and the frame aft of the gearbox had to be modified to make room for it, incidentally, also creating the space through which to run a twin-pipe exhaust system.

One inevitable outcome of the US market taking the major share of XK production was that the cars were eventually offered with a 3-speed Borg-Warner automatic transmission. The XK140 was the first variant with this option, for the 1957 model year, and it was continued into the XK150 (but not for the SE).

Chassis comparisons

On the chassis front, it is worth comparing the principal figures for the XK120 and its admired predecessor the SS100, which are as follows:

SS100: wheelbase 104in, front track 52.5in, rear track 54in, kerb weight 2,603lb, 5.50–18 tyres

XK120: wheelbase 102in, front track 51in, rear track 51in, kerb weight 2,912lb, 6.00–16in tyres

Thus despite being noticeably more compact than the SS100 – shorter in wheelbase, substantially narrower in track – the XK120 was substantially heavier, partly because post-war customers demanded more in the way of creature comforts and equipment, partly because its new styling made it both longer and wider overall. A visual comparison of the two cars shows how much more volume is enclosed by the XK120 body, creating extra surface area which in turn translates into extra weight. True, there should have been some savings, in the front suspension for example, while the XK engine did not weigh all that much more than the OHV engine. The Mark V chassis, however, was hefty (with the benefit that it was much stiffer than in any earlier Jaguar) and in any case, there was no arguing with the weighbridge.

Unfortunately in some respects, the XK-series bodies were built in the manner of the 'steel saloons' up to and including the Mark V. That is, they were constructed from a relatively large number of pressings from a number of suppliers (although predominantly from Pressed Steel), although at least the front and rear wings came complete. One has to remember the speed with which the design was conceived; production engineering was left to catch up once the decision had been taken to manufacture the XK120. The early months – indeed years – of the car's story is among other things that of a struggle to source the steel body components, filling the gap until these came on-stream with a trickle of cars whose bodies were aluminium, much easier to form (in small volume) with minimal machinery.

Eventually final assembly of the XK and of the Mark VII saloon took place on parallel production lines at the new (for Jaguar) Browns Lane factory. Thus only the earliest production XK120s were aluminium-bodied, and built at the old Foleshill plant in a trickle to keep important customers happy, while the steel panel supply network was sorted out and the transfer to Browns Lane – a wartime Daimler 'shadow' factory – was carried through. Inevitably, it is these aluminium-bodied cars, lighter and therefore with slightly better acceleration, which are now regarded as the ultimate classics. Jaguar's records show that 240 such cars were made (in well over a year) before body production switched to steel.

The new manufacturing facilities resolved many headaches and resulted in much more consistent body quality. The heavy reliance on Pressed Steel meant that Jaguar was largely tied to a single supplier – no longer able to play one off against another – and in the eyes of some Jaguar engineers the delivered quality of components was not only consistent, but consistently mediocre. At least, however, it meant that when new body styles were evolved, Jaguar did not have to tackle quite such a jigsaw of panels coming from different places. And the body styles did evolve. The XK120 was launched as an open sports car, followed in course of time by the handsome fixed-head coupé. Then a demand arose for a drophead coupé, in other words a car distinct from the 'roadster' in retaining the higher coupé door sills, A-pillars and windscreen arch, plus wind-up windows. Because the body was carried on a chassis rather than being unitary, such developments could be carried through at body level without having to worry about what modern engineers would call 'the platform'. The same went for running and series changes, by far the most visually obvious of which was the adoption of a one-piece windscreen for the XK150 which was also, for the sake of improved elbow room, slightly wider; this change increased the car's frontal area from 17.5 to 18.2 square feet, which also had its effect on maximum speed. Less evident, but just as important was the 3in forward movement of the engine in the XK140, to create a little more legroom, which had already been improved by sinking a shallow footwell into the originally flat floor. The XK120 had indeed been rather cramped and became more so in a post-war world where many customers were becoming more bulky.

In terms of steering, handling and ride comfort, the XK120 was inevitably superior to the SS100. The independent front suspension (IFS) alone would have seen to that. Apart from reducing the unsprung weight, to the benefit of both roadholding and ride comfort, IFS deleted the link via which disturbing forces could be transferred from one front wheel to the other, not that there is any suggestion that the SS100 ever suffered from the dreaded 'wheel wobble' of some small, cheap cars with beam front axles (notably the Austin Seven). It must also be admitted that even in the XK120, with large and heavy wheels and high performance in relation to the size and specification of some of its suspension and steering components, the wrong combination of incorrect alignment, out-of-balance wheels and a degree of steering joint wear could lead to a disturbing shimmy, with forces transferred through the steering system itself. Independent front suspension is not, indeed, an engineering panacea, merely a better starting point – something the early XK120s were far from alone in discovering.

The new layout made the installation of the steering, the Burman recirculating-ball system which was becoming a byword for lightness and freedom from kick-back (if not, even then, for positive centre-feel) much easier. Today, the actual layout with its long steering column and steering box mounted ahead of the engine in the car's crush-zone, would give any safety engineer nightmares, but this was the mid-1940s. Possibly to counter criticisms of vague steering feel around the straight-ahead, the change-over to the XK140 brought with it the adoption of rack and pinion steering, a fairly bold move at a time when many chassis engineers still feared the problems of kick-back and felt that any rack and pinion system would need to be damped. At least the XK series never needed power-assisted steering. Narrow cross-ply tyres (6.00–16 remained the standard fit right through to the XK150S) meant the loads could always be managed by the average driver, even with little more than three turns lock-to-lock. For the same reason, steering feel and feedback were always beyond reproach.

The IFS itself was a double wishbone layout, with longitudinal torsion bar springing, laid out by Bill Heynes following a study of the available and practicable options. Heynes was especially impressed by the torsion-bar front suspension in the Citroën *Traction Avant*; he was not alone, since Alec Issigonis adopted a similar layout for the Morris Minor which first appeared in 1948, and Riley had been using it in the RMA/RMB saloons for some time. Essentially, the XK carried over the suspension from the Mark V which had been the first IFS-equipped Jaguar, but the XK chassis was not, as is sometimes suggested, simply a cut-down Mark V. Most obviously, its front track was 5in narrower and the tyres, carrying far less load, were narrower – the Mark V ran on 6.70-16 covers. But one virtue of IFS, compared with a solid axle, is that its main components can be transferred corner to corner, so to speak, without worrying too much about the space between.

However, the front end had in essence to consist of the Mark V chassis rails, to carry over the suspension mounting points including the rear attachments of the torsion bars, which had the advantage of taking a large part of the suspension load into the structure well aft and thus efficiently. The XK frame was made very strong in this area, with a major

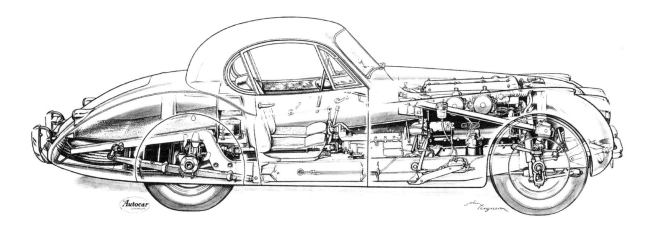

Left: The Laycock-de
Normanville overdrive
was installed in a unit with
the 'short-shaft' gearbox.
The overdrive operated
only with top gear engaged,
unlike the units used on some
smaller-engined cars.
(JDHT/Paul Skilleter)

Above: This cutaway shows
details of chassis, suspension, and engine installation
in an XK sports car, empha-
sising the simplicity of the
design by modern standards.
The engine was originally
installed well aft, but extra
cockpit space was eventually

achieved by shifting it further forward. The steering
column position would end
the career of any 21st
century safety engineer ...
(LAT)

Below: A detailed view of
the XK120 front end shows

attachment of wishbones
and dampers to the front
ends of the chassis rails via
fabricated brackets. The
front end of the engine is
positioned comfortably aft
of the front axle line –
and of the steering box!
(JDHT/Paul Skilleter)

When the need for an XK140 replacement was acknowledged, one of the proposals was this device, seen outside Wappenbury *Hall. It was not proceeded with, proving once again that Sir William Lyons knew a bad thing when he saw it …* (JDHT/Paul Skilleter)

cross-member running between the two main rails immediately aft of the gearbox. The Mark V chassis was heavily cross-braced but with its narrower track and shorter (by 18in!) wheelbase the XK120 needed no such elaborate measures. Its rear chassis rails kicked up abruptly over the rear axle – the pre-war penchant for 'underslung' chassis had long since succumbed to concerns about accessibility, ease of assembly, and rear suspension travel – and then tapered rearwards and slightly downwards to support the tail structure and the spare wheel, housed beneath the boot floor. They also carried the rear attachments for the semi-elliptic 'cart' springs which located the rear axle without any form of assistance – no radius arms or Panhard rod, merely a couple of lever-arm dampers (which were exchanged for telescopic dampers in the XK140/150, as also in the later Mark VIIs).

If the early XKs had an Achilles' Heel, it was their brakes. The cars had high performance, they were not light (as we have seen) and originally they were fitted with steel-disc wheels of relatively modest size by the standards of their day, meaning that 12in drums were the biggest that could be fitted, and that these were not well ventilated. It soon became clear that XKs driven competitively along winding roads, to say nothing of down Alpine passes, could suffer very badly from brake fade. An obvious palliative was to fit spoked wheels to improve brake drum ventilation but at best this alleviated the problem. It certainly didn't

... and the actual replacement for the XK140, pending the eventual arrival of the E-type, was the XK150, seen here in this US publicity photograph. It was more substantially re-engineered in some respects than its outward appearance might have suggested. (Jaguar)

provide a cure. It is also worth noting that contemporary road testers, notorious for their tendency to deliver bad news in veiled Delphic tones, were unanimous in their condemnation of the handbrake.

Once Jaguar's competition activities had helped to focus attention on disc brakes, it could only be a matter of time before they arrived in a version of the XK. Sadly, it was only in 1957, four years after the great Le Mans victory which had been largely attributed to the then-new disc brakes, that they finally appeared with the transition from XK140 to XK150. It had taken that long to turn an expensive racing prototype system into something which was cheap and durable enough for proper series production. When they arrived, however, they made a huge difference to the verve with which the car could be driven. The sad thing was that by then, the XK had lost its sporting edge and become rather more of a grand tourer. It was only with the very late arrival of the 3.8 engine in the XK150S – of which fewer than 1,500 were built – that performance edged back towards the standard set by some of the earliest cars in the series.

By that time it was already clear that a significantly superior product could result from adopting a modern body structure – no more separate chassis – and a better rear suspension, whether independent or with a much better-located live back axle. In 1961 the result of these cogitations emerged in the form of the E-type (Chapter 7).

4 The **XK** becomes the **standard engine**

n 1951, the Mark VII appeared to replace the old Mark V, not that it was that old, dating back only to 1948 as we have seen. The designation Mark VI was skipped because Bentley had already appropriated it.

There were two reasons only for the Mark VII, but they were both good ones. The first was the deletion of the old OHV engine and standardisation on the DOHC XK, and the second was to move the appearance of Jaguar's staple big saloon decisively into the post-war era.

As we have seen, the Mark V may have looked like something Jaguar had on the drawing board when the war began, but it was actually carried through as an interim measure when the plan for Pressed Steel's Oxford plant (next door to the Morris works at Cowley) to build the Mark VII body complete, slipped disastrously – not by months but by years. The Mark V was perforce a combination of a con-servatively styled body assembled using the largely discredited pre-war system, with the new chassis which had already been developed by the team under William Heynes and which included features such as double-wishbone independent front suspension and hydraulic brakes, vital ingredients for a post-war car. Once everything was ready for the Pressed Steel supply chain to begin operating, the Mark VII body and the XK engine could be mounted in the existing chassis with the minimum of disruption (the majority of XK development road-running had been accum-ulated in Mark V 'mules' by this time). The two cars had identical chassis dimensions – 120in wheelbase, 56in front track, 57.5in rear track – because the chassis themselves were identical, or as nearly as made little difference. The only chassis changes of note in the Mark VII were the installation of a revised braking system, including a servo, in deference to its extra weight and higher performance, and a switch from Burman worm-and-nut steering to the recirculating-ball type, as in the XK120. Despite this, the sheer weight on the front wheels meant that to keep steering effort within reason, the gearing gave four and a half turns of the wheel between locks. The car also gained a 'fly-off' handbrake of the type fitted to the XK120, in place of the then-orthodox 'umbrella-handle' in the Mark V.

Seen from the 21st century, the braking system change seems like something out of the Stone Age – the adoption of a better kind of flint, perhaps – but at the time it was significant. The front brakes of the Mark VII had two trailing shoes per drum, rather than the conventional two leading shoes. The difference is that while leading shoes tend to pull themselves into contact, creating a servo effect, trailing shoes depend entirely on the application pressure exerted through the system. The catch is that, to quote *The Motor* in its review of the new Jaguar, the servo effect 'is bought at the price of a considerable change in braking characteristics with rise in temperature.' So the trailing-shoe arrangement was adopted in a quest for more consistent characteristics, quite important in a car weighing close to two tons and capable of 100mph. But the trailing shoes considerably increased the necessary operating pressure, hence the system had to include a Clayton-Dewandre vacuum servo to bring pedal efforts within bounds. It all points to the way in which, at the time, braking performance was becoming a real headache in heavier and higher-performance cars. Today, solutions are available for almost any braking system challenge, but (as we saw with the XK120 in the previous chapter) this certainly wasn't the case in the early 1950s. Despite this, the Mark VII enjoyed its competition successes – in the hands of sympathetic drivers with strong right legs, and with non-standard brake lining materials – including one victory in the Monte Carlo Rally.

The Mark VII replaced the immediate post-war Mark V, introducing the XK engine and far more modern styling to the big saloon range but retaining a separate chassis and a 120in wheelbase. (Jaguar)

Regarding the engine, it may at the time have seemed strange to outsiders to take a unit which was beginning to make a name for itself in an admired sports car, and install it in a hefty saloon. Yet the saloon was what the engine had first been intended for, the sports car application coming about (as we have seen) almost by accident. The whole image of SS/Jaguar immediately pre-war, not just of the low-volume SS sports series, was of cars which performed well above the average for their class and which looked wonderful – even under the bonnet. That had always been the XK's job, from the moment of its conception. It only became a 'sports car engine' because the XK120 happened to appear first, and because twin overhead camshafts had long been associated with sporting marques like Alfa Romeo.

As we have already seen when discussing the XK120, the virtue of the DOHC engine lay less in its torque output, which was only marginally better than that of its 3½-litre OHV predecessor, than in its

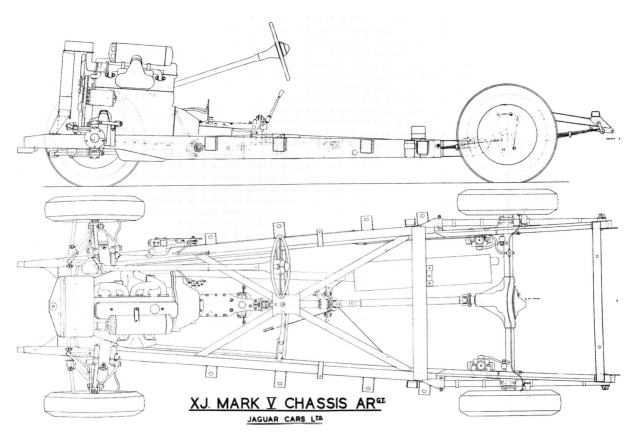

XJ. MARK V CHASSIS AR^{GT}

JAGUAR CARS L^{TD}

The Mark V chassis – here intriguingly labelled on a Jaguar drawing as the 'XJ Mark V' – was developed after the war to incorporate the independent front suspension devised by Bill Heynes, with springing by longitudinal torsion bars anchored in the region of the front bulkhead. Note the cross-bracing which was needed in the saloon but omitted when the basic chassis was shortened and narrowed for the XK120. In the Mark V, the engines remained the old OHV 2½- and 3½-litre, replaced for the Mark VII by the then-new XK 3.4. (JDHT)

much better peak power output – 160bhp instead of 125bhp – achieved at significantly higher engine speed but without loss of refinement. This gave Jaguar engineers a choice when it came to gearing. Did they leave it the same as in the Mark V, for similar acceleration but better maximum speed, or did they lower the final drive for better acceleration? The engine's characteristics were not the only factors here. Weight and aerodynamic drag also came into the picture. The Mark VII was roughly 150lb, or 4 per cent heavier than the Mark V, the difference being accounted for by the new engine, the higher standard of equipment (including that brake servo) and the more enveloping bodywork with its bigger surface area. That argued for a slight lowering of the final drive from the Mark V's 4.3:1.

On the other hand, although no definitive figures are available, it is clear that the Mark VII had lower aerodynamic drag. As *The Motor* said when reviewing the Mark VII on its introduction, 'the new body shape … should have a substantially lower drag than the Mark V with its separate mudguards' and it would have been a shame to throw away the potential for a 100mph maximum speed through gearing the car so that peak power was reached in top gear at some lower speed, even though mid-range acceleration would have benefited. This was the case for retaining the existing gearing or even raising it. As *The Motor* pointed out, the potential existed for Jaguar to offer not only the fastest production sports car (the XK120) in the market at that time, but also the fastest 4/5 seater saloon in the form of the Mark VII. Again, this was a time when maximum speeds, especially the 'magic hundred' still counted for a great deal in the selling of cars, and William Lyons and his marketing men needed no reminding of this.

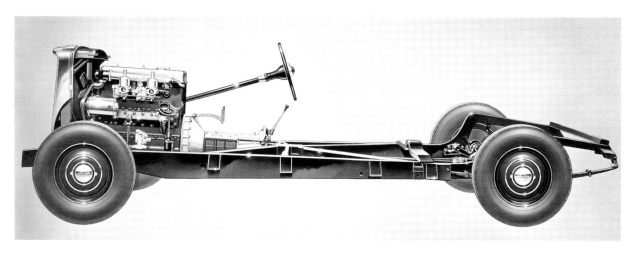

Top: The Mark V chassis seen from the side: apart from the change of engine to XK, the layout remained similar in principle through to the Mark IX. The abrupt kick-up of the rear chassis rails above the axle is also characteristic of the XK120. Not visible here is the braking system, one of the most continuously developed aspects of the big saloons as their weight remained high and their performance steadily increased. (JDHT)

Above; Bill Heynes's independent front suspension, showing how the lower wishbones picked up beneath the chassis rail (and clamped to the front end of the longitudinal torsion bar) while the upper wishbones were mounted on brackets above, together with the long-stroke dampers. The steering linkage is substantial but the steering box tended to isolate the column from feedback of shock-loadings. (JDHT)

In the end, sure enough, the final drive was left virtually the same (actually 4.27 instead of 4.3), enabling the lower aerodynamic drag, and the XK's higher operating speeds and maximum power to take the big saloon on to its coveted 100mph maximum.

Performance comparisons, therefore, are interesting. Testing the Mark V in 1950, *The Motor* achieved a mean maximum speed of 90.7mph, and 0–30 and 0–60mph times of 4.9 and 14.7sec respectively. The magazine had to wait until 1952 before getting its hands on a Mark VII, and that car recorded a mean maximum of 101mph, as well as 0–30 and 0–60mph times of 4.6sec and 13.7sec respectively, in other words not slightly slower as might be expected, but usefully quicker. To some extent this was due to the higher speeds which could be achieved in the intermediate gears before changing up – 51mph and 74mph in second and third in the Mark VII, 46mph and 67mph in the Mark V – but it was also due to some painstaking and surprisingly long drawn-out development work to establish exactly the right settings to match the XK engine to the bigger car, at least to an acceptable standard for press testing.

Notes contributed by Bob Berry to the Jaguar archive detail some of the earlier tests. On 16 October 1950 – well before the car's launch – he speaks of a maximum speed of 102/103mph achieved on the Oxford-Bicester road (then perfectly legal, although probably rather daunting) with a 0-60mph acceleration timed at 13.9sec, and 0–100 in 55.7sec! This car however 'could not be considered satisfactory' with a suspicion that it was fitted with the wrong carburettor needles. There was 'lots of pinking, vibration, brake judder and exhaust boom' – clearly not a car to be offered to the public, let alone press testers. The following four tests were even worse, with the maximum speed on one occasion down to 89mph. More satisfactory results were achieved early in 1951 with a second prototype in which the compression ratio was raised from 7:1 to 8:1, with a note that the 10–40mph time was 12.6sec instead of 13.6sec, while the maximum speed was 2.5mph better. This note also mentioned that the higher-compression car achieved better fuel economy at low speeds, but the lower-compression example was better at high speeds. It is worth noting that there was at this period a very proper concern with fuel economy, since Britain was still suffering from petrol rationing. The more economical your car, the farther you could go on your ration. The big Jaguars were not good in this respect. Tested by *The Motor*, the Mark V achieved 18.2mpg and the Mark VII, 17.6mpg, the figure dragged down both by its extra weight and by use of its higher performance.

The Mark VII body, compared with the Mark V, was distinctly modern in the sense that, in the American idiom, it abandoned running-boards and swept the front wings smoothly aft to blend with the rear. However, if you flip back and forth between front three-quarter pictures of the Mark VII and the Mark V it makes an interesting case study in the evolution of William Lyons's approach to design. Even though you can see at once that they are completely different, any attempt objectively to list the points of obvious difference, stops when you have noted that the 'pre-war' downward sweep of the Mark V wing into a vestigial running-board has given way to a properly 'integrated' series of side panels with not a running-board in sight. The other changes are subtle. The headlamp configurations, for example, are not all that different. The main headlamp units are not completely integrated within the front wings, as in so many contemporary designs. Yet here one also sees the 'Jaguar line' which was to last, especially in side view, through to the mid-1980s and the breaking, or at least the re-arrangement of the mould by the XJ40. Internally, the car was spacious, as indeed it should have been on a wheelbase of that length. It is interesting to note that even more space was created because compared with the XK120, the XK engine in the Mark VII was mounted 5in further forward. One new Mark VII feature which became almost a Jaguar tradition for many years was the division of the 17-gallon fuel capacity (the Mark V was 14 gallons) into two separate tanks, one on either side, each with its own filler and pump – fully duplicated systems!

The Mark VII was indeed generally well received and it is worth noting that according to Andrew Whyte[1] slightly more of these cars were delivered between 1951 and 1957 than the total number of XK sports cars made between 1949 and 1961. When examining the division of engineering effort, the relative importance of the saloon and sports car programmes to Jaguar's fortunes must always be borne in mind. That said, from the big saloon's arrival in 1951 until 1954, it saw little apparent attention. However, the big car was potentially capable of exploiting all the changes made to the XK engine and in 1954 there appeared the Mark VIIM, in which the compression ratio was raised to 8:1 and the power output rose to 190bhp. In other words, the Mark VII had progressed from an 'XK120' engine to an 'XK140' – although the engines were not entirely the same, since details such as SU carburettor needles and ignition timing curves were adapted to the saloon's much higher inertia. Things happened more slowly in the Mark VII. To counter the occasional complaint of 'float' and excessive roll angles leading to passenger nausea, spring rates were increased and the front anti-roll bar stiffened, but wheel and tyre sizes remained the same.

By this time too, a watershed had been crossed on the transmission front, with the offering from early 1953 of optional Borg-Warner automatic. This was almost entirely for the benefit of the US market in which the rise of the automatic could no longer be

1   Andrew Whyte, *Jaguar, the Definitive History*, Appendices

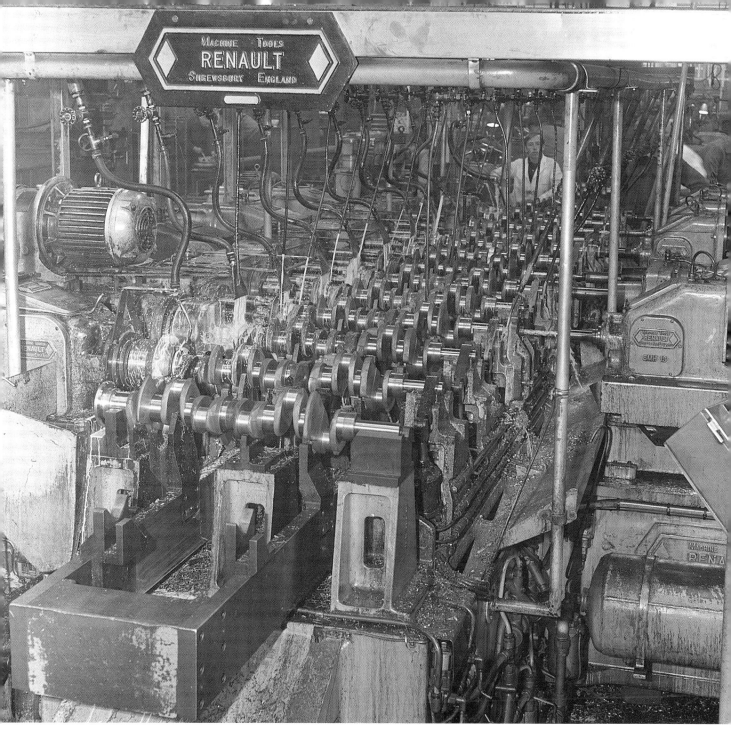

ignored, especially by a maker of large luxury saloons. By the time the big Jaguar progressed another couple of stages, automatics would become the US-market standard and manual gearboxes supplied to special order only (it would be 1956 before Jaguar offered automatic transmission to its British customers, after Borg-Warner had built a British factory in Letchworth and began production there). Borg-Warner's automatics for Jaguar were always 3-speed (although some American contemporaries, leaning on the huge torque output of their increasingly large V8 engines,

Crankshaft production at Jaguar in the late 1940s or early 1950s. It is interesting that Renault supplied the machine tools involved, even though these appear to have come from Shrewsbury!
(JDHT/Paul Skilleter)

made do with 2-speed units like GM's Powerglide for quite a long time). The experience gained with Borg-Warner automatics in the big saloons, and the demands of the US market, eventually led to similar transmissions being offered in the XK140 and the later XK150.

Meanwhile, in 1954, the Mark VII was offered with the option of overdrive on top gear, bringing the benefits of more relaxed cruising and better economy. Normally (this was a time when in theory at least, customers could choose from a range of final drives) the overdrive was combined with a lowering of the final drive ratio to 4.55:1, so that maximum speed – which remained about the same – was achieved in overdrive rather than direct top, but mid-range acceleration was improved. When combined with the extra 30bhp of the Mark VIIM this should have resulted in a worthwhile improvement in performance but somehow it didn't happen, at least if *The Motor* road test of 1955 was any guide. Mean maximum speed was 104.3mph, an improvement of less than 4mph on the older version, while the acceleration figures remained virtually the same,

Above: XK cylinder head machining at the stage of valve guide holes and seat recesses. Machining on a one-by-one, stage-by-stage basis like this would be unthinkable today even for a small-volume engine – but these were days when the ratio of labour to machinery cost was very different. (JDHT/Paul Skilleter)

Right: Setting up the XK engine depended on achieving the correct valve clearance by inserting 'biscuit' shims beneath the bucket tappets – requiring a plentiful supply of accurately measured shims, at that time a manual task ... (JDHT/Paul Skilleter)

THE XK BECOMES THE STANDARD ENGINE

with the VIIM needing 19.5sec to cover the standing-start quarter-mile compared with 19.3sec for its predecessor. The weights as tested were near identical, so one has to assume either that the 1952 test car was a particularly good one or that the 1955 example was below par. There must have been some discussion at Jaguar but so far, no evidence has emerged from the archive. At least the overall fuel consumption improved to 18.8mpg, so the overdrive proved its worth in that respect.

The process of steady improvement continued and 1957 saw the launch of the Mark VIII with 210bhp, and thus from the engine point of view related to the XK150 as the Mark VIIM had been to the XK140 (in a further XK150 parallel, the Mark VIII also abandoned a 'split' windscreen in favour of a one-piece design). It was, nonetheless, something of an

interim measure because 1959 saw the arrival of the more definitive Mark IX which brought three major engineering advances rather than the additional chomework which had been a Mark VIII feature. Just as in the last of the XK150 sports cars, the engine capacity was increased to 3.8 litres, enabling the maximum power output to be modestly raised to 220bhp without any sacrifice in driveability. The other two significant changes were the adoption of disc brakes all round, finally overcoming the limitations of drum systems, and of power-assisted steering, increasingly well-tried and established in Jaguar's lucrative US market and thus incorporated more or less by popular demand. The gearing of the steering system was reduced so that only three and a half turns of the wheel were needed to get from one lock to the other.

The brakes were generally admired, as well they might have been, for their consistency of performance and fade resistance, but road testers encountered a new phenomenon, that of 'knock-back' in which, during cornering, the pads were pushed well clear of the discs. This resulted in an alarming split-second of free brake pedal travel before anything happened, the next time the brakes were applied. The effect was upsetting rather than serious, and remedies were soon found. The brakes needed to be good, because the evidence is that the 3.8 engine with its usefully higher

Above: Anxiety over operating refinement quickly led Jaguar to balance the entire crankshaft assembly dynamically, including the torsional vibration damper and flywheel. The original idea had been to balance each component in isolation prior to assembly. (JDHT/Paul Skilleter)

Right: In the early days of production, crankshafts were still fettled and rough-balanced by the simplest possible means. Simple – but a task for a skilled operator. In the 1950s, Coventry had enough such people to make this approach viable, but it couldn't last. (JDHT/Paul Skilleter)

THE XK BECOMES THE STANDARD ENGINE

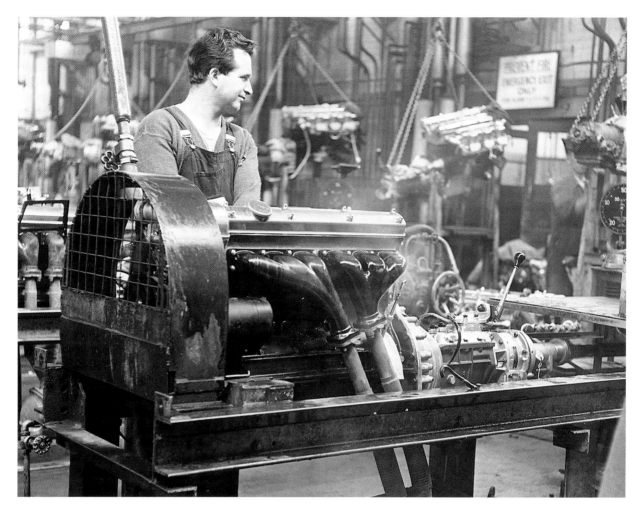

torque gave a genuine boost to the performance in all respects. The highest reliably recorded mean maximum speed seems to have been *The Motor*'s 113.5mph, in a car which also reached 60mph in exactly 11sec. However, there was a payoff when it came to fuel consumption which *The Motor* testers edged down to 13.5mpg. This was not good, even at a time when petrol rationing was a thing of the past and the stuff was fairly cheap. At this remove, one shudders to think what the hydrocarbon and carbon monoxide emissions must have been in some circumstances.

The 'big Jaguars' had enjoyed a good run for ten years, always technically in the shadow of the sports cars and the successful racers, but making a vital contribution commercially, with over 47,000 examples delivered from the first Mark VII to the last Mark IX. To an increasing extent, as time went on, they were hamstrung by their separate-chassis construction and by 1960 it was clear, just as it was

with the XK150, that a lighter, stiffer car with the same or better level of performance could be created by throwing away the chassis and taking loads through the body shell. The solutions adopted by Jaguar in these two cases, though, were rather different.

As an aside, it is well worth noting that in 1960, Jaguar purchased Daimler from its parent, BSA. Thus in a way full circle was turned, since Jaguar now operated out of Browns Lane which had once been a Daimler factory. With this purchase (for £3.4 million!) Jaguar inherited the Radford works which were to become a principal engine manufacturing and machine shop, freeing extra space at Browns Lane, while on the product side it brought with it four cars, the 101 Majestic, the Majestic Major and its DR450 limousine derivative, and the SP250 sports car. It also brought three engines, an ancient OHV 3.8-litre 6-cylinder (for the Majestic) and two OHV V8s from the drawing-board of Edward

Turner, a nominal 4½-litre – actually 4,561cc – unit producing 220bhp for the Majestic Major, and a 2½-litre (2,548cc) unit delivering 140bhp for the SP250.

Rationalisation was called for but not immediate wholesale destruction. The Majestic and its ancient engine was the first to go, in 1962, while the SP250 made an uncomfortable bedfellow for the XK150, let alone the E-type, and was gone by 1964. The Majestic Majors had a following and a certain presence – the hefty saloon with its 114in wheelbase was renowned for making most sports cars look foolish on the Silverstone circuit during the annual Guild of Motoring Writers' Test Day – and they were retained until 1968, together with the big V8 engine which was greatly admired but which, sadly, was virtually hand-manufactured at great cost, without the aid of dedicated production tooling. In some ways these cars, especially the limousine, sat well with the existing Jaguar saloon range but for the 1970s, they were replaced by a single Jaguar-derived model (Chapter 8). The other Daimler 'survivor' was the smaller and more modern V8 engine which, with the demise of the SP250, found its way into a version of the new, compact Jaguar saloon first introduced in 1955 (Chapter 6). This ensured the V8 enjoyed a useful, if hardly mainstream future.

Left: The original Jaguar XK production practice was to start-up each engine as it emerged from the line and run it briefly on town gas (safer than petrol in a confined workshop). The check was applied to 100 per cent of production. Today, the quality of engine build is taken so much for granted that the first time most engines fire is at the very end of the vehicle production line … (JDHT/Paul Skilleter)

Above: The Mark IX was the last of the big Jaguar saloons to have a separate chassis. Its successor would move to unitary construction, following in the footsteps of the 2.4/3.4 series. (JDHT)

5 Racing
technology

The XK120 may have happened almost by accident but it soon began winning races and rallies, its successes now exhaustively documented. For a while the Jaguar attitude seemed to be that if owners wanted to compete, that was up to them and if they won, that was all to the good; but there were too many keen competition engineers in Jaguar for that attitude to survive. Most of its top engineers had at some stage been directly involved with motor racing or with developing engines and chassis for racing.

One thing all these people, including William Lyons himself and William Heynes as his engineering chief, were conscious of was that even in the 1950s, 'sports car' competition was edging away from carefully prepared road cars and towards specialised racers. If Jaguar was going to go racing seriously, there was only one sensible target and that was the Le Mans 24 Hours, where a good performance, let alone a victory, did more good than acres of conventional advertising. And there was no way the XK120, however carefully prepared, was going to win Le Mans. To stand any chance of victory, the company needed a car which looked as though it might be a stripped-down XK120 but which, underneath, would be far more modern and in particular, much lighter. Work therefore proceeded in what amounted to a new car under the designation XK120C (for Competition) whose only carried-over features from the XK120 itself were a general similarity of line, the front suspension design, and the XK engine. Even the principal chassis dimensions were different, the XK120C wheelbase being a full 6in shorter than that of the 120.

The key to lightness lay in structural efficiency, and even more specifically in the stiffness of the body between the points at which the front and rear suspension loads, including the driving and braking loads, were carried into the body. This provided one good reason, if any were needed, for throwing out the rear semi-elliptic 'cart' springs and locating the live rear axle by means which did not involve a pair of highly stressed mounting points many inches aft of the axle centre-line. If an independent suspension was even considered at this stage, there is no surviving indication, but there is no doubt that a de Dion arrangement was considered.

The structure was indeed stiff and efficient although it would probably not please a modern designer with access to a good computer. The approach is two-dimensional rather than three, but

the triangulation of frames is good and the relationship between tubes and diaphragm bulkheads is clever. The tubular side frames, the fabricated bulkheads and the floor, consisting mainly of pierced channel-section members, certainly created a central structure of satisfactory torsional stiffness. The forward extensions of the side frames carried the engine mountings together with those of the front wishbones. As in the original XK120, the front springs were longitudinal torsion bars, thus feeding their loads mainly into the very stiff front bulkhead area. A 'front face' was formed in the plane which accepted the loads from the front dampers and also housed the steering box and rack of the rack-and-pinion steering.

For that important back end, Heynes arrived at an interesting arrangement which not only fed all the loads into the rear bulkhead of the torsionally stiff centre section but also compensated for the tendency of the torque effect to transfer load between the driven wheels, encouraging wheelspin and 'tramp'. Heynes's elegant-looking solution was to use a single transverse torsion bar, anchored at its centre, as the springing medium with a trailing arm at each outer end to provide fore-and-aft axle location, while sideways location was provided by a rather serpentine-looking Panhard rod running from the left of the rear bulkhead to a bracket beneath the axle on the right. Immediately above this bracket was another from which a reaction arm ran directly forwards to the rear bulkhead. This reaction arm resisted rotation (nose-up or down) of the axle but the cleverness of the arrangement was that its asymmetry enabled the force created by torque reaction of the axle to cancel out – or at least, to greatly reduce – the normal load transfer effect between the wheels, so improving traction. Although Heynes may not even have thought about it, it also avoided the risk of a conventional A-bracket – locating the axle both sideways and against torque – imposing loads which would distort the final drive casing and lead to oil loss (a danger of which some later designers fell foul). The only penalty, a very minor one, was that the rear roll centre, determined by the pivot point of the reaction

The C-type was purpose-engineered to win Le Mans, and duly did so. The XK engine was part of the formula, but body and chassis engineering were far more advanced than in the XK sports cars, even though a live axle was retained. By any modern standard, the power output with which success was achieved was modest. (Jaguar)

link, was not symmetrical; but on a racing circuit where, by definition, there is 360° more right than left turn per lap, even this might be considered an advantage. As an additional bonus, careful detail design of the linkage enabled the suspension to be adjusted so as to optimise the handling. Finally, massive telescopic dampers fed their loads directly into the upper corners of the very stiff rear bulkhead. Everything aft of that – if one excepts the huge (182-litre) fuel tank sitting where the luggage would go in a road car – was essentially cosmetic, or at least aerodynamic, and attached to the main structure only by four bolts.

This structure, driveline and running gear, clad in a light aluminium body (the main structure was steel, the welding of aluminium at that time still being considered a black art), weighed-in at less than 2,100lb compared with around 2,900lb for the

RACING TECHNOLOGY

The D-type was the radical successor to the C-type, with monocoque centre section and great attention paid to aerodynamics, although with the benefit of hindsight, they may not have been as good as is usually assumed. The stalwart XK engine continued to supply the power but its ultimate potential was always hampered by its long stroke which limited maximum revs, even with a steel crank and other modifications. (Jaguar)

standard XK120 roadster. This was good news in every respect, not only for acceleration and cornering ability but also for the brakes. Add the superior aerodynamics, which Jaguar suggested had reduced the power needed to sustain 100mph from 75bhp to 60bhp, dial in the additional power of the race-tuned XK which, with 9:1 compression ratio and an optimised cylinder head, delivered 210bhp, and the result was a spectacularly fast car for its day. Given reliability, the XK120C always stood an excellent chance of winning Le Mans in 1951, and sure enough it did, even though two of the three cars went out with oil system failure, blamed on the rupture of copper pipe flanges which were then replaced with steel.

As so often in the history of sports car racing, the regulations of the time stipulated, after a fashion, that cars should be 'production'. Accordingly, Jaguar prepared to put the XK120C into small-volume production, although the process was delayed by the move to Browns Lane and, it is claimed, by material shortages during the Korean War period. Eventually, however, 53 cars were produced and sold. There was no cheating: apart from the XK engines being in a slightly gentler state of tune, delivering 200bhp, any of these cars could in theory have won the 1951 Le Mans event. Cars were even provided for test by the top magazines, *The Motor* registering a mean maximum speed of 143.7mph, a 0–60mph time of 8.1sec and the relatively modest overall fuel consumption of 16mpg. The magazine complained that the weather during its maximum speed runs, on the already famous Jabbeke straight in Belgium, was 'of a very low order indeed' but that sadly, the road could only be closed for two days! More worryingly perhaps, the maximum retardation achieved in the brake test was only 0.8g, and this for a pedal effort of 125lb.

The production cars might well have fared better in the 1952 event than did the works team, for a misguided essay in aerodynamics, a longer nose and radically revised tail section in search of a lower drag

coefficient and higher speed on the Mulsanne straight, played havoc with the cooling system. Why, one still asks, was it not picked up in testing, given that Jaguar ran extensively at Silverstone before the event? As a result, all three cars retired early in the race. For 1953 the cars reverted to the successful 1951 bodywork, but lightened, while in other respects, there were substantial modifications. Under the bonnet, the engine now breathed through three twin-choke Weber carburettors but the power output was still, at least supposedly, only 220bhp. The rear suspension was revised, the fuel was now contained in an aircraft-type rubber bag tank, and most important of all was the 'secret weapon', the six-pot power-assisted Dunlop disc brakes, which meant that conservative braking distances for the sake of avoiding fade were a thing of the past, and led to slightly misguided talk about 'being able to brake 200 metres deeper into corners'. The result (Jaguar first, second and fourth) was crushing.

After the great success of 1953, there was a strong feeling at Jaguar that to continue winning 'their' race, a better car than the C-type (as the XK120C had logically become known) would be needed. From the engineering point of view, the ways forward were obvious: reduce the weight and the aerodynamic drag still further, increase the power still further – and refine those wonderful disc brakes. There was some debate – and some competitive testing – about the need for such a 'full-house' solution but it was resolved in favour of an all-new car which was, naturally, christened the D-type.

In the new car, the weight was reduced through the use of a new and even more efficient structure. This consisted of a semi-monocoque centre-section with a tubular front extension and, just like the C-type, a 'tacked-on' and essentially unstressed rear. The centre section was not a true monocoque, which is a pure shell, with no discontinuities, in which stresses are evenly distributed in all directions. It was however a carefully designed and fabricated 'tub' of light alloy, closely resembling a section of aircraft fuselage, in which every panel contributed to strength and above all to stiffness. The front frame carried, as in the C-type, the main engine mountings and the front wishbone mountings. The rear suspension of the C-type was modified, and instead of the Panhard rod for sideways axle location there were now two angled lower tubes meeting beneath the final drive, while four trailing arms, 'blade'-type so as not to create upsetting transverse loads, now located the axle fore

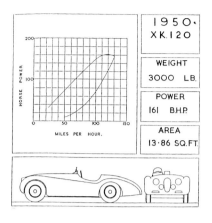

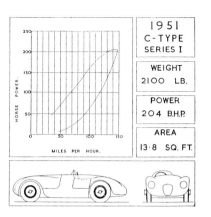

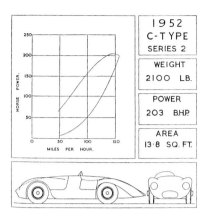

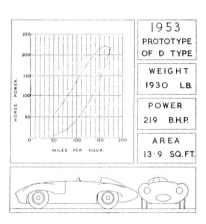

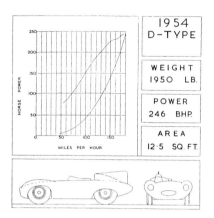

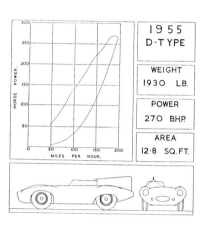

Left: The XK-SS was a 'road-going' version of the D-type, but in fact, all Jaguar's 1950s Le Mans winners were road-legal and were driven to France from Coventry. Its structure was similar and so, naturally, was the now highly developed XK engine. Many production XK-SS were caught in the great fire of 1957 which destroyed much of the early Browns Lane site. (Jaguar)

Above: A chart, originally prepared by Bill Heynes himself, showing power output and power consumption curves for the standard XK120 and for five competition cars from the 1951 C-type to the final 1955 D-type. The power requirement is crucially influenced by aerodynamic drag above 100mph or so. Gearing is the other major consideration: note how in each case the power-required curve intersects the power-available curve just after its peak. In theory this is the result of under-gearing, but in practical terms it means full power can be used for a respectable part of the time – so long as drivers can be trusted to observe the red line! (JDHT/Paul Skilleter)

and aft and in rotation while also providing some extra roll stiffness. The lower two arms were connected to the transverse torsion bar spring, which was retained, while the upper ones served as radius arms resisting torque reaction. Astonishingly, the tyres were still 6.50-16, as they had been from the earliest days of the C-type, although they were low-profile radials from Dunlop and the rims had been increased in width from 5.0in to 5.5in.

The question of aerodynamic drag was tackled by Malcolm Sayer, recruited from what was then the Bristol Aeroplane Company. He had already penned the C-type's shape, and for the new car he insisted on lowering the bonnet line, something which could only be achieved by dry-sumping, allowing the engine to be lowered by most of the depth of a conventional sump. Dry-sumping also allowed for a substantially greater oil capacity, since oil consumption between the minimum laps at Le Mans had become a serious concern. The engine was also installed at a canted angle, although its top-end width meant this did not in itself reduce the overall height.

Just as concerned with stability as he was with drag, Sayer also called for the rearward extension of the driver's headrest into a vestigial fin, even though it added to the wetted area and caused a small drag increase. Also, although the nose air intake looked exceedingly small, Sayer placed it at the point of maximum pressure and thus ensured that cooling flow would indeed be sufficient (although it is not recorded how unhappy he is likely to have been at the installation of a single driving lamp slap in the centre of this intake, shown in some photographs of the D-type prototype; it doesn't appear in any subsequent picture of the car!).

As for the engine, everything possible was done to ensure the survival of its bottom end at peak operating speed. The usually quoted output for the 'production' D-type – there really was a production line, one picture has least 14 cars visible – was 250bhp at 6,000rpm, and long life called not only for a nitrided steel crankshaft but also for high-strength big-end bolts, among other measures. Then again, the power output of the car which won at Le Mans in the tragic year of 1955 is given as 285bhp at only 5,750rpm, with the aid of a revised cylinder head with a larger included angle between the inlet and exhaust valves. In the end, the optimum layout was settled upon as inlet valves inclined at 35° from the cylinder centre-line, and exhaust valves at 40°, creating the so-called 35–40 head.

The mystery of power outputs is compounded by the fact that most authorities quote the power output of the works cars for the 1956 event at Le Mans as 275bhp, and this with Lucas fuel injection replacing carburettors. The race turned out badly for the works team, since two of the three works cars were eliminated by Paul Frère's crash in the opening laps. The third was delayed by a cracked injection pipe although in reaching sixth place it proved itself easily the fastest car on the track. However, the race was still won for Jaguar by an 'old' car entered by the Ecurie Ecosse. It was left to the Ecurie to wind up the D-type's Le Mans career on a high note in 1957. On this occasion the winning car was running a fuel-injected works 3.8-litre engine delivering a claimed 285bhp at 5,750rpm, enabling it to outrun the remaining D-types which were still Weber-carburetted 3.4s; but altogether the D-types claimed a clean sweep of the first four places in the race.

That triumph to all intents and purposes marked the end of the D-type's career and of Jaguar's direct interest in racing. New regulations threatened to impose a 3-litre capacity limit for sports car racing. According to Andrew Whyte, 87 D-types were built in all, including the works cars, plus a further 16 which were turned into the rather ugly XK-SS series during 1957 – an odd way of using up left-over stock, some might think.

Although it no longer ran a works team, Jaguar certainly developed 3-litre power units to comply with the revised regulations, and prepared engines for the various entrants who raced at Le Mans under the 3-litre regulations, notably Hamilton in 1958, Lister, the Ecurie Ecosse from 1958 through 1960, and ultimately Briggs Cunningham with the E2A in 1960, whose engine achieved 294bhp at 6,750rpm. The engineering archive contains one report on a 1960 test run on one such 3-litre XK with dimensions 85mm bore by 88mm stroke, for a capacity of 2,996cc, running the 35–40 cylinder head with high-lift (7/16in) cams and Lucas fuel injection. This engine peaked at 304bhp; almost as significantly the peak came at 6,500rpm, because with the stroke reduced from 106mm to only 88mm, piston speeds and bottom-end loads were considerably reduced and the engine could be revved higher. But the highest BMEP ever recorded in an XK, according to the archive, was the 207lb/sq in seen (again in 1960) at 4,000rpm in a 3.8-litre 'Gold Head' with ⅜in cams, again with a Lucas injection system.

Good though these figures were, experience had taught Jaguar to be very wary of the Lucas system. The archive contains a copy of a letter from Bill Heynes to a Lucas manager, dated 22 May 1962: 'I am very concerned that we have over the past six months made no advance in the use of Lucas Fuel Injection … The position remains that the chief advantage of fuel injection is to enable us to use an exaggerated valve timing or port design that cannot suitably be covered by carburettor equipment, especially in respect to the low end of the power curve.' The record further shows that Jaguar was at that time contemplating a combination of Lucas PI and the 35/40 head to offer a production car with a reliable 280bhp, but nothing came of it and the Lucas system eventually appeared elsewhere, in the Triumph TR6 and 2.5PI.

As for Jaguar's racing efforts, they went on the back burner for many a year although, given the company's history and the inclinations of many of its engineers, they never ceased completely. Some effort was still devoted to evolving power units like the fuel-injected all-aluminium 3.8-litre used in the competition E-type from 1963, an engine which delivered a best output 344bhp at 6,500rpm. But the only truly major racing project of the 1960s famously emerged from the rather strange decision to develop the XJ13, a mid-engined design powered by a 4-cam, 5-litre version of the V12 engine. As is well known, a single car was built but it was not long into its test programme when Sir William Lyons – as he had been since knighthood in 1956 – ordered a halt, as it was already clear the car had no future in the rapidly evolving world of sports car racing at that time. Norman Dewis once told the author how the development team continued virtually to smuggle the car out of Browns Lane on Sundays and take it illicitly to the MIRA test track for further work. Inevitably, Sir William came to hear about this and Norman was hauled in for a lecture. 'He gave me one hell of a roasting,' Dewis remembered, 'and then he said: "Well? How did it go, anyway?"' It had gone pretty well by most yardsticks, but it made no difference to the shelving of the project.

From an engineering point of view the XJ13 was advanced in some respects but 'pre-ground-effect' in its design, one of the things which would have made life very difficult for it. Its construction owed something to the D and E-types although, of course, the engine was in a different place. Like the Cosworth DFV, the V12 in the XJ13 was a stressed member, capable of carrying the rear suspension loads through to the tub.

One reason why the XJ13 remained a dark secret for so long was the length of time it took to perfect the production V12 engine. Jaguar management suffered a fear that widespread knowledge of a V12's existence would kill the market for the XK-engined E-type. When, eventually in 1971, the V12 was ready for announcement, initially in the E-type, it was proposed that a film should be made of the sensational-looking old racer that never was. The car was nearly written off in the process as Norman Dewis recalls that towards the end of a full day of filming, he was persuaded to do 'just one more run' and suffered a tyre failure on the MIRA high-speed track banking, rebounding from the safety barrier at the parapet and rolling the car into a ball of metal in the infield. Norman emerged virtually unhurt and the car was eventually rebuilt – if not re-created – by body maker Abbey Panels and Jaguar apprentices. The author, then a frequent visitor to MIRA as an *Autocar* road tester, can vouch for the fact that the terrifying skid-marks from this incident were still visible weeks later.

In any event, what emerged from Jaguar's racing efforts? Neither Sir William Lyons nor Bill Heynes ever denied that the objective was favourable publicity, the kind that came with winning. Some manufacturers treat racing activities as a hard but effective school for their engineers: ('In Formula 1,' Honda's former Chairman Nobuhiko Kawamoto once told the author, 'there are no excuses, only results.'). Jaguar never took that view as most of the senior people in its racing programme had already established strong technical records in competition. For the most part they made their contributions not quite in their spare time, but in addition to their 'legitimate' jobs at Browns Lane. In the days of the C and D-types it was always a small but nimble team, capable of drawing conclusions and applying lessons very quickly. But the racing programme always consumed talent and money which might have been devoted elsewhere, and when favourable results with their sales-boosting publicity could no longer be more-or-less guaranteed, that was the finish.

In pure engineering terms, the C and D-type programmes showed what could (then) be achieved with a surprisingly simple product and a limited amount of power, so long as the objectives were clearly laid down and understood. Success came despite rather than because of the XK engine which, as we have seen in this and previous chapters, was limited by its design in the extent to which power could be wrung from it – although admittedly it was mostly very reliable and provided strong mid-range torque. A great deal of the credit goes to weight-saving design, clever but sound chassis work, excellent aerodynamics at a time when it was an under-appreciated virtue, and of course the emergence of those disc brakes, which Jaguar alone had the foresight to develop in conjunction with Dunlop. Norman Dewis in particular devoted enormous testing time and effort to taking the idea from the stage of contemplating a road version of an aircraft disc brake, to that of a practical (if still expensive) race-winning system.

Jaguar would, eventually try, and even win Le Mans, again, but that would take place in another world and many years later, and is the story is told in a later chapter.

6 The Morse Code

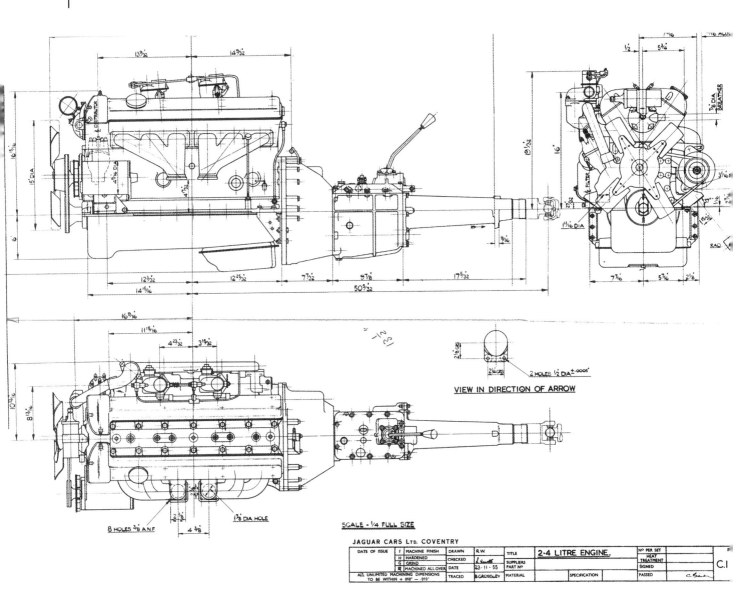

8 HOLES ³⁄₈ A.N.F   1⅞ DIA HOLE

VIEW IN DIRECTION OF ARROW

SCALE - ¼ FULL SIZE

JAGUAR CARS LTD. COVENTRY

DATE OF ISSUE	F	MACHINE FINISH	DRAWN	R.W.	TITLE	2·4 LITRE ENGINE.	N° PER SET		P
	H	HARDENED	CHECKED				HEAT TREATMENT		C.1
	G	GRIND	DATE	23·11·55	SUPPLIERS PART N°		SIGNED		
	R	MACHINED ALL OVER							
ALL UNLIMITED MACHINING DIMENSIONS TO BE WITHIN + ·010″ — ·010″			TRACED	B.GROSSLEY	MATERIAL		SPECIFICATION	PASSED	

In the mid-1950s there was one product missing from the Jaguar line-up: a compact saloon, of the type which had once been represented, one might argue, by the 1½-litre which had been made before and just after the war. The 1½-litre had indeed made up the majority of production until its withdrawal, with the rest of the pre-war range, upon the introduction of the Mark V in 1949. It had no successor at that time because, unlike the 2½-litre and 3½-litre engines for which Jaguar now held the tooling, the smaller 4-cylinder engine still had to be bought from Standard. With the intention to standardise on the XK engine for the post-war range, there was no place in the plan for a smaller car.

Yet by the early 1950s, it was becoming clear that if Jaguar wished to use its new base at Browns Lane for substantial expansion – and William Lyons certainly wanted to – then it would have to broaden its customer base. The only realistic way to do that was to develop a smaller, lighter car which would sell for less money to more people. One of Lyons's major concerns in drawing up his outline specification was that the car would have to maintain Jaguar's high-performance reputation, which meant above all that it must have a maximum speed of at least 100mph.

Several engineering conclusions emerged immediately. The first was that a smaller car would need a smaller engine. Here there was a choice. Sitting on the shelf was the 4-cylinder, 95bhp, 2-litre XK which would have powered the stillborn XK100 sports car. Would it do for a small saloon? If not, the 6-cylinder XK would need to be made smaller. The evidence (see Chapter 2) is that the 4-cylinder was actively studied for a while but rejected for two reasons. The first was simple. It would take Jaguar too far down-market. It had already become an 'XK company' and the 4-cylinder would be out of sympathy with that image. Second and more important, the car which began to emerge from studies was substantially smaller than the Mark VII but still not all that small – the 120in wheelbase of the big saloon left a lot of scope for shrinkage without coming down to the level of a 'family' car of that era. Thus the 2-litre 4-cylinder engine would be too small to cope anyway, not only in terms of power output but also – given the likely weight of the new, smaller saloon – of torque also. Consequently it was not even left on the shelf, but consigned to the museum.

So how was the XK to be shrunk? There was only one sensible way to do it. Reducing the bore of the already substantially under-square 3.4 would create a monster. The crankshaft stroke would have to be shortened, which would have the advantage of reducing piston speeds and bottom-end loads, and hopefully of making the engine even more refined. The choice seems to have fallen fairly quickly on a 28 per cent reduction from the 106mm stroke of the 3.4 to 76.5mm, creating a nominally 2.5-litre engine (2,483cc) which, for marketing reasons, would go into a car designated 2.4, to emphasise the link with the 3.4-litre XK. It was certainly significant that at a stroke – a short stroke, indeed – the XK had been turned from an engine which was well under-square in the old tradition into a comfortably over-square unit whose dimensions do not look out of place today. It is interesting, at this remove, to read *The Motor*'s comment, in its first 2.4 road test, about the engine 'having exceptional piston area in relation to its size'; the fixation with piston area, in a generation whose thinking had been conditioned by the RAC taxable power rating system, took a long time to die. That test confirmed that the maximum speed target had been comfortably met (101.5mph mean maximum, in overdrive) with acceleration to match that of the Mark VII (0-60mph in 14.4sec). Overall fuel consumption, at 24.4mpg, was around 30 per cent better than that of the big car, if hardly admirable in absolute terms.

Another unavoidable engineering decision was that the new car would need to employ unitary construction, for the first time in a Jaguar. It was not simply that the entire industry was moving in that direction. It was not even that unitary construction would enable the new car to be made substantially lighter, therefore with high performance even with the 2.5-litre engine and with better economy too. If the car was to be made in the kind of numbers being planned, the unitary approach was the only one which would allow bodies to be produced at a sufficiently high rate. To be economical, the new car

A dimensioned three-view drawing of the 2.4-litre XK engine. All the measurements are interesting, yet potentially the most interesting of all, the distance from crankshaft centre line to cylinder block face, is not to be seen. Having created this much smaller-capacity unit by shortening the stroke (narrowing the bore would have been ridiculous, creating a grossly under-square monster) Jaguar also substantially lowered the block height, saving a bit of weight and allowing shorter connecting rods to be used. Yet the only time the lower overall engine height was really exploited was not in the small saloon, but in the E1A prototype of the E-type. (JDHT/Paul Skilleter)

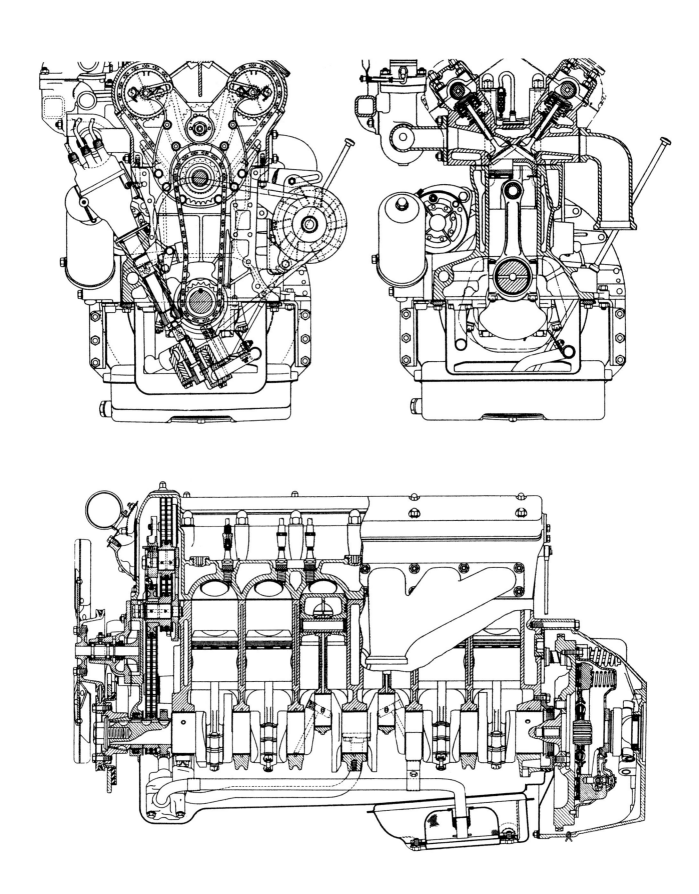

Above left: Cross-section views through the 2.4-litre engine show not only the lower deck and shorter connecting rods, but other interesting details, such as, the chain drive to the twin overhead camshafts with intermediate pinion, and the skew drive to the distributor and oil pump. While the cylinder head looks good from a gas-flow point of view, the rest of the induction system is less admirable. The shorter stroke meant the 2.4-litre engine could be revved higher than its parent 3.4-litre, but its Achilles' heel was the base of the block which was level with the crankshaft centre-line resulting in oil-sealing problems, among other drawbacks. (JDHT/Paul Skilleter)

Left: The lengthwise cross-section of the 2.4-litre engine emphasises its close resemblance to other members of the XK family despite the shorter stroke (which, as can be seen, called for a raised piston crown in order to maintain compression ratio, creating what would be seen today as an appalling crevice volume for the creation of HC emissions). The much wider main bearing and coolant passage between cylinders 3 and 4 is clearly visible. This was the feature which enabled the 4.2-litre version of the long-stroke engine to be created when the bore centres were re-spaced at five equal intervals. (JDHT/Paul Skilleter)

Above: The original 2.4 was meant to re-introduce a smaller Jaguar saloon, for a market abandoned when production of the old 1½-litre ceased. It was not all that small, with a 107in wheelbase, and it used a short-stroke version of the (by now) well-tried XK 6-cylinder engine, rather than reverting to a 4-cylinder. Equally important, it was the first Jaguar to use unitary construction – fine in principle, but creating a lot of problems in practice because of poor body-build quality control. (JDHT)

would need to achieve at least 10,000 units per year – double the rate of the Mark VII at its best – and hopefully it would do substantially better. The idea of creating a production facility to make 10,000 per year of a completely new separate chassis, to be clothed with an unstressed body which would have to come from Pressed Steel anyway, was a nonsense. Much better to create a unitary body and leave the whole thing to Pressed Steel, so that operations at Browns Lane would be confined to painting and simplified (without the chassis) final assembly.

As for the size of the car, it was decided that it needed to be more than a foot shorter than the Mark VII, as well as substantially narrower and lower. As the layout developed, with Lyons working on the styling as always, the 'compact saloon' emerged with a wheelbase of 107.4in. Since the wheelbase largely determines the 'real' size of a car and the amount of space inside, this meant the new model would be compared with such contemporaries as the Rover 75, the Humber Hawk, the big Morris Isis and even, in size if nothing else, with the biggest contemporary British Ford, the Zephyr. But Jaguar was aiming at a different market from the volume manufacturers, at people who would, 15 years later, be looking for an 'executive car'.

As a complete car, the new model ended up 181in long overall, 67in wide and 57.5in high. To put it into Jaguar context, that was 15.5in shorter than the Mark VII, 6.5in narrower and 5.5in lower – a substantial shrinkage by any standard and more than enough to ensure the new car would not 'poach' customers from the existing one. The styling was accepted as handsome and distinctly Jaguar, complete with fairings which filled the rear wheel arches. The one odd and slightly jarring feature was that the original 2.4 tapered very noticeably towards the rear, with a front track of 54.7in but with a rear track of just 50in. Alongside the saloon, there existed at one stage, mock-ups for a 2-door coupé derivative of the 2.4, one of which subsequently had its roof and rear pillars removed to see how a convertible might have looked. While the former would have added further headaches to the unhappy relationship between Jaguar and Pressed Steel, the latter ought to have proved too frightening. To a team which had only just created its first unitary body, the implications of then chopping off the roof would surely have been too much to bear.

The body construction was in no sense unusual, being based on a 'platform' with channel-section longerons, cross-members and sill sections welded to it to form box sections. To this platform was attached the front wheel inner arch and scuttle assembly and the rear assembly – wheel arches, rear bulkhead and seat pan. Commentators of the time, still coming to terms with the new approach, made little mention of the importance of the pillars in transmitting loads or of the roof in contributing to torsional stiffness although a glance at the 2.4 shows that the B-pillars in particular were substantial by modern standards.

However, the body certainly was lighter, and the car as a whole emerged with a kerb weight of around 2,800lb compared with the 3,864lb of the Mark VII. In other words, the ratio of weights was not very different from the ratio of engine capacities, suggesting that acceleration performance would be of the same order. As for achieving the required 100mph maximum speed, that too was assisted by the car's reasonable aerodynamics and much smaller frontal area.

The XK engine in the new car was not merely shorter in stroke by 29.5mm, a good deal more than an inch, as this alone would have called for longer connecting rods, but in fact, Jaguar went the other way, with the result that the block height was reduced all the way from 11.5in to 8.85in, making the unit usefully more compact and slightly stiffer. All important machining could still be carried out on the same tools, so the economy of scale was considerable. This was really the point at which the XK became a major production engine, with output running at a rate sufficient to support production of at least 20,000 cars a year. The short-stroke engine used Solex rather than SU carburettors and the initial power output was quoted as 112bhp at 5,750rpm, making it even clearer that the 4-cylinder engine simply would not have been up to the job. The engine drove through the familiar 4-speed Moss gearbox and the initial choice of final drive ratio was 4.55:1, allowing for the fact that the 2.4 had smaller wheels than the Mark VII (the standard size was 6.40-15in). Quite soon in the car's career overdrive would be offered as an option, operating on top gear only, and eventually – moving with the times – a 3-speed Borg-Warner automatic option would also appear.

The 2.4 was radically different in the chassis department as well as in its body structure. Bill Heynes was well aware that a drawback of the unitary body was the relative ease with which mechanical and road noise could be transmitted into the body shell, without having to pass through a chassis frame and a set of body-to-chassis mountings which could be tuned to take out vibrations which might lead to body panel resonation. For this reason Heynes abandoned his well-tried system of double wishbone front suspension with longitudinal torsion bars, which was serving well in the Mark VII and the XK120 as well as in the C and D-types. He felt it would be difficult to feed loads from the rear end of the torsion bar into the unitary body – just about where the scuttle would be mounted – and at the same time keeping things quiet. Therefore, while retaining double wishbones (although of a completely new and more satisfactory geometry), he went for conventional coil springs and mounted the entire front suspension on a fabricated steel sub-frame, in turn mounted to the body via flexible bushes which could be tuned to prevent the transmission of the most annoying road-generated frequencies. Thus began an engineering approach which would be a key to future success, not least in the XJ6 and its successors. The hydraulic dampers were co-axial with the springs and mounted into the sub-frame's spring turrets.

At the rear of the car, Heynes went for an extremely unusual layout using cantilevered semi-elliptic leaf springs – in other words the front and centre of each spring was mounted to the body while the axle was carried on the extreme rear. In theory, the centre of each spring was clamped (with rubber interleaving) and loads were fed into the body at the front end where there was even more rubber. By these means, plus the use of rubber insulation within the actual axle-to-spring attachments at the rear, Heynes hoped to keep out any really objectionable road noise, and the design meant the springs did not intrude into the luggage or back seat space. The rear suspension was completed by radius arms to locate the axle against torque rotation, a Panhard rod to locate it sideways, and angled hydraulic dampers connected the wheel hubs to the rear bulkhead.

With the benefit of half a century of hindsight the whole rear suspension arrangement looks quite frightening from an NVH (noise, vibration and harshness) point of view, with nine distinct pathways via which disturbance could feed into the unitary structure – two spring mountings per side, two radius-arm mountings, two upper damper mountings, and one Panhard rod attachment, all in different places, with some of them – those of the forward spring mountings and the upper damper attachments – almost guaranteed to cause trouble. At that time, it must be said, the whole business of NVH and its relationship with unitary structures was still being

sorted out and the ability of noise, like water, to seek out any point of weakness was not fully appreciated. The benchmarks did not exist.

At least when viewed primarily as a suspension the layout worked well, enabling the 2.4 and its successors to become, for many years, successful and respected competitors in saloon car racing. As for the odd narrowness of the rear track, that was partly to achieve the 'tear-drop' shape which was the basis of William Lyons' styling approach, but also represented a deliberate attempt to reduce understeer at a time when it was felt that customers with a sporting approach to driving – which was one of the things that rather summed-up the target audience – wanted to feel that the back end was actually 'doing something'. Whether it was really best to achieve this by deliberately reducing the rear roll stiffness – which is the primary result of narrowing the track – is open to debate. *The Motor*'s road test comments were that '… the handling of the car, although sensitive to tyre pressures, is very good despite the need to turn the wheel four-and-a-half turns between locks … the cornering power is very high with only a trace of understeer.' The idea that consistent understeer in moderation was the characteristic best suited to the average driver had yet to penetrate, either among the opinion-formers or in Jaguar's chassis development department. The 2.4 steering was Burman recirculating-ball, as in the XK120, but Lockheed provided its new Brakemaster braking system, still drums all round although all-round discs would soon become an option, and a worthwhile one.

As soon as the 2.4 was established, the inevitable question was whether the taller-block 3.4 engine would fit. The question came not only from British enthusiasts but also from the US market where the 2.4 was felt to be distinctly 'under-gunned'. The answer was two years coming, although it might have been a few months sooner without the disastrous fire of early 1957 at the Browns Lane factory, which destroyed a great deal of stock including most of the launch items for the 3.4, which was in essence a 2.4 with the larger-capacity and much more powerful engine. When it arrived, the 3.4 was a formidable proposition, its engine carried over more or less directly from the XK140 and providing 210bhp. The rest of the car did not remain the same, since the rear suspension especially had to be strengthened to cope with the greater torque throughput – those who had entered the 2.4 in competition already knew that the rear spring mountings needed beefing-up to avoid premature wear and eventual failure. The final drive, a heftier Salisbury unit, was 3.54:1 (3.77:1 when overdrive was fitted). The manual gearbox was amply strong enough: its one great virtue.

From a performance point of view the 3.4 was a great success. A road test by *The Autocar* in 1958 recorded a mean maximum of 120mph in overdrive (although one wonders how many runs it took to achieve that) with direct top rev-limited to 119mph. The 0–60mph time was 9.1sec, excellent in its day – but the overall fuel consumption of exactly 16mpg was anything but. *The Autocar* merely added its customary caveat about hard driving and added that a fuel capacity of more than 12 gallons, in other words a range of something better than 200 miles between brims, would be a good idea! The test has a fair amount to say about the quality of the steering ('the self-centring is unusually pronounced … even at medium speeds appreciable effort is required at the wheel when sharp turns are made…') but is suspiciously silent where the actual handling is concerned. The point is made that Jaguar – not alone at that period – recommended different tyre pressures for different types of driving. *The Autocar* felt that the lowest, 'normal use' pressures produced 'directional stability of a lower standard … a dead feel to the steering' and recommended readers to the intermediate pressure settings (31lb/sq in front, 28lb sq in rear). However, Porter and Skilleter[1] show that Sir William Lyons himself was far from happy with the handling of the prototype 3.4, heavily criticising its transition from moderate understeer to roll-induced oversteer 'calling for quick correction' in long, fast corners; and it is sad to recall that Mike Hawthorn met his death on the public road, in a 3.4. Small wonder, perhaps, if the chassis engineers dialled a little more castor into the front suspension geometry, even at the expense of higher effort, both to help 'quick correction' and to discourage the need for it in the first place! Those using the car in competition could of course set up their cars to suit their own preferences.

In his critique of the 3.4, Sir William also remarked on the noise level as being 'quite unaccept-able … almost twice as bad as the 2.4'. According to *The Autocar*, however, 'a feature of this twin-camshaft engine is it is lack of fuss … a pleasant, subdued boom results from wide throttle openings in the intermediate ratios.' Boom, indeed! A word to make any modern NVH engineer reach for his short sword … This is not to say the test was trouble-free, for the magazine comments on the automatic choke which clearly played up, on a degree of over-damping or stiction when the accelerator was released, and a possibly related tendency for the idling speed to edge upwards throughout the test period. As for the Moss gearbox, 'first and second … are not always easy to engage when the car is at rest … quick changes may be accompanied by a grinding noise unless careful and accurate double declutching is employed.' Of the optional extra all-round Dunlop disc brakes ('available at an extra cost of £36 15s') *The Autocar* rightly says that 'it would be a false economy to specify a 3.4 Jaguar without disc brakes' which rather begs the question of why they were not standard. In the tradition of the late 1950s, serious criticism is confined to trivia: 'The unmelodious horns are out of keeping with the model, and their penetrating power was not as great as one would expect in a fast car.'

Horns aside, there was clearly enough wrong with the 2.4 and 3.4 to justify further development effort. Demand for the car remained strong even though news of early defects – the blame for some of which could be laid firmly at the door of the suppliers – had filtered out, while deliveries were interrupted by strikes at Pressed Steel which caused the supply of bodies to dry up. This was the adverse side of being tied to a single major supplier. Even when supplies were flowing, Jaguar body engineers were highly critical of what they found when they inspected incoming bodies. Porter and Skilleter[2] quote a report for Sir William which complained that 'the lack of welding and general fitting of mating surfaces is really frightening … on the cantrail, the number of welds was found to be 60 per cent short of designed requirements.' With standards like this, it is not surprising that the 2.4/3.4 was gaining a reputation as a car whose excellent basic refinement could be ruined by persistent squeaking and rattling. Yet all Jaguar could do was remonstrate with Pressed Steel. The company had nowhere else to go, and could not hope to set up its own press facility even if it had the space.

It could however improve the basic car, and in 1959 it was carried some way forward with the announcement of the Mark 2. This was a clever adaptation of the original body which at first glance,

1 Philip Porter and Paul Skilleter, *Sir William Lyons, the official biography*, p.149

2 Philip Porter and Paul Skilleter, ibid, p.167

didn't appear to change it very much. Yet the side window and windscreen area had been significantly increased, making the cabin much lighter inside; in the earlier version, those in the back seat had felt distinctly shut-in. In addition, the whole back end had been subtly reworked to accommodate a widening of the rear track by 3½in, so that it was now only 1½in narrower than the front. This increased the rear roll stiffness and produced more consistently understeering handling. Luggage space was slightly increased but the fuel tank capacity remained at 12 gallons. All-disc brakes were now standard, while overdrive remained an option, along with 3-speed automatic transmission, while power-assisted steering joined the options list in 1961. The changes increased the weight by 50lb or so.

The Mark 2 emerged in 2.4 and 3.4 forms, the former still with Solex carburettors but now with 120bhp. Even so, there were ugly rumours, fuelled by Jaguar's consistent unwillingness to make one available to any authoritative magazine for press testing, that the Mark 2 2.4 could no longer achieve a genuine 100mph. A gain of 8bhp should have been more than enough to compensate for any extra rolling resistance, and the drag coefficient could not have changed all that much. Acceleration would have been more likely to suffer. My own feeling is that the 2.4 could probably still achieve 100mph – just; but 'just' was no longer good enough for Jaguar which wanted to push its performance image rather than that its 'base' car. It was therefore much easier to persuade Jaguar to cough up the new Mark 2 3.8 which was added to the range as its flagship, the bigger engine (as in the XK150) delivering 220bhp but with valuable extra torque, 322Nm instead of 290Nm. This made the Mark 2 into a real express, *The Autocar* recording a mean maximum speed of 125mph in overdrive in a 1960 test, with 60mph reached in only 8.5sec. Overall test fuel consumption on the other hand plumbed new depths, at 15.7mpg. Never had that 12-gallon tank seemed so small.

One interesting feature of the 3.8 was the standard fitting of a Powr-Lok limited slip differential, with the result, according to *The Autocar*, of 'the complete elimination of the rear axle hop or tramp which handicapped some earlier models when using full acceleration from a standstill.' Now it could be told … As to the steering and handling, the magazine's testers contented themselves with talk of 'pronounced understeer' and 'quite powerful self-centring', this being a car devoid of power assistance

and with five full turns of the wheel between locks. Of equal interest is the advice that '(in third gear on wet roads) care has to be taken to use only light throttle when coming out of bends or away from corners … should the back end of the car slide, lifting the accelerator foot is usually enough to check it at once.' To the careful reader, that 'usually' speaks volumes. To avoid offending advertisers, 1950s road tests could be masterpieces of subtlety and faint praise. This test car (YHP 790) was driven by Sir William after its return from the magazine, prompting his comment[3] that 'This car was gone over very carefully before it was handed over for test. I drove it this weekend on an indifferent road. It sounds as though it is falling to pieces.' As an ex-*Autocar* tester of a slightly later period, the author hopes this was a comment on the car rather than the care exercised by the testers, but we have already been into Jaguar's problems with Pressed Steel and the persistency of the rattle-and-squeak situation with the small saloons.

Despite these problems, the value for money represented by the Mark 2 made it extremely popular within its target audience, not least in the British home market. The series ran with few changes – other than the introduction of the new and infinitely superior all-synchromesh 4-speed manual gearbox in 1966 – until 1967, being joined in 1962 by an up-market version powered by the Daimler 2½-litre V8 engine referred to in Chapter 4. Installing the neat little pushrod V8 in the Mark 2 engine bay posed no problems, and the car was discreetly distinguished by a mock-Daimler adaptation of the radiator grille, and different badging. Since the engine was very little larger than the short-stroke 2.4 XK (although it delivered a useful 140bhp, an increase of 20bhp over the Jaguar 2.4) the Daimler's performance was just a little superior to that of its 6-cylinder stablemate. As though to confound direct comparison, the Daimler was listed with automatic transmission as standard. A *Motor* test of 1963, carried out on a Daimler with the then-new Borg-Warner 35 3-speed automatic transmission, showed a respectable maximum speed of 109.5mph, and a 0–60mph time of 13.5sec, but with an overall fuel consumption of 16.4mpg. Automatics in those days tended to be thirsty beasts.

The smaller-engined Mark 2 ended its days, after a minor 1967 facelift, as the 240/340 alongside their cousin the Daimler V8-250. All were withdrawn by

3 Philip Porter and Paul Skilleter, ibid, p.167

1969. Towards this latter stage of their careers, the XJ system of project numbering had come into existence and two such numbers were allocated to Mark 2-related projects. The first, XJ7, covered work in 1964 relating to the replacement of the Solex carburettors in the 240 with SU instruments. The minutes of one MPM include the note that 'road testing of the prototype vehicle continues and the improvement in performance is considered adequate … slow running is very unsatisfactory and cannot be set lower than 700rpm … noise level is considered passable, but the air silencer arrangement is expensive and complicated.' Evidently these problems were overcome because the final-series 240 did indeed have SUs, along with the 'straight port' cylinder head also used by the 340. The other project number allocation, XJ15, covered engineering work to make the new 4-speed all-synchromesh gearbox compatible with a 'compact overdrive' which would enable the existing propeller shaft layout to be retained.

Meanwhile, though, an interesting hybrid had emerged with the project number XJ3, in the form of the S-type, in which the Mark 2 was given an independent rear suspension similar to that fitted to the E-type. This involved substantial engineering of the back end which, instead of the widely separated attachment points associated with the live axle, now had to accept loads via the E-type (or Mark X, see Chapter 8) sub-frame. The whole back end was restyled in consequence, gaining rear wings with strong overtones of Mark X, complete with a 7-gallon fuel tank in each: at last, a little more fuel capacity. Body production remained in the hands of Pressed Steel, and a Jaguar programme meeting minute of 27 September 1963 relating to XJ3 prototype build notes that 'the Pressed Steel standard of body finish is poor', indicating that little had changed on that front.

The S-type was introduced in both 3.4 and 3.8 form, the latter proving substantially more popular, at least overseas. The extensive changes made it substantially heaver than the Mark 2 and it could not hope to perform as well. On the other hand, the independent rear suspension provided better roadholding and more predictable handling, especially with the adoption, at last, of radial-ply (185-15 Dunlop SP41) tyres. *The Motor* tested a 3.8 S-type with Borg-Warner Model 8 automatic transmission at the end of 1964, recording a maximum of 116mph, a 0-60mph time of 11.8sec, and the expectedly dreadful fuel consumption of 15.3mpg overall. Two years later the magazine tested a manual version of the car – with the new all-synchromesh gearbox – and this time saw 121mph maximum, 0-60mph in 10.2sec, and fuel economy still down at 15.4mpg.

There was one final twist to the long story of the 'small saloon' with the introduction of the 420 (project number XJ16) in 1967. As the name implied, the XJ16 used the newly-stretched 4.2-litre evolution of the XK engine, out of the E-type and for

this application delivering 245bhp with, again, useful extra torque. This went beneath a completely restyled nose, creating (still on the original 107in wheelbase) a car which looked like a slightly shrunken Mark X. The marketing people, looking at the relative success of the 'Daimler' V8-250, decided it would be worth badge-engineering a Daimler version of the 420 also, under the 'twinned' programme number XDM16 but this time without even the excuse of a Daimler-designed engine. Thus was born the first Daimler Sovereign of the new era. The MPM minutes of 27 April 1966 reveal that Sir William Lyons was insistent that the launch of the XJ16 and the XDM16 should take place simultaneously. The extra output of the 420/Sovereign just about compensated for the extra weight and the clearly inferior aerodynamics of the new nose with its forward-sloping grille, and performance remained much the same. *The Motor* managed one test of the 420 in automatic form, with Borg-Warner transmission as ever: maximum speed was 115mph, 0–60mph time was 9.4sec (so the extra torque counted for something) and the overall fuel consumption – no surprise here – was 15.4mpg.

All these later, heavier and more complex derivatives of the 'small saloon' line were short-lived and essentially stop-gap in nature, while work proceeded on the 'small saloon' to end them all – the XJ6, which would arrive in 1968 (see Chapter 9). That is certainly not to decry the importance of the series as a whole. Andrew Whyte[4] suggests a grand total of 185,200 cars built on the 107.4in wheelbase between the first 2.4 in 1956 and the final Daimler Sovereign (420) in 1969. Apart from providing Jaguar with its real volume and therefore its financial foundation through a critical period, it also taught the company about unitary construction, and that would be very important in years to come.

4 Andrew White, *Jaguar, the Definitive History*, Appendix

7 The E-type

By the mid-1950s, it was becoming clear that however much they were admired, the XK sports car series could not go on for ever. The engine was still seen as splendid but the chassis was beginning to creak with age. In some respects the chassis harked back to the pre-war SS with its 'cart-sprung' live rear axle. Plans were therefore developed for a successor which would be able to exploit the output of the XK engine to the utmost, and also be compatible with the new engines, V8 and V12, which were even then on the drawing board.

To the engineering team this meant three things above all. First, the new car would discard the separate chassis and adopt the structure of the successful Le Mans racing cars – an ultra-stiff monocoque centre-section with tubular front extension to form the engine cradle, and a lightweight tail. This would save weight and thus improve performance but it would also, through superior torsional stiffness, improve handling and refinement. Sadly, as some long-term E-type owners eventually discovered, it also meant that corrosion in the central monocoque, its strength crucially dependent on box-sections along the sills and in an arc over the scuttle, would be both disabling and expensive to put right. Second on the list of requirements, the new car would have to have independent rear suspension. The team may have won Le Mans with carefully located live axles but its members still appreciated their limitations in terms of handling and ride comfort. They were however determined not to do the job on the cheap – no swing axles for them – but to create a suspension system which would be well behaved in all circumstances and in the hands of less-than-expert drivers. Third, the car would exploit all the technologies proved during the Le Mans campaigns, most notably of course the disc brakes but also the aerodynamics.

Logically therefore, the development programme started from the basic concept of a 'civilised' D-type with the addition of an independent rear suspension. As such, the first prototype in the E-type programme was run in 1957. This car, the E1A, owed a lot to the racing D-type but had a recognisably E-type body shell made of aluminium (much easier to hand-form for prototyping). It was powered by the short-block 2.4-litre engine because the bonnet line was so low, but having only 120bhp did not matter because the two main aims of the car were to prove the effectiveness of the aerodynamics and of its completely new independent rear suspension, the first to be developed by Jaguar, and as it turned out, an engineering classic. Sadly this epoch-making little car, which would sit so well in today's Jaguar Daimler Heritage Collection, was simply chopped up and thrown away when it was felt to have fulfilled its purpose.

The E-type's aerodynamics were the ultimate expression of Malcolm Sayers's expertise before his untimely death. Air entered the smoothly unified shell only via a single pitot intake in the extreme nose, and great care was taken in the shaping of the wheel arches, the cockpit opening and the windscreen. The result was not only moderate drag – later wind-tunnel testing showed the E-type was not as good in this respect as its looks suggested – but also low lift and good side-wind stability, without a spoiler in sight. Despite this, the car was far from purely aerodynamic. William Lyons, as ever very much his own head of styling, certainly made sure the lines swept and balanced so beautifully, and that the shut-lines and detailing added to the effect. When the production E-type eventually emerged in 1961, the lines were apparently little changed, if one acknowledges the revised bonnet line and the alterations necessary to create the fixed-head coupé (the prototypes having been roadsters). The quarter-bumpers and overriders of the production car were little more than gestures, and any positive contact by the extreme nose –

As early as 1959, the E-type had achieved something like its definitive production form, as seen in this detailed mock-up, with quarter-bumpers and pitot air intake. Was anyone overlooking the sports ground at the time? Presumably the driver of the mower was in the company's pay ... (JDHT)

invisible from the driving seat – was an expensive business. The apparently smooth, one-piece nose, which hinged upwards around a hinge at the front to give access to the engine, was actually made from several small pressings carefully welded and lead-loaded. More specifically there was an upper nose/centre section assembly, a lower nose, and the two wings which were bolted into place. Some of the internal members, including the air duct trunking, were, interestingly, bonded in place.

Even today, with higher-capacity machines, better materials and with a generous tooling budget, pressing the E-type nose as a single piece would be extremely difficult and expensive. As it was, repairing even a minor 'ding' could cost a lot of money. By the time the production car emerged, the completely smooth bonnet of the E2A prototype had gained the now familiar central hump which gave clearance over the

taller 3.8-litre engine. It made the bonnet shape even more complicated but probably also, through the swaging effect, usefully stiffer.

As for the rear suspension, it was a classic not only of engineering but also of William Lyons's skill, not to say ruthlessness, in handling people. According to Bob Knight, Lyons simply bet him £5 that he couldn't design an independent rear suspension inside a month. Suitably riled, and with several ideas festering away in his brain, Knight set to – mainly on Saturday mornings – and presented his boss with a complete set of layout drawings within the deadline. 'Bill took out his wallet and handed over the £5 without a murmur', said Knight, 'and I realised that I had £5 and Bill had his independent rear suspension!' The suspension in question, as others including Knight himself have since pointed out, owed something to a modification of the Porsche swing-axle layout which Georges Roesch had suggested in

1933. Knight's adaptation used a wishbone, hinged to the final drive, beneath (rather than above) the fixed-length drive shaft which therefore became – looking lengthwise – the upper member of a double wishbone geometry without any need for splines to accommodate changes in drive shaft length. The twin co-axial spring and damper units ran one either side of the drive shaft, each to pick up on one 'tine' of the lower wishbone, a nicely symmetrical arrangement which also helped to react torque. The layout was completed by a long trailing link to locate the wheel fore-and-aft without unduly disturbing its geometry in other axes.

One might argue that it was not an ideal layout, but it was far superior to the swing axle, simple, relatively cheap, and didn't take up huge amounts of space inside the body shell as would a conventional double wishbone system. On the debit side its geometry, especially the control of camber and of roll

centre height, was constrained because the two 'wishbones' were of necessity much closer together than in a conventional double wishbone layout, and even a small alteration in the relationship between the inboard mountings (at least, the mountings of the wishbone, and the inboard universal joint of the drive shaft) could make a big difference to the way the car behaved. From a stressing point of view, there was also the challenge of taking brake torque reaction out of the wheel and back into the body. Knight solved this by adopting inboard rear disc brakes, which had the further advantage of reducing the unsprung weight.

Even then, trials with the E1A showed the desirability of spreading the distribution of loads into the body by mounting the final drive – complete with lower wishbone attachments – on a separate sub-frame which was in turn secured to the body. Otherwise there were too many direct pathways by which noise could enter the central monocoque, which in turn could react to some frequencies almost like a crude loudspeaker. In short, the E1A was almost painfully noisy. Compared with a separate chassis, the new body structure was technically superior in almost every way but you could not carry loads into it in quite the same carefree way. Nor indeed could you have asked the tubular front frame to accept impact loads in the manner required by modern safety regulations, but such considerations were well in the future. In any event, a rear subframe was built into the subsequent E2A prototype, which was powered by a 3-litre D-type racing engine with linered aluminium block, dry sump and fuel injection, and proved the point. Sub-frames, already adopted for the front end of the small saloon, were to become part of Jaguar's engineering approach, used to great effect for example in the Mark X and eventually and supremely in the XJ6.

The E-type front suspension followed in the line of the XK120 and the racing cars, with double wishbones and longitudinal torsion bars. As always this made sense in that the spring loads were thus fed directly into the monocoque section of the hull, reducing the loads where the wishbones were mounted to the tubular front frame. Another important chassis engineering move was to switch to smaller wheels, the E-type being launched on 6.40-15 tyres rather than the familiar 6.00-16 of all XKs. The difference in rolling radius is not all that great but the change gave Jaguar's designers – primarily Sir William Lyons – the lower ride height they were looking for, without compromising the suspension geometry. It also usefully lowered the centre of gravity.

Engine considerations

It would have been foolish to offer the E-type with anything but the most powerful XK engine available, and as we have already seen, by the time the new sports car emerged the engine had been stretched to 3.8-litre capacity, bored-out from 83mm to 87mm to take the actual capacity from 3,442cc to 3,781cc. For the E-type, with three 2in SU carburettors, the quoted power output was 265bhp (gross) at 5,500rpm.

This leads to an immediate worry. Aerodynamic the E-type might have been, but the mean (two-way) maximum speeds achieved in road test by the two leading British magazines were no less than 150.4mph (by *The Autocar*, running the LHD fixed-head coupé 9600 HP on Dunlop R5 racing tyres in Belgium), and 149.1mph (by *The Motor*, running similar tyres on the RHD roadster 77 RW). The R5s were supposed to be a listed extra, the standard tyre being the Roadspeed RS5, as we have seen with dimensions 6.40x15, absurdly narrow by any modern standard, and not cleared for 'sustained' operation at 150mph. The problem is that no matter how gross one assumes that gross – rather than net – power figure to have been, calculations lead one to suspect that the power output in the road test cars must have been substantially more than the paper figure. Even on the R5s with their larger rolling radius, a speed of 150mph equates to around 5,800rpm in top gear, and there is more than a suspicion that the cars were very

The XK engine ready for E-type installation looked magnificent, with a deep cast-alloy sump as a visual balance to that famous twin-cam cylinder head, and three side-draught SU carburettors, a challenge to the art of the flow-balancer. Modern engine designers would immediately take issue with the relative shallowness of the cylinder block, but this was after all an engine designed in the immediate post-war years, and which had been 13 years in production by the time the E-type emerged – and it was destined to survive for three more decades after that! (JDHT)

specially prepared to ensure they reached (or came very close) to the magic 150mph. Extending the power curve to peak at 5,800rpm instead of 5,500rpm would mean an increased top-end (gross) power output of perhaps 290bhp, the extra 25bhp being worth at least another 5mph of maximum speed, if not more. It would also be relatively easily achieved with a little tweaking of the cylinder head – a smoothing of ports, the careful selection and matching of camshafts with lift and timing overlap at the top end of tolerance, and some tweaking of the ignition timing curve. Further fuel is added to the fire of suspicion by *The Motor*'s comment in its road test that 'the 9:1 compression ratio caused a trace of pinking in the 2,000-2,500rpm band even with 100-octane fuel.' It is also worth noting that the R5 tyres suffered less rolling resistance than the standard road tyres, which would have made a further small but significant contribution to reaching the magic 150mph.

This all fits in with the widespread tendency, among contemporary press road testers, to refer to Jaguar test cars as 'Bob Berry Specials' in deference to the company's then PR Manager (and notable competitions driver in his own right), who at the very least ensured that his cars performed to their utmost even if they were not actually 'blueprinted'. This would have been especially true of those first two E-types, since Bob Berry (and Sir William Lyons) would have been acutely aware of the publicity value of a 150mph maximum achieved by the premier British motoring magazines of the day. It remains doubtful if many customer cars straight off the production line would have achieved even 145mph, but the legend had been established and in 1961 there were far fewer motorways on which owners could hope to check such a high maximum.

Aside from considerations of maximum speed, the E-type chassis was deservedly admired. The road

tests had nothing but praise for the handling and steering. The latter was rack-and-pinion, another Jaguar first, and felt not to be too heavy despite being geared at two and a half turns lock-to-lock (if modern readers find this surprising, remember the virtually even weight distribution with the engine so far aft – a 'front-mid engine layout' long before the idea became fashionable – and the narrowness of those cross-ply tyres). Understandably, there was far less praise for the carried-over 4-speed Moss gearbox, for the interior space and even for the all-disc brakes, which lacked bite when cold and needed a huge, 115lb effort on the pedal to achieve a 1g stop (or, according to *The Autocar*, a 0.87g stop). There were also complaints about upwards light 'spill' from the beautifully faired headlamps in misty conditions.

By the time the two leading road tests appeared, the E-type had already created a sensation at its unveiling during the 1961 Geneva Motor Show. Demand was inevitably high not only because of the way the car looked but also because it was priced initially at around £2,100 including purchase tax – Ferrari performance for one-third the price. Even so, the criticisms in those road tests gave the product

planners a few things to consider, like a better gearbox, more interior space, better brakes (discs notwithstanding) and less 'leaky' headlamps.

Many of these requirements were addressed at the same time as the amendments needed to enable the E-type to accept the final enlargement of the XK engine, with a cylinder bore of 92.07mm which, with the familiar 106mm stroke, gave a nominal capacity of 4.2 litres (4,235cc). This was no simple stretch, since, as already observed when describing the last XK150, even the increase to 3.8-litre capacity needed dry liners to ensure cylinder wall integrity. Fortunately, there was one shot left in the XK engine's locker. In the original design, the crankshaft's seven main bearings were not evenly spaced. The centre bearing and the end bearings were significantly wider than the others, with the result that the cylinders in the earlier XK engines were in two groups of three, with a wider coolant passage between No. 3 and No. 4. Now, the only way to create the scope for boring-out the engine beyond 3.8 litres was to re-space the cylinder bores evenly along the length of the block, using as much of its length as was feasible. The trouble was that this called for a completely new

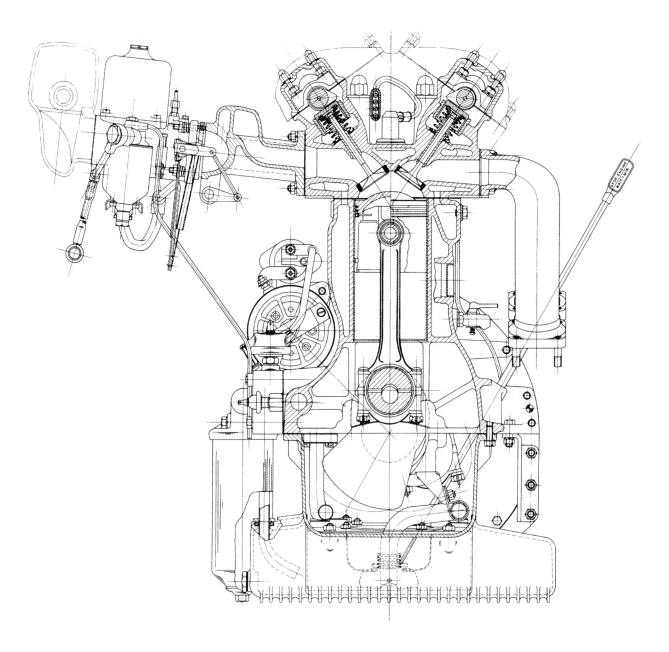

Above: A cross-section through the 4.2-litre engine (in this form, as fitted to the E-type 2+2) shows how thin-walled liners were inserted within the cylinder bores when these were taken out as far as anyone dared. Helped by the revised spacing of the bores with equal centres, these did away with the larger gap that had previously existed between cylinders 3 and 4. Apart from the shallowness of the bloc, already referred to, students of modern engine design would certainly question the generosity of the coolant passages extending all the way down to the bottom of the bore. (JDHT/Paul Skilleter)

Right: Although the XK engine began life with a symmetrical cylinder head, the inlet and exhaust valves both inclined at 35° from the vertical, it was eventually discovered that leaving the exhaust valves a further 5° outwards resulted in a power bonus. Thus was created what became known as the 35/40 head, used in most of the later, larger and most powerful versions of the XK. (JDHT/Paul Skilleter)

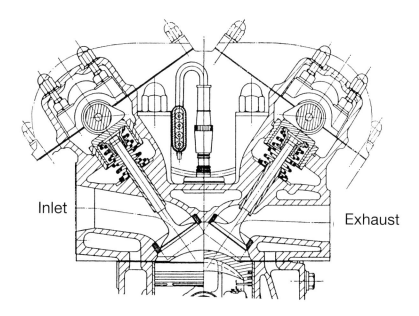

CYLINDER HEAD 35/35 PRODUCTION

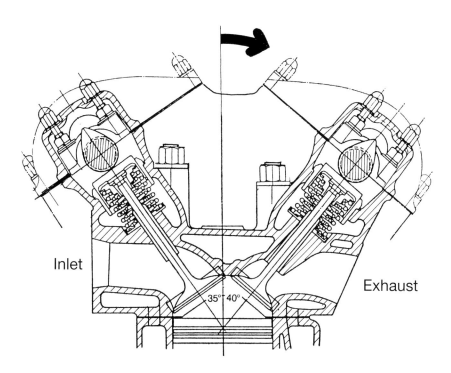

CYLINDER HEAD 35/40 "WIDE ANGLE"

The exhaust valve angle is increased
from 35° to 40° to enable the inlet valve diameter
to be increased.

crankshaft, but since there was no alternative, this was done, and rather well done at that. The new steel crankshaft was admirably stiff, but to make absolutely sure there was no damaging resonance, a new Metalastic vibration damper was mounted on the nose. Remarkably – for those of delicate engineering sensibilities – the cylinder head castings remained unchanged, which meant the nominal centres of the combustion chambers in the head no longer aligned precisely with the centre-lines of the re-spaced cylinders. Astonishingly, this seemed not to matter – given that the diameter of the combustion chamber was smaller than that of the cylinder, the difference creating a squish effect as the pistons neared top dead centre. And there was the distinct advantage that no action needed to be taken on the design either of the cylinder head or of the camshafts (and that 3.8 and 4.2 cylinder heads were interchangeable).

The result of all this work was not only the biggest, but arguably also the best of the XK engine range. It needed to be, because it still had a lot of work left to do. It could not very well be made any bigger

Above: Not all studies for the 2+2 were successful or admirable. There is clear evidence here of an intention to distance the larger car from the sports 2-seater, and little imagination is needed to see in this mock-up some of the spirit of the later XJ-S. (JDHT/Paul Skilleter)

Right: By the time the final V12 E-type rolled off the production line, in 1975, some 13 years after the first

3.8-litre, it had put on substantial weight and frontal area, and even the roadster was built on the longer wheelbase originally created for the 2+2. The faired-in head lamps were an early casualty, not only of American requirements but also of poor optics. Although the V12 was still a fast car, late-series 4.2-litre 'E's were no match for the early-series 3.8s. (Jaguar)

because at over 700cc per cylinder it was already close to suffering 'big banger' syndrome, the point at which lack of refinement caused by small differences in cylinder-to-cylinder conditions becomes more evident. With their greater diameter the pistons were heavier still and the loads they imposed were considerable. The 6,000rpm speed

limit remained firmly in place, in fact the standard red line discouraged owners even from coming close to it.

Perhaps perversely, or so it seemed to enthusiasts at the time, this increase in capacity brought no more power for the E-type. On paper, the output remained 265bhp although now at 5,400rpm rather than 5,500rpm. Torque output, on the other hand, was up from 349Nm to 380Nm, a thoroughly worthwhile increase which allowed the standard final drive to be raised to 3.07 from 3.31, for better refinement and (hopefully) better economy. Interestingly, the higher final drive meant that the 5,400rpm power peak came at almost exactly 150mph which remained the claimed maximum speed. Possibly the most welcome move was a pensioning-off of the despised – although tough – old Moss gearbox in favour of a new all-synchro-mesh unit which was almost ecstatically greeted ('a lightweight lever can be whisked into any gear as fast as the hand can move', said the 1965 *Motor* road test of the E-type 4.2, which sure enough recorded a mean maximum speed of exactly 150mph, again achieved on special racing tyres). The test also noted that more space had been found in the footwells and that the seats now moved further aft, making the car's interior a more toler-able environment for drivers more than around 70 inches tall. A larger and more conventional brake servo had brought pedal pressures out of the Tarzan league, with only a 60lb push now needed for a 0.97g stop. The standard tyres were still 6.40-15 crossply, although Dunlop 185–15 SP41 radials were an approved alternative and were made standard during 1965.

In 1966, the E-type programme undertook the considerable step of adding a 2+2 version. This was the first E-type variant to be allocated an XJ project number (XJ8), covering the major revisions to the monocoque needed to fit a small rear bench seat able to accommodate children up to – perhaps – ten years of age, or a single agile adult twisted side-ways. Even this required increasing the wheelbase from the original 96in to 105in, although a shorter rear overhang meant the overall length was only 2in greater. To give the cabin a generally roomier feel, the roof was raised by an inch and a half and the wind-screen rake reduced. The doors were lengthened almost as much as the wheelbase, to make access to the rear feasible.

As an aside, it is interesting to see that the 'Bob Berry Special' approach to press test car preparation continued. In the minutes of an MPM held on 4 February 1966 it is noted that 'Mr. Knight informed the meeting that no provision has been made for the special engines that were necessary for press performance tests. Mr. England will arrange.' The same meeting also noted 'quality concerns over Jaguar-produced gearboxes' with 'standards no higher than Rover or BMC'. Gear tooth-cutting machines were having to be reset every 20–25 components. Serious consideration was given to the fitting of a 5-speed ZF gearbox – mentioned several times in MPMs – but nothing came of it. Other XJ8 problems which emerged in the early stage concerned the exhaust system, with 'up to 12 per cent power loss in prototype installations' and baffle collapse.

Inevitably, the changes which created the XJ8 added around 280lb to the E-type's weight and some 5 per cent to its frontal area. With exactly the same engine and gearing, its maximum speed was reduced by 14mph according to Jaguar, although 136mph may seem quite fast enough when one has one's young offspring in the back. Aside from the larger dimen-sions, major engineering changes included the switch to radial-ply tyres (Dunlop SP41, 185–15) as standard and in deference to family/touring customers, the option of Borg-Warner's 3-speed Model 8 automatic transmission.

Purists suggested the changes made to create the 2+2 ruined the visual balance and the overall line of the car. Many customers apparently begged to differ, and sales of the 2+2 and the 2-seat fixed-head coupé soon became more or less equal, though always running behind the 2-seat roadster. However, further moves were already afoot and in 1968, although overshadowed by the arrival of the XJ6, the Series 2 E-type made its appearance at the London Motor Show – preceded by a fair number of slightly curious 'Series 1½' cars. By now the XJ project number series was moving on apace, and the Series 2 was developed as the XJ22 (2-seater versions, still with 96in wheelbase) and the XJ23 (2+2), the latter with the base of the windscreen moved forward in an attempt to lose some of the 'uprightness' of the original 2+2 shape.

It was much easier to decry the Series 2 as a retrograde step, not least because its develop-ment team was beginning to be weighed upon by the safety and exhaust emission regulations beginning to come into force in its largest market, the USA. The situation was destined to get much worse. In

November 1971, Bob Knight was even moved to write a memo to the soon-to-retire Sir William Lyons complaining that the engineering manpower needed to run all the validation testing for the US market in particular left almost nothing to spare for new model development. He needed more people to accomplish everything that was now technically demanded, but this was a time when Jaguar was regarded as a small part of the large British Leyland empire, and seen as such by a corporate team sitting not in Coventry, but in Berkeley Square, London.

The visible changes to the E-type Series 2 included a larger air intake (thus significant alterations to that complicated one-piece nose assembly) to provide extra flow for the second radiator which would serve the optional air-conditioning system, rather heavier and at least slightly more effective bumpers, and deletion of those lovely but flawed headlamp fairings in favour of sealed-beam units in 'troughs' which certainly did nothing for the car's aerodynamic quality but provided much better headlamp beam control. Under the skin, power-assisted steering made its appearance, essential for the American market and worth standardising now that radial-ply tyres had been adopted.

In terms of the American-market car itself, the Series 2 changes were more fundamental. In the face of what now seem laughably lax emission requirements the 4.2-litre engine had to switch to twin dual-choke Stromberg carburettors rather than the classic triple SUs, and power output came tumbling down to 245bhp (gross) which, it now emerged, was equivalent to a mere 171bhp (net). Other manufacturers were in the same boat, however, and the era of the high-performance car in the USA appeared to be coming to an end.

Jaguar had long had other ideas, which by 1971 crystallised into the V12 engine for the E-type Series 3. The V12 engine deservedly has Chapter 10 to itself, but the E-type remains notable for having been its 'launch pad'. The Series 3 emerged, under the Jaguar programme numbers XJ25 (2+2) and XJ26 (2-seat roadster), for a fairly short production run which ended when the last of a final batch of black, right-hand-drive roadsters came off the line in March 1975 (although delivery-mileage cars were certainly sold in Britain much later that year). The relative ease with which the big engine slotted into the E-type goes a long way to justify the decision to adopt single-cam cylinder heads. A 4-cam engine would have made the job far more difficult. Transmission

choice continued to lie between Jaguar's 4-speed manual gearbox and a 3-speed automatic. Engine room apart, the 105in wheelbase was now standardised, even for the roadster, the air intake grew larger still, and the front suspension was revised with the angling of the wishbone mounting axes to provide an anti-dive reaction during braking, a trick first successfully employed on the XJ6. Ventilated front discs made their appearance, adding to the effectiveness of a system which had been generally admired – once the heaviness of the under-servoed early brakes had been rectified. By now, the tyres had perforce become wider (E70-15 Dunlop SP Sports on 6in rims were standard wear) and the wheel arches were subtly bulged to cover them – subtly, but enough to spoil the original purity of line.

The result of installing the V12 in the E-type may not have been quite as vivid as some were expecting and hoping, but the emphasis was much more on refinement and flexibility than on high-end power. By way of proof, as an unscheduled addition to the *Autocar* road test figure-taking session at the MIRA test track, my colleague Michael Scarlett insisted on engaging fourth gear in our manual-gearbox car while at rest and switched-off on the one-mile horizontal straight, then floored the accelerator and operated the starter motor until – astonishingly quickly – the engine became self-sustaining. When it was time to lift off and brake at the far end of the straight, the car had exceeded 120mph. That was flexibility allied to exceptional performance. Despite this, *Autocar* could only persuade this car to a genuine two-way mean maximum of 143mph, so the 150mph days had gone – and with automatic transmission the V12 E-type would have been slower still. It didn't really matter, especially since the car's demise was hastened by the political events of the early 1970s. Sports cars with a road test fuel consumption of 15mpg were not going to enjoy any great success with oil being used as a political weapon. Even so, over 15,000 V12 Series 3s were built out of a total of around 72,500 cars in total.

Having waved goodbye to the E-type, the world of the motoring enthusiast waited to see the shape of the F-type. Generally, opinion was that it would need to be smaller, lighter and more nimble than the E-type had become in its later years. What actually came next – the XJ-S – was nothing like that. Once or twice in the subsequent quarter-century we have come close to glimpsing a proper F-type, but we are still waiting.

8 **High technology** for the **big cars**

It is instructive, looking at the Jaguar record, to realise how little of significance seemed to happen between the end of the racing programme in 1956/57 and 1961. In four years, the only product announcements were some gentle up-dating of the XK150 and the much needed evolution of the original 2.4/3.4 into the Mark 2. The reason for this apparent inactivity was that almost every design, development and experimental engineer was working on one or both of two new cars, the E-type (Chapter 7) and the Mark X. Both represented breaks with the past, but they had more in common than that. Naturally, both were powered by the XK engine. Both had independent rear suspension, and both used new methods of body construction.

The big saloon series, up to and including the Mark IX of 1958, could not be extended for ever, or even for very long. Cars with separate chassis were beginning to be regarded as distinctly old-fashioned. So, indeed, were 'prestige' cars with live rear axles. Jaguar had sought to keep abreast of the most obvious technical developments, so that (as we have seen) the Mark IX emerged with disc brakes and power-assisted steering, but some matters could only be addressed via a fundamental rethink. The Mark X was the car intended to put the situation right. At that time, a really big and impressive car was still seen as essential to serve the upper echelons, and to appeal to the important US market in which, during the 1950s, really big cars (by European standards) were beginning to look medium-sized alongside their American counterparts.

It would not have been entirely out of the question to have continued with some form of chassis, even a 'perimeter frame' such as was tried in some American models, but Jaguar's engineering team had tackled one major unitary project in the 2.4/3.4, and felt this structural approach was the way ahead. To have done the new car any other way would have been to risk taking half a step forward instead of a whole one.

That said, it must be admitted that as an exercise in unitary construction, the Mark X was not a whole-hearted success. The main object of the unitary approach is to save weight by eliminating the separate chassis and distributing stress throughout the entire body, making each panel take its share. Yet the unitary-construction Mark X weighed 182lb or 4.5 per cent more than the chassis-based Mark IX, taking a like-for-like comparison of 3.8-litre automatic test cars weighed by *The Autocar*. Was this because the

Mark X was bigger? Not really. Its 120in wheelbase was the same, its front track 1½in wider, its rear track identical. True, the new body was nearly 6in longer than that of the Mark IX and it was three inches wider; but it was also 8½in lower, and probably therefore enclosed less actual space.

That it was beyond dispute heavier is almost certainly because of the conservative engineering approach, adopted for two possible reasons. First, it made sure the body would accept the stresses fed into it by an all-new suspension system, and even more, perhaps, that it would be stiff enough not to suffer the apparent fragility, the squeaks and rattles, which plagued the 2.4 and 3.4, Jaguar's first unitary-construction models. The kind of customer who would buy the Mark X simply would not put up with that kind of thing, and the Mark X body would again be manufactured at, and delivered from, Pressed Steel at Cowley because there really was nowhere else for Jaguar to go. Oddly enough, the apparently quiet interval from 1957 to 1961 had seen a lot of business activity: Jaguar had acquired Daimler and Guy Motors (and in 1963, added Coventry Climax to its local empire). Sadly, it did not in the process acquire any meaningful panel-pressing capacity.

In any event, the Mark X body was unitary but not as unitary as some. As a foundation, it still had two massive longitudinal box-sections beneath its floor, and these were joined by a hefty scuttle assembly which also incorporated box-sections of considerable area. The loads carried into the more remote parts of the body, especially the roof, were less significant, which at least meant it was possible to keep the pillars slim by the standards of the day (it also made it possible to contemplate a future pillarless coupé derivative or even a convertible, although neither idea ever made it into metal). One good reason for this conservative structural approach, not to make too fine a point of it, was Jaguar's concern that the Mark X would be stiff and quiet despite the worst that Pressed Steel quality control could do, and to judge by the 2.4/3.4 (Chapter 6) that was pretty bad. But

The Mark X retained the massive yet streamlined look which Jaguar had made its own, and it was indeed a massive car in most respects, although substantially low-built compared with its large-saloon predecessors. By modern standards the wheels were small, the aerodynamics were dreadful and the car weighed far too much, with dire effects on fuel economy, but by early 1960s standards it was highly competitive, especially at its asking price. (Jaguar)

there was also that new suspension, front and rear. At the front, in contrast with the E-type, the reliable old torsion bar spring arrangement was discarded in favour of conventional double wishbones, coil springs and telescopic dampers, all mounted on a fabricated sub-frame, as in the small saloons. The sub-frame accepted and transmitted (through isolating flexible mounts) all the main suspension loads. It also, logically, housed the steering gear, but the full evolution of the front subframe into a complex system which would also involve the engine mounts was yet to come.

At the back, the Mark X used almost exactly the same layout – adapted, naturally, to the 8in wider track – as did the E-type. This was the effective double wishbone arrangement devised by Bob Knight with a 'proper' lower wishbone but with the fixed-length drive shaft forming the upper link, and the disc brakes inboard, the whole thing being mounted to a subframe complete with the final drive unit, before being offered up to the body. Bob Knight's own story of how the suspension came into being, as the result

Above: While the XK engine was – of course – carried over, the Mark X was radically different in two respects, first its use of unitary construction and second in its independent rear suspension, using basically the same layout as in the E-type but with a wider track. Sadly the unitary construction was almost an essay in how like an old-fashioned chassis you could make it – most of the stiffness came from box-sections rather than skins. (LAT)

of a bet with Sir William Lyons, is related in Chapter 7; although in truth he did not, in its telling, say for which car the layout was first intended. It could have been either. As it happened, the E-type came first chronologically, launched at Geneva in March 1961 while the Mark X had to wait for an 'in house' press event at Browns Lane in the autumn of the same year. Since both programmes had proceeded in parallel for a number of years, it is fair to say that the suspension was developed for them both. There is no indication that any other form of suspension was considered, the test results having proved generally satisfactory: Jaguar accorded great importance to pounding around the reproduction Belgian pavé circuit at the MIRA proving ground, an exercise which could, in the 1950s, render some cars fit for the scrap yard in a few hundred miles and which was especially hard on suspension components and mountings. In the case of the Mark X, a great deal (by 1950s standard) of durability mileage was also built up in France, the first time a Jaguar had been subjected to anything like a formal Continental proving exercise.

As it turned out, the sub-frame arrangement for locating and attaching the rear suspension and driveline was to prove highly efficient at reducing noise and vibration, but with the Mark X, Jaguar could afford to take no chances. In other respects, the chassis engineering agenda had been set by the

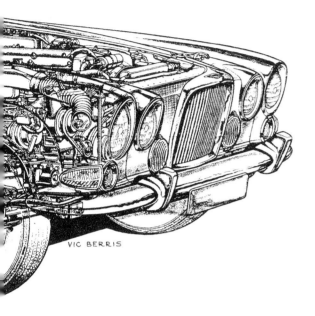

Below: Whatever accusations could be levelled against it in some crucial respects, the Mark X successfully maintained Jaguar's image when it came to performance and handling. Motoring journalists frequently criticised lack of sideways support from the seats when the car was driven hard, but the typical owner probably never used even half of the chassis' considerable potential. (Giles Chapman Library)

Mark IX which was already equipped with disc brakes and power-assisted steering as standard (so, no excuses for additional weight there, either). With suitable alterations, such as the moving inboard of the rear brake discs, systems could be transferred. All the same, the combination of the new body and the new suspension meant a far greater development engineering load than had been the case even when moving from the Mark V to the Mark VII.

Naturally, there was scope to lower the Mark X body because the independent rear suspension meant there was no need to leave space for propeller shaft articulation. But one of the styling tenets of the time (and for long afterwards) was that low meant sleek, and one further change was made to bring the Mark X closer to the ground. This was a switch to significantly smaller diameter wheels, the 6.70-16 tyres of the Mark IX giving way to 7.50-14s on the Mark X. This was, you should bear in mind, a time when wheel and tyre sizes were growing smaller, on the premise that big wheels took up a lot of space within the body shell (which is true). The minimum point had been reached in 1958 with the BMC Mini, launched on 10in wheels. Fashion dictated that cars with big wheels looked old-fashioned, and that simply could not be afforded in the Mark X, even if ground clearance suffered. One effect was that the Mark X tyres had a smaller rolling radius, with the result that the standard final drive ratio had to be drastically lowered to 3.54, from 4.27 in the Mark IX. Perhaps oddly, Jaguar thought it worthwhile fitting a Powr-Lok limited-slip differential in the Mark X, as they had in the XK150S and the Mark 2 3.8 – even though the big car had independent suspension rather than a live axle. It seems the doubts arose from the combination of very high inertia and the smaller wheels.

Some adjustment of final-drive ratio was also called for because compared with the Mark IX, the Mark X would have a higher maximum speed, to which the gearing needed matching. There was probably little to choose between the two cars in terms of drag coefficient. Although most of its body was smooth enough, the front end of the Mark X was aerodynamically terrible, with a forward-leaning radiator grille which was also one of the current fashions. There is no record of what Malcolm Sayer thought of it. But because it was so much lower, the Mark X had a significantly smaller frontal area and this guaranteed that the total high-speed drag would be reduced. A rule-of-thumb calculation (0.8 x

overall width x overall height) suggests the Mark X had an effective frontal area of almost exactly 23 square feet, while the much taller Mark IX was 25.55 square feet, so the reduction in aerodynamic drag would have been around 10 per cent. One notable feature of the Mark X body was that it began a long Jaguar tradition of having twin fuel tanks, one on either side of the luggage compartment, each with its own filler and electric fuel pump. For the Mark X, total fuel capacity was 20 gallons.

What was more, the Mark X had extra power. While the 3.8-litre XK was carried over, for the new car it was taken to its highest state of production tune, similar to that in the XK150S, with 'straight-through' cylinder head porting and three SU carburettors, one for each cylinder pair. The gross power output was thus lifted from 220bhp in the Mark IX to 265bhp (at 5,500rpm) in the Mark X. There was also a useful increase in maximum torque, from 322Nm to 349Nm, underlining the comments made in previous chapters about improving the XK engine's mid-range BMEP through close attention to breathing.

What one would logically expect to find, therefore, was that the Mark X would have a usefully higher maximum speed because of its lower frontal area and higher maximum power, while its acceleration – except at higher speed – would be about the same because the extra weight would just about be compensated by the extra torque. This indeed seems to have been the case. As already mentioned, *The Autocar* tested both cars in 3.8-litre form with automatic transmission in late 1958 and late 1962 respectively; the mean maximum speed figures were 119.5mph for the Mark X and 113.5mph for the Mark IX. On the other hand the Mark IX was actually quicker from rest to 60mph, achieving it in exactly 11sec while the Mark X needed 12.1sec. Overall test fuel consumption, also weight-dependent, fell marginally – in fact, by 2 per cent – from 14.4mpg in the Mark IX to 14.1mpg in the Mark X.

The Autocar may have given the game away just a little in its preamble to the road test, in which it said that the test car 'had already covered over 13,000 miles, including two Continental trips, when handed over, but had obviously received proper maintenance in the Jaguar works and was in near-perfect condition. There was not a body creak or rattle.' Were they, then, expecting some? But the magazine was full of praise for the car, and especially for the brakes and the 'almost neutral steering characteristics (that) have been achieved', although slightly less enthusiastic about the Borg-Warner DG 3-speed automatic transmission and some aspects of the ride, of the power-assisted steering and of the heating ('but it is a big advance over previous Jaguar systems'). Real condemnation, in the spirit of the times, was reserved for things which didn't really matter ('one could do with further places inside the car to stow the odds and ends that go with travel').

We have to turn to *Motor* (by 1963, no longer *The Motor*) for figures on the Mark X 3.8 with manual transmission and overdrive. This car just managed a mean maximum speed of 120mph, but manual gear shifting, and a kerb weight of just over 4,000lb (175lb lighter than *The Autocar* automatic) managed to bring the 0–60mph time down to 10.8sec. On the other hand, the overall fuel consumption figure was down as well, to only 13.6mpg – not quite what one might have expected. By this time it was open season on the Moss gearbox and thus it is no surprise to find the test saying 'it is justifiably fashionable to be rude about Jaguar gearboxes and we must echo yet again [again?] the criticism that the manual box is unworthy of the car.' However, the magazine goes on to point out the obvious: that by the mid-1960s, most customers for this type of car wanted automatic. The writers were also less than gentle when it came to the fuel consumption, not only the overall figure but also their careful measurement during '17 miles of gentle driving over country roads, averaging 36mph' which yielded just 23.3mpg, by implication about as good as you could ever hope to see. In fact, on this occasion the magazine put the boot in to an extent which clearly worried Jaguar, since it also criticised the lack of sideways support from the seats, the pedal layout, and the lightness and lack of feel of the steering ('the impression transmitted through the wheel when cornering fast is that of driving on a wet road with the front wheels about to break away …'). In vain, one fears, had Jaguar tried to explain to British road testers that this was what American customers preferred, and the company was not going to indulge in the complication of completely different steering systems for its two biggest markets. The company may have tried to explain, summoning *Motor* road tester Roger Bell – later to become the editor of the magazine, and a well-respected competition and test driver – to a meeting at Browns Lane at which a lively discussion ensued with Bill Heynes, flanked by many of his senior engineers. Bell recalls that 'I

don't think it's quite right to say the company tried to explain. The explaining was mainly by me to them. In other words, I was there to justify my (i.e. *Motor*'s) criticisms, not to hear their excuses.' Evidently the meeting failed to create mutual understanding, because *Motor*'s then-editor Richard Bensted-Smith ended up writing an apologetic letter to the factory.

Whatever the feelings provoked, help was at hand, although the benefits were limited when it came to the steering. Soon after the *Motor* test appeared, the Mark X was heavily revised with the substitution of the 4.2-litre engine for the 3.8, Jaguar's new all-synchromesh gearbox in place of the frequently cursed Moss unit, and the then-new (but still 3-speed) Borg-Warner Model 8 automatic transmission to replace the DG. Marles Varamatic steering was adopted. With its variable ratio, this sharpened the steering reaction during cornering, but did sadly little to overcome the mushy feeling about the straight-ahead position. Radial-ply tyres, size 205-14, also became standard. Other welcome refinements included an alternator to replace the DC generator (so, at last a chance to keep up with the current consumption of those four powerful headlights when driving slowly) and a pre-engaged starter. The sum of all these changes in fact represented a substantial engineering programme which fully justified the allocation of a project number (XJ5) from the list which was then coming into being.

The scale of Jaguar's production at around this time is shown in a programme file issued in May 1964 and held in the archive. This gives the vehicle production rate during 'Mark X phase-out, XJ5 phase-in' at 75 cars a week (compared with 100 E-types a week, the balance of production being the Mark 2 in its various forms). Engine production targets were 355 per week of 'present Jaguar types' plus 175 per week of the 4.2-litre, made in Building 2 – in other words, sufficient for the XJ5 and the 4.2 E-type (XJ8). Mention is also made of 120 engines a week for the XDM2, which means the Daimler 2½-litre V8 for the Mark 2 derivative. The production target for the new all-synchromesh gearbox is given as 355 per week (to which automatic transmissions from Borg-Warner must of course be added) but it is also noted that '122 old gearboxes a week are to continue on the Mark 2', so clearly there was considerable stock of the Moss box to be used up!

The XJ5 challenge was that the Mark X chassis, like that of the E-type, had proved extremely capable and would have no trouble handling more power and torque. The problem was how best to give it more, and the 4.2-litre engines beginning to flow from Building 2 (the old Daimler works at Radford) were the answer.

There was, it is said, a time when Jaguar contemplated using the Daimler 4½-litre V8 from the Majestic Major to answer the need to add more urge to the Mark X. It might have served well, for in its existing form it offered 220bhp with formidable torque output. In many respects it was a splendid engine despite its pushrod OHV layout (with a clever cross-over arrangement which enabled it to have vee-opposed valves in hemispherical combustion chambers, all operated from the one camshaft) and it would apparently have fitted without any problem. Sadly, as explained in Chapter 4, it was hardly an economic proposition. It would have taken a lot of investment, and a certain amount of further development to make it compatible with the Mark X. In any case, Jaguar's engineers, not only Bill Heynes but also Walter Hassan when he returned to the fold as part of the Coventry Climax takeover, could not be expected to feel enthusiastic about using someone else's engine in the company's 'top' car. As a clinching argument, development of the V12 was already underway. Indeed, before too long, XJ5 'mules' were on the road powered by early V12 engines, under the programme number XJ10. The interim solution – although in the case of the Mark X it proved also to be the final one – was therefore to fit the 4.2-litre XK whose evolution was explained in Chapter 7.

As in the E-type, the 4.2 brought extra torque rather than extra power. The stated power output remained at 265bhp but the torque output, for the Mark X 4.2, rose from 349Nm to 380Nm. This was enough to provide noticeably improved performance, as seen in the test carried out by *Autocar* (also now devoid of the definite article in its title) late in 1964, on Mark X 4.2 automatic AWK 134B. On the weighbridge, this car scaled just 28lb less than the 3.8 automatic. It reached a mean maximum of 121.5mph, although the road test notes that this involved transgressing the 5,500rpm red line. Thus a higher final drive, perhaps 3.31 rather than 3.54, might have been a good idea except that it would probably have prevented the car from breaking the '10-second barrier' from rest to 60mph, when in fact it managed it in 9.9sec. Intriguingly, overall fuel consumption emerged as 14.5mpg which is hardly a

creditable figure but which even so represents a 2.8 per cent improvement over *Autocar*'s 3.8. There is no clear reason why it should have been better, since the final drive remained the same and the magazine measured the steady-speed fuel consumption at 30mph as 22.4mpg.

The test makes little direct reference to the quality of the Borg-Warner Model 8 transmission as compared with its predecessor the DG, other than to mention that it 'helps by allowing quite a lot of 'slip', and when the throttle is opened abruptly the tachometer shows the quick jump in engine speed which the converter provides without changing down.' Any such statement would appal a modern transmission engineer who takes top gear lock-up for granted, but it helps to explain why the big Jaguar's fuel consumption was so poor. The Varamatic steering was generally welcomed although there is still an implied criticism of over-lightness, plus the observation that the variable-ratio feature – achieved through careful design of the steering rack – 'is not noticed in ordinary driving' which could be either genuine or faint praise.

Motor had to wait the best part of a year before testing a similar car (CLB 526B) and for some reason recorded a significantly lower maximum speed of 118.2mph, a worse 0–60mph time of 10.3sec, and the worst recorded road test fuel consumption of any Mark X, at 13.4mpg. *The Motor* test broadly agreed with that of its rival where the car's dynamic qualities were concerned, but it roundly condemned, both directly and by implication, the lack of sideways support in the front seats: 'Some of our drivers – particularly the lighter ones who had the greatest trouble staying in place without clinging to the wheel – complained that no road feel whatever was transmitted.' To this, Jaguar would surely have replied that where the seats were concerned, the magazine road testers wanted sports seats in everything, while some less than athletic customers appreciated being able to slide in and out of place with ease. Where the steering was concerned, the clash of interest between the road testers, who always wanted more feel and feedback, and the American-market customers who wanted to be able to steer as they would in a Cadillac, with one finger on the wheel, would take a long time to resolve.

It is interesting that the *Motor* test, while generally praising the revised Mark X heating system, ventures the criticism that 'like all but a few of the most recent designs, [it] lacks sufficient ducted ventilation to be driven with the windows closed in summer.' For those too young to remember, this complaint came at about the time when Ford, in an update of the humble Mark 1 Cortina, had shown that highly effective through-flow ventilation was actually possible. Jaguar, and most other manufacturers, took a while to catch up.

One final authoritative test of the Mark X, carried out by *Autocar* late in 1965, raises again the question of ideal gearing. This was a manual transmission car with overdrive, therefore with a 3.77 final drive rather than 3.54, the overdrive ratio thus giving an overall gearing of 2.94. As the magazine observed, this meant that direct top was rev-limited to 107mph, while the mean maximum of 122.5mph (the best ever authoritatively attributed to the Mark X) was achieved at only 4,700rpm, suggesting that an 'in between' gearing might have yielded up to 125mph. Sure enough, with the higher gearing the car was slightly slower from rest to 60mph, managing only 10.4sec. On the other hand, the very high gearing (with overdrive taken into account) is mainly to thank for an overall test consumption of exactly 16mpg, by far the best ever seen in a Mark X.

The final incarnation of the Mark X came in the form of the 420G, which it became in 1966. Despite the change of name, this was really no more than a minor facelift, with some interior changes – some smoothing of edges, some padding – which were nods in the direction of the new science of passive safety. It is probably significant that the 420G seems never to have been allocated a project number from the XJ series, although admittedly there are one or two 'unclaimed' numbers from around this period, especially XJ9 and XJ11, which might have fitted. It is more likely that the changes were not great enough to justify the allocation of a number. The 420G lingered on until 1970, a little after the introduction of the XJ6 (Chapter 12). There was no new 'big Jaguar' because the altered socio-economic circumstances of the 1970s meant there was no prospect of such a model ever being economic to produce. Its place was taken, to a certain extent and as we shall see, by the long-wheelbase versions of the XJ6 and its successors; but the last 420G to leave the factory also marked the end of an era.

Perhaps oddly, the Mark X/420G was never badge-engineered into a Daimler, unlike the smaller Mark 2-derived 420 which spawned the first Sovereign. There was, however, one Daimler postscript to the big-car story. In 1968, the Daimler limousine, the DR450 inherited with the 1961 takeover, was replaced by a new limousine intended to offer a similar specification – and a similarly grand image – at lower production cost. This was the DS420, built on a stretched Mark X/420G platform (as we have seen, the platform itself was very strong, almost to the point of being self-supporting), powered by the 4.2 XK engine and clad with a body which enjoyed considerable design input from Sir William Lyons. The project was given its own programme number, XDM3 (DM for Daimler rather than J for Jaguar, XDM2 having been the 2½-litre V8-engined Mark 2). The graceful DS420, usually known simply as the Daimler Limousine, enjoyed an astonishingly long life, due in part to the waiving of some safety regulations because of its low volume and likely use. In 1981, Jaguar announced that assembly of this model had been switched to a specially created 40,000 square foot facility in Browns Lane, following the closure of the specialised London body plant (Mulliner, Park Ward as it had once been). Assembly at Browns Lane took place on a unit assembly basis rather than on a production line, with individual cars passing from one specialised team to another in an assembly process which occupied around two weeks. At the time, unit assembly was a rather fashionable concept, but in the case of the Limousine it was surely making a virtue of necessity. As one of the only two purpose-built limousines in the Western World – the other being the Rolls-Royce Silver Wraith – the big Daimler survived until 1992 and was phased-out only after some 5,000 had been built, a number which considerably exceeded original expectations. It even enjoyed some later engineering interest, since the allocated project number list includes XDM62, 'Projected limousine for Middle East markets' and XDM65, 'Limousine to US Federal requirements'. By the time the limousine was finally withdrawn, it was the only car still using the XK power unit.

9 The **XJ6** and **XJ12**

By the early 1960s, it was becoming clear to Jaguar's management that it could not continue independently with the manufacture of three distinct product lines. At that time it was producing the Mark 2, the E-type and the Mark X, but the sports car was to some extent a separate consideration. The two saloons had become widely regarded as the 'small Jaguar' and the 'big Jaguar', which itself rather suggested that an all-embracing new 'Jaguar' should be something in between the two. Sir William Lyons, introducing the XJ6, said the decision to produce a completely new car, 'superior in all respects to existing models, which would be so advanced that it could remain in production for a minimum of seven years after its introduction' had been taken in 1964. Since the XJ6 was launched towards the end of 1968, Sir William was in effect giving it until 1975. He did not quite live to see the launch of its true successor, the XJ40, which took place in 1986, a year after the father of the company had passed away.

In fact, the beginning of the XJ6 story goes back a little earlier than 1964. In 1969, when *CAR* magazine presented its Car of the Year award to the XJ6 (the 'other Car of the Year award' went to the Peugeot 504) the author – who was then the magazine's assistant editor – interviewed Bill Heynes at some length while preparing the in-depth coverage which would appear in the award edition[1]. Heynes admitted that first thoughts on what became the XJ6 had revolved around a fastback saloon evolved from the E-type. However, he went on, 'the present design soon emerged as a more practical form within the dimensional limits of the specification.' Heynes was emphatic that the specification had not called for specific, quantified improvements on any aspect of the 420 – although tacitly acknowledging that this was the in-house benchmark – and insisted that they had set out to do 'the very best they could in all respects, without necessarily deviating from accepted practice, but bearing in mind the car must have reserves of strength and road behaviour sufficient to meet the demands imposed by the new engines which would eventually be fitted.' He would be drawn no further on the subject of those engines although rumours of both a V8 and a V12 had been flying around for months (see Chapter 10).

Serious studies were first drawn up under the allocated project number XJ4 for a '4/5 seater saloon'

1 *CAR* magazine, March 1969, p.21

which indicated the aiming point clearly enough, since the Mark 2 back seat could scarcely be regarded as providing room for three abreast, whereas the Mark X was generously endowed in this respect. By 1966, the company was deeply committed to the programme although the minutes of a project progress meeting dated 27 April 1966 (with Sir William Lyons himself present, which was not always the case) noted among other matters that the XJ4 'was running three months late'.

It is not entirely clear at what point the XJ4 designation was dropped in favour of XJ6, the number originally allocated to the V12/V8 engine programme, but it was a late one and probably impelled by the marketing consideration that it would be a bad thing to call a 6-cylinder saloon 'XJ4'. There was of course no precedent for calling it XJ-anything, but 420 had already gone, Mark 3 might imply a throwback, Mark XI would give entirely the wrong impression that the new car was an extension of the big-saloon range, and T-type (as a successor to the S-type) risked confusion with the then-new Bentley T and possibly even with the old MG sports cars. Besides, XJ had something of a ring to it and XJ numbers were already being bandied about in the enthusiast press. Despite this, as late as December 1967, reports were being filed on strength and stiffness tests conducted by Pressed Steel on the first representative XJ4 (not XJ6) body shell, revealing a torsional stiffness of 4,815lb ft per degree for the shell 'in white' and 6,740lb ft per degree with glazing installed, which among other things, points to the contribution of the glass to the stiffness of any modern unitary body shell – an improvement of almost exactly 40 per cent in this case, even in the days before windscreens were bonded into place.

As to specification, the new car was to be much closer to the Mark 2/S-type than to the Mark X in general size. In its original form the XJ6 had a wheelbase of 109in, less than 2in longer than that of the 420, while its front and rear tracks of 58in and 58.6in respectively differed only by fractions of an

The XJ6 grew out of the idea of replacing both the small saloon and the Mark X with a single intermediate-sized car to be produced in economic volume. In its initial form it proved a great success from most points of view but was criticised for lack of back seat space, especially by anyone used to the Mark X. Consequently, a 4in stretch was inserted in the wheelbase, initially for 'long-wheelbase' versions, but eventually made standard. (Jaguar)

inch from those of its predecessor. The new car was never in any real sense a replacement for the 'big Jaguar' even when its wheelbase was stretched, following early mutterings about cramped back seats in the otherwise laudatory road tests, by 4in to 113in.

One of the principal engineering targets was exceptional refinement, achieved mainly through the adoption of a new front suspension to complement the carried-over (with modifications) E-type rear suspension and sub-frame. The front suspension would be double wishbone and coil spring, as in the Mark X, but this time the axes of the wishbone mountings would be slightly nose-up, to create an anti-dive effect under braking, while the front sub-frame would be bigger, and would carry not only the suspension mounting points but also the front engine mountings. This sub-frame was carefully and cleverly located to the body shell at four widely spaced mounting points, each of which constrained its movement in some senses while leaving it free in others. The combination of wide spacing and flexibility maintained accurate location while creating longitudinal compliance, something we now take more or less for granted, but which made the XJ6 astonishingly free from road noise, and especially from low-frequency bump-thump, by the standards of its day. Meanwhile the mounting of the engine to the sub-frame meant that a great deal of power unit mechanical vibration from the engine also had to pass through what amounted to a double isolation if it was to reach the cabin. In describing the complete front suspension and sub-frame installation, Heynes pointed with some pride to the fact that the front suspension and sub-frame mountings incorporated six different mixes of natural and synthetic rubber, each with a different frequency characteristic. One of the early headaches in XJ6 production was to maintain those characteristics within tolerance. Even so, Jaguar always favoured rubber mounts to the steel-mesh bushings of the type Rolls-Royce had recently introduced on the Silver Shadow, fearing the effect on the latter of dirt-clogging on poor roads.

At the same time, the author observed (as he now writes) 34 years ago, Jaguar was relieved to discover that some of the problems which might have been expected to arise, with so much rubber between the suspension and the body, simply did not manifest themselves. Bob Knight, interviewed at the time when his position was Chief Development Engineer, cheerfully expressed a certain amount of surprise that everything worked out so well, first time. And, as he put it: 'If we didn't come across problems, we

certainly didn't go looking for them.' For the XJ6, Jaguar fitted a new Adwest rack and pinion power-assisted steering system. It was a sign of the safety-conscious times that it was mounted at the extreme rear of the front sub-frame; no more would Jaguars have long steering columns aimed at the driver's chest. Reaction to the new system was generally favourable although the road testers still complained about over-lightness leading to lack of feel.

For the rear suspension, Heynes said Jaguar had considered fitting self-levelling but had good reason for deciding against. The more internal loads and the emptying of the fuel tank moved the centre of gravity forwards, he explained, thus increasing the tendency to understeer, so the rear roll centre rose, creating a compensating roll oversteer effect and ensuring that the handling remained consistent whatever the load state – something a self-levelling system would actually have spoiled.

In the engine department, the original idea had been for the XJ4/6 to use a 3-litre version of the XK engine, with the shorter-stroke dimensions of the 3-litre competition units. However, as the programme progressed and the car inexorably gained weight, it was decided that sufficient performance to maintain the Jaguar image could only be achieved with an engine of larger capacity. It could only be an XK, because the V12 engine programme was still far from complete and the unit which would eventually take over from the XK, the 'slant-6' AJ6, was a long way in the future. The logical conclusion was that the XK 4.2, at that time still a comparatively recent 'stretch', should be carried across as the top-range power unit, delivering 245bhp with two SU carburettors. In this form the XJ6 was a genuine 120mph car, the *Autocar* achieving 123mph mean maximum in the manual/overdrive version and exactly 120mph in the automatic. The corresponding 0–60mph times were 8.7sec and 10.4sec, showing where the automatic transmission was most of a performance liability, and the overall test fuel consumptions were 16.0mpg and (amazingly) 16.4mpg respectively, suggesting in retrospect – or even at the time, truth to tell – that the automatic must have been driven somewhat differently at some stage of its test mileage.

However, apart from the trusty 4.2-litre there was also a 2.8-litre aimed at two distinct markets: on the one hand, the British buyer who might be tempted away from a volume manufacturer's top model into an entry-level Jaguar, and on the other, European customers who, in some markets, were subject to

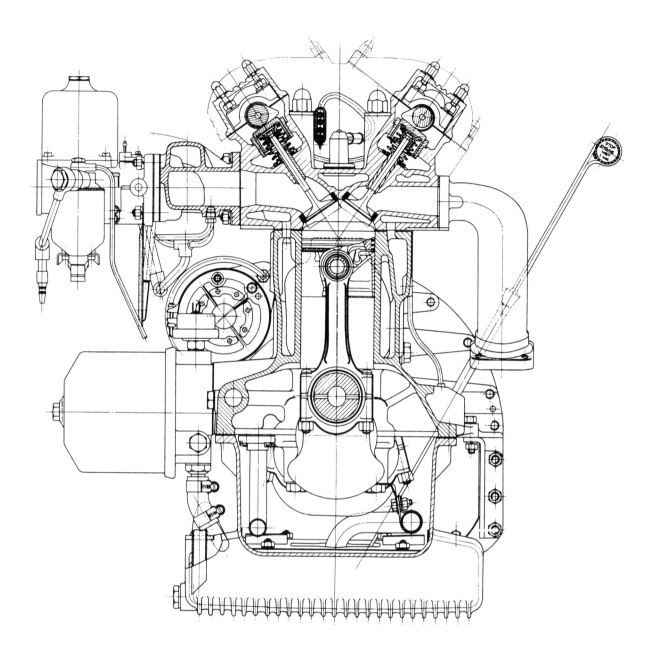

One of the less-successful aspects of the early-series XJ6 was the offering of a new 2.8-litre derivative of the XK engine. This version, seen here in cross-section, was intended for 'budget price' customers in the UK home market and for fiscally constrained European

markets. For reasons which have never been properly explained, the 2.8 proved unreliable as well as less economical than some owners may have hoped. It was quickly withdrawn, eventually replaced by a more satisfactory 3.4-litre. (JDHT/Paul Skilleter)

penal taxation rates on cars with engines of more than 3-litre capacity.

The 2.8 was created not by altering the 4.2 but by going back to the old short-block 2.4 and lengthening the stroke by 9.5mm, the new dimensions of 83mm bore by 86mm stroke giving an actual capacity of 2,791cc. The power output was given as 142bhp, although this was measured on the more conservative DIN basis and cannot be directly compared with the 133bhp (gross) of the 2.4. As it turned out, the 2.8

was a thoroughly unsatisfactory engine whose performance seemed mediocre without delivering any economy benefit. It also proved relatively unreliable, suffering a number of piston failures, and was somehow never available when either *Autocar* or *Motor* wanted to discuss the scheduling of a road test. Word went around the British market that the 2.8 was to be avoided and in 1972 it became 'export-only' to European markets where it had a supposed fiscal advantage. In fact, most of the XJ6s one saw in Europe around 1970 were 4.2s, suggesting that if customers were rich enough to buy the Jaguar, they were rich enough to pay the higher annual vehicle tax in places like France and Italy. Sure enough, in 1973 the 2.8 vanished altogether, to be replaced by a 'new' 3.4-litre XK which can be tracked through a series of mentions in Model Progress Meeting minutes. On 12 October 1971 it was said to be 'now giving 186bhp, well up to previous 3.4 standard.' The minutes from 6 April 1972 include the note that 'the decision has been taken to replaced the 2.8-litre engine with the 3.4', and on 9 May it was confirmed that the engine 'continues to make progress.'

To make matters more confusing, the new 3.4 was not a simple revival of the original XK engine, even though it had the familiar 83mm bore and 106mm stroke, but was in effect a small-bore derivative of the later 4.2 block, with the evenly spaced main bearings and stiffer bottom end, and with a straight-port cylinder head. It delivered 161bhp at a peak of only 5,000rpm, indicating that it was to some degree economy-tuned, and its torque output was far superior to the 2.8. With so much more clearance between the cylinder bores, it did not need the liners which had been a feature of both the 3.8 and the 4.2. In the hands of *Autocar*'s testers the XJ 3.4 achieved a mean maximum of 117mph in overdrive top – well below 5,000rpm – and 115mph in direct top, equivalent to 5,350rpm. Its 0–60mph time was a respectable 10.9sec and its overall fuel consumption was 16.7mpg. This seems scarcely to reflect an 'economy' engine but comparisons with earlier XJ6s could be misleading. The *Autocar* road test rightly points out that 'since 1971 the compression ratio has been reduced (to 8.8:1) to avoid the need for five-star (101RON) fuel, while the ECE15 emissions

Once the V12-engined E-type had been announced in 1971, speculation became rife as to when the unit would be fitted to the XJ saloon. The announcement came quite quickly, but production was extremely slow to ramp up. As explained in the text, doubts linger as to how fast the early XJ12 really was, since the engine delivered less than 300bhp, but sadly there could be no doubting the model's prodigious thirst – and unfortunately 1973 saw the eruption of the first great 'energy crisis' following war in the Middle East.
(Haynes Archive)

regulations have forced changes in ignition timing and carburettor settings.' Further proof of the situation came in a 1977 *Autocar* test of an XJ4.2 automatic which managed 117mph maximum, 0–60mph in 10.6sec and an overall fuel consumption of 15mpg. By this time, emissions engineering had seen the SU carburettors replaced with a pair of Strombergs for US-market cars, and the 'honest' DIN power output for these 4.2-litre cars was down to 180bhp at only 4,500rpm, with 315Nm of torque at 3,000rpm.

But the 'entry-level' engine, whether 2.8 or 3.4, was hardly the most burning issue where the XJ6 was concerned. To begin with, everyone was agog to know when the new engines promised at the time of the car's announcement would actually appear. In addition, there was the sad and long drawn-out episode of the 2-door coupé version.

The **V12** arrives

As we have already seen, the long-awaited all-alloy V12 engine (whose development story has Chapter 10 all to itself) made its first appearance in the E-type Series III in 1971, but it was clearly intended for wider application. In fact the XJ6 engine bay had been designed from the outset to accept the V12, something which was more or less obvious to enthusiasts even though they could not know exactly what size the V12 would be. Sure enough, the new car duly appeared in 1972 as the XJ12. This was another case of market-inspired XJ-renumbering, because the project number 'XJ12' had originally been allocated to the Series 2 E-type with 4.2-litre engine and all-synchromesh gearbox. As it was, the choice lay between XJ12 and XJ6 V12, and the view was that most speakers would shorten the latter into the former anyway.

It is interesting, now, to find an archived copy of a memorandum from Bob Knight to Lord Stokes, dated 10 June 1971 which lays out the planned new model and variant introduction dates for the coming three years. These included a target of March 1972 for the XJ12, May 1972 for the long-wheelbase versions of both XJ6 and XJ12, October 1972 for the XJ6 and XJ12 2-door coupé, and March 1973 for the XJ6 and XJ12 4-door 'Mark 2' (Series II). It goes on to suggest September 1973 for the XJ27 (the XJ-S) and March 1974 for the XJ28 (XJ-S convertible). With the benefit of hindsight it all looks horribly optimistic in terms of engineering load, but perhaps Bob Knight was creating an opening to plead for more Group resources to get the job done.

True, the V12 application was announced during 1972 but few prospective customers stood much chance of laying their hands on one until 1973. According to Andrew Whyte[2] a mere 326 XJ12s were delivered in 1972, plus 70 examples of a badge-engineered Daimler derivative, the Double Six. This was not because of unforeseen problems with the installation or in the new production facility in the Radford factory, still known in Coventry as 'The Daimler'. The main cause of the delay was the dreadful industrial relations which Jaguar seemed to have inherited as part of its merger with BMC, to become in turn part of British Leyland. Almost the whole of the 1970s were to see serious trouble on this front, aggravated by Sir William Lyons's effective retirement (he actually relinquished his directorship in March 1972, becoming the figurehead President, a title he retained until his death 13 years later) and the weakness of Jaguar management thereafter. It could be argued that Jaguar in this period suffered from British Leyland-style industrial relations because it had become far too integral a part of British Leyland; but its engineers were still striving away and there was nothing wrong with the basic product, only with how (and how often) it was put together.

From the outset, the XJ12 was available only with automatic transmission (the 3-speed Borg-Warner Model 12) which certainly took the edge off its ultimate potential performance. As discussed in Chapter 10, work proceeded for some time on a 5-speed manual gearbox of high quality which would have had the torque capacity to cope, but this project was shelved when it was realised that the vast majority of XJ12 customers would want automatic anyway. It would not have been worth tooling-up for a manual gearbox which would only ever have been made in small volume. The argument was that if a sufficient 'niche' demand arose, a gearbox could be

2 Andrew White, *Jaguar, the Definitive History*, Appendices

outside-sourced – but it never was, at least where the XJ12 was concerned.

The first test of an XJ12 carried out by *Autocar* is a source of contention, at least for the author who was on the magazine's technical and road test staff at the time. A full set of acceleration, braking and other figures was taken at the MIRA test track, one result being a 0–60mph time of 7.4sec. However, the car's maximum speed was too high to allow safe lapping on the MIRA high speed circuit and the time had arrived when trying to measure very high two-way mean maximums on British public roads reliably was asking for trouble. The then Managing Editor, the redoubtable Wing Commander Maurice Smith, DFC, volunteered to take the car on a long Continental trip during which he would establish the mean maximum speed, and he returned with a figure of 146mph which was duly published. Maurice was undoubtedly convinced of his figure and was not a man to be gainsaid, but the acceleration curve, mathematically extrapolated, suggested nothing more than 140mph. To this day, the author regards that as the real maximum, but at least the overall test fuel consumption of 11.4mpg was sadly credible. In the teeth of the changing political situation in the Middle East and the first energy crisis, it would do nothing to enhance the XJ12's chances of selling in any volume.

The early history of the XJ12 is somewhat confused because the long-wheelbase (LWB) alternative was announced shortly after – not coincidently with – the arrival of the new engine, and not much more than a year later, in 1973, the Series II XJ was announced with a wide range of improvements. As already mentioned, the LWB was a 4in stretch, the whole of the extra length going into the formerly cramped back seat – the back doors were also lengthened by 4in, the easiest way to recognise the LWB. Stretching a unitary body shell is never an easy exercise but at least in this case it was done as simply as possible, the main affected components being the floorpan (and thus also the exhaust run), the rear doors and the roof panel. The extra weight of the LWB was given as 80kg (176lb) which naturally had a small adverse effect on performance and economy. On the other hand, as is often the case, most test drivers thought the LWB handled better. Eventually, the LWB body was to become the standard for all 4-door XJs.

The changes which created the Series II were not mechanical although they did involve some substantial structural engineering. The first priority was to meet the coming wave of impact safety requirements in the US market, which involved more substantial bumpers sitting higher and on stronger mountings, in turn resulting in a shallower radiator grille with a larger auxiliary intake beneath it. The second priority was a radical improvement of the heating and ventilation system, with an airmix heater control unit replacing the old water-valve type, and better ventilating through-flow. This in turn enabled the optional air conditioning to be improved. The changes were accompanied by a new minor control layout which was not universally admired.

With the introduction of the Series II, the XJ6 and XJ12 designations were officially dropped in favour of new ones based on engine size. Thus we had the XJ3.4, XJ4.2 and XJ5.3 (with the V12 engine). Almost coincidentally with this came another announcement, from the Leyland Group, that Jaguar engineering would remain autonomous rather than being subsumed into the Rover-Triumph office, and that Bob Knight – who had fought hard for this independence – would be in overall technical charge with Harry Mundy responsible for powertrain development.

The change of nomenclature came about partly because within Jaguar, XJ6 and XJ12 had been superseded. It became policy not to discuss XJ numbers, because it inevitably gave clues to future model plans and also because the XJ6, in all its various guises, had caused an explosion of project numbers which could be misleading unless you were familiar with them all. Thus XJ29 and XJ30 were allocated to LWB versions of the 'Series I' XJ6 and XJ12 respectively. These were immediately followed by XJ31 and XJ32 for the equivalent LWB Series II cars, and then, confusingly, by XJ33 and XJ34 allocated to the short-lived standard 109in wheelbase Series IIs.

The saga **of the 2-door** coupé

Following on from this list, XJ35 and XJ36 referred to the 2-door XJ Coupé versions derived from the Series II cars, 6-cylinder and V12 respectively, which actually reached production. Confusingly, XJ37 and XJ38 were allocated to coupé versions of the Series I, which only ever existed in prototype, or perhaps pilot-production form. Also of interest, in passing, is the allocation of XJ42 to an XJ3.4C which never

The 2-door coupé version of the XJ6 was undeniably beautiful, but missed its target. Aimed at the growing demand for 2-door cars in the USA, it took far too long to enter volume production, and the relatively few cars to emerge were sold in Europe and especially in the UK home market. The requirement to make the 2-door body pillarless led to fundamental flaws (door sealing, aerodynamic noise) which were never overcome. Eventually, the 2-door was killed off in favour of the more profitable XJ-S with which it would otherwise have competed. (Haynes Archive)

happened, the number passing on to the convertible counterpart of the XJ41 Coupé (Chapter 12).

The outstandingly attractive 2-door coupé deriv-ative of the XJ was first exhibited in 1973, with the explanation that production would actually begin in 1974. In the event, based on Andrew Whyte's figures, only six XJ4.2Cs and nine XJ5.3Cs were actually delivered in 1974, although in the subsequent three years to 1977, production ran into four figures.

The reasoning behind the Coupé was simple: the American market had developed an avid taste for pillarless 2-door bodies. The car was therefore conceived on the shorter 109in wheelbase, with the rear doors deleted together with the centre pillars (the B-pillars) from which they hung, while the front doors were lengthened to meet up with a shortened structure on either side of the back seat. This rear structure played an important role because it had to transmit the loads set free by the deletion of the B-pillars, through the strengthened rear quarter panels (the C-pillars) and so into the roof. This was not a simple undertaking although the minutes of an MPM from 6 January 1972 note that 'the first full (XJ6 2-door) prototype should be ready to run by the end of January 1972.' The basic idea was praise-worthy, but these were the days before computer-aided design, and some optimistic assumptions seem to have been made about the ability to transfer loads not only through the doors, but some of the joints in the revised structure. It may also have been that the body team may have miscalculated the effect, even of small amounts of additional flexure on door and window sealing, aerodynamic noise and general refinement.

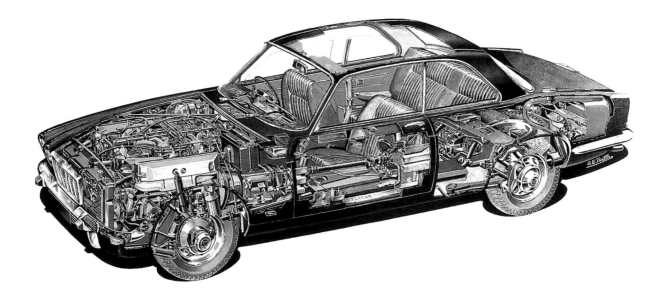

The problems proved intractable without further major work, and the XJC never 'made it big' in the USA. Many more of them were bought by home-market enthusiasts who simply loved the look of the car, but by the time production ended in late 1977, only around 10,500 (just over 20 per cent of them V12s) had been built, while production of the 4-door at that stage already ran deep into six figures. It was felt, among other considerations, that the XJC ran the risk of 'cannibalising' XJ-S sales, and that new car (Chapter 11) was seen as far more important not only as carrying E-type genes but also as being technically (if not aesthetically) more successful. In many ways the definitive XJC 5.3 road test was that conducted by *Autocar* late in 1975. By this time the V12 engine had lost its carburettors and gained D-Jetronic fuel injection by Lucas out of Bosch, and was delivering 285bhp (DIN) at 5,750rpm on a 9:1 compression ratio, with 399Nm of torque at 3,500rpm. Still with the Borg-Warner Model 12 transmission, this car reached a mean 147mph, ran 0–60mph in 8.3sec and achieved an overall test fuel consumption of 13.6mpg. Interesting, one might think, that the maximum speed achieved by this undeniably more powerful – and higher-geared – car only just exceeded that of the earlier saloon …

Above: A cut-away drawing of the XJ12C shows most of the general principles of the XJ body. A unitary shell, structurally far more efficient than the old Mark X, used front and rear sub-frames not only for suspension and front engine mounting, but also to provide effective insulation against noise transmission. In its day the XJ was reckoned to be almost peerless in terms of refinement. Although V12 engine was first seen in the E-type, it fitted the XJ's unitary-walled engine bay with no serious problems. (Author's archive)

Top right: By 1979, the XJ6 had already been in production for 11 years, but the travails of the Leyland Group through the 1970s and failure to bring the more advanced XJ40 project to fruition led to the creation of the XJ6 Series 3 which, while embodying useful improvements, was too close to the 1960s car to achieve a real step forward. The Series 3 also tried to embody, without great success, answers to some of the quality problems which had dogged Jaguar through the previous decade. (Jaguar)

Right: In addition to road testing, XJ4/XJ6 prototypes were extensively checked on 4-poster vibration rigs as seen here. (Giles Chapman Library)

One of the less fortunate aspects of the V12 version's career was its choice – by the Leyland Group – as Jaguar's contender in Touring Car racing (Group 2 of the European Touring Car Championship). True, it was a little lighter than the 4-door but it was still hideously heavy by comparison with its deadly racing rival the BMW 6-series, not as stiff, and extremely complex. Broadspeed did their best, but the car never achieved any results of significance, and in truth it never stood a chance. Beautiful it may have been, and most impressive on the road, but on the race track, hardly ever – although at times it was extremely quick while it lasted, which was never long enough. Perhaps one more season would have seen Broadspeed sort out its oil surge problems and its other causes of unreliability, but we shall never know. Its end came in the latter half of 1977 when it was announced that 2-door production would end imminently. As *Autocar* put it, 'it appears that it is to become a victim of the drive to streamline XJ production by rationalisation. The coupé still used the old short-wheelbase platform, whereas all other XJs now use the long-wheelbase body and have done for three years.'

As already indicated, that was really only part of the story. Through 1976, the minutes of Model Progress Meetings reveal an ongoing discussion about a Series III 2-door, the final kiss of death being the observation that 'a Series III 2-door would add substantially to engineering effort and programme investment. There is no evidence as yet of incremental sales from the 2-door model.' This came with the recommendation that 'the 2-door should be deleted at Series III launch' although in fact it didn't even last that long. It is worth noting, as a marketing factor behind this decision, that while British and European customers were prepared to pay extra for a 2-door coupé version of a 4-door saloon, American customers quite logically expected it to be cheaper!

Final essay: Series III

It was thus without the 2-door derivative that the original XJ series continued towards its final evolution, as the Series III, announced in 1979. This was developed using a further rash of XJ project numbers including XJ50 for the V12, XJ51 for the 3.4 and XJ52 for the 4.2 (although why in that order is not clear). Separate numbers, XJ53 and XJ54, were allocated to the Daimler Vanden Plas versions in 4.2 and V12 form respectively.

Now we were back to just three Jaguars, 3.4, 4.2 and 5.3, with Daimler Vanden Plas equivalents where appropriate. From the bodily point of view the Series III had an all-new 'glasshouse' with a subtly flattened roof and larger glass area, and therefore with more headroom and a lighter interior. In addition, the A-pillar bases were moved 3in further forward, making the windscreen flatter. This may have had a slightly adverse effect on aerodynamics, but it meant better visibility and more effective windscreen wiper action. The front and rear appearance had also been altered, the new, larger rear lamp clusters being a noticeable recognition feature. On the powertrain front, the V12 had been revised yet again to accept the Lucas interpretation of Bosch L-Jetronic simultaneous fuel injection, which was also applied to the 4.2, while both of the larger engines now used Lucas OPUS solid-state ignition. The 3.4 alone retained carburettors, plus conventional ignition. Claimed DIN power outputs were 287hp, 205hp and 162hp respectively. There were changes on the transmission front too, with General Motors' GM400 3-speed automatic now fitted to the V12, while as an alternative to the Borg-Warner 65 transmission in the 6-cylinder cars, the 5-speed '77mm' transmission from the Rover 3500 (SD1) had been successfully adapted. From Jaguar's point of view this must have been the only worthwhile thing that ever came out of British Leyland.

The GM400 transmission was not a new introduction for the Series III but was in effect a running change consolidated into the Series III launch. In mid-1976, the Model Progress Meetings (MPMs) were being told that stocks of the Borg-Warner Model 12 were being consumed at 220 per week and that they would all be gone by the end of October. Its replacement with the GM400 was 'proceeding according to plan' even though 'the introduction decision was to be confirmed.' Evidently it was. Other intriguing engineering points arising from the MPMs at this time included a serious proposal that the Series III body should incorporate the XJS boot arrangement, in which the spare wheel sat upright against the rear bulkhead. The reaction was that the change would cost too much, and that the existing arrangement could be made US Federal safety-compliant. It was also noted in 1976 that 'Product Planning and Marketing were in favour of EFI [Electronic Fuel Injection] for the Series III' – a recommendation which, as we have seen, led to EFI being adopted for the 4.2 (in fact US-market

The introduction of the XJ Series III saw the XK engine take one of the final steps in its career as a production engine, now equipped with fuel injection supplied by Lucas, but using Bosch technology. The under-bonnet view, shorn of carburettors, looked unfamiliar but mechanics soon learned that this was a complex system which opened a new era in terms of trouble-shooting and maintenance. (JDHT)

Series II cars had EFI from 1978) but not for the entry-level 3.4.

Once the Series III was in place, it was really a matter of holding the fort until the completely reworked XJ40 could be introduced some time in the 1980s (Chapter 14). There was one final twist to the story, however, and that came in 1981 with the introduction in the V12 engine, of a completely revised cylinder head which allowed the compression ratio and thus the engine's thermal efficiency to be raised. This reduced its fuel consumption which, with the world struggling to emerge from the second great energy crisis in less than a decade, had become barely acceptable. The new unit was ushered into being by an equally new product team. As recently as

the Series III launch in 1979 Jaguar's literature included a 'team photograph gallery' which included Bob Knight and Harry Mundy, both of whom retired in 1980, the last of the 'old guard' at Browns Lane (Walter Hassan had retired in 1972, alongside Sir William Lyons himself, and Bill Heynes had departed soon after the original XJ6 launch, in 1969). Thus the introduction of the HE (High Efficiency) version of the V12 fell to new Chairman and Chief Executive John Egan, assisted by Jim Randle as Director of Vehicle Engineering and Trevor Crisp as Group Chief Engineer, Power Units and Transmissions.

The full story of the V12's transformation into HE form is told in Chapter 10. Suffice it to say that the advanced thinking of the Swiss engineer Michael May enabled Jaguar to transform the V12, essentially by moving away from the Heron-type combustion chamber layout and re-engineering the formerly flat-faced cylinder head, to create a configuration in which an approximation to stratified combustion took place in a new chamber carefully shaped around the valves. As a result, the new high-compression V12 produced 299PS (DIN) at 5,500rpm compared with the former 287PS at 5,750rpm, while its maximum torque rose spectacularly from 383Nm to 432Nm, an increase of nearly 13 per cent. This not only increased the engine's efficiency but also allowed the final drive to be raised to 2.88:1, improving steady-speed fuel consumption still further. Now Jaguar could claim fuel consumption figures for the HE V12 saloon of 26.8mpg at 56mph, 21.5mpg at 75mph, and 15mpg in the urban test cycle, compared with the previous 21.2mpg, 18.2mpg and 12.5mpg respectively. The V12 had been given a final, and considerable, lease of life.

All that remains to note of the public life of the Series III is that although it was for the most part replaced by the XJ40 series in 1986, one survivor soldiered on until 1993. This was the top-line Sovereign V12 which survived simply because it took so long to install the engine into the new car. Indeed, in 1992 there appeared one final iteration on the XJ6 theme, this being the XJ Majestic LWB – a further 5in stretch of the original body shell, with a wheelbase of 118in. The modification of the body was out-sourced (to the Coventry company Project Aerospace) and included a higher roof and new window glass. This final model was current only for a year, because the V12-engined version of the XJ40 eventually emerged in 1993.

Oddments of a long career

Alongside the long-running production story of the XJ6 series, there were some episodes which understandably never saw the light of day at the time. There was for example, the allocation of project number XJ39 to 'Series III special bodies', covering the development of cars armoured and otherwise security-equipped to various standards. More fundamentally, there was an ongoing interest, encouraged by recurring energy crises and growing demand in Europe, in a diesel-engined XJ6. As early as 1984 the Austrian specialists Steyr fitted their advanced M1 unit-pump direct-injection diesel, with two-stage injection, into a demonstrator XJ6. The author was invited to drive it in Austria, where the vehicle seemed to perform extremely well and with remarkable refinement by the standards of the day. It is clear from documents in the archive that Jaguar evinced considerable interest in this installation and it is likely that the project foundered more on the question of cost and the size of the market than on technical grounds.

At about the same time the Italian diesel specialist VM was deeply involved in a project to create an XJ6 Series III diesel, using the company's 3.6-litre (92 x 90mm, 3,588cc) 6-cylinder turbodiesel, under the project number XJ44 ('XJ30 with 6-cylinder VM diesel engine'). It was a time when the US car market had entered into what turned out to be a short-lived whirlwind romance with the diesel engine, following the energy crises of the 1970s which had resulted in panic-stricken Americans spending a lot of their time queuing at filling stations. For a short time this was a serious programme involving the running of up to 14 development vehicles, but it was quickly terminated as the US market regained its normal gasoline-based equilibrium.

However, the question of the diesel engine would not altogether vanish. By the early 1990s the European executive car market was moving decisively in that direction. Mercedes had the longest history of all of building diesel passenger cars, and during the 1980s BMW joined in. By this time any legitimate interest should have been linked to the XJ40 rather than the XJ6 Series III, but alongside XJ44 the archive throws up another XJ project number, XJ59, 'projected XJ6 Series III with BMW 6-cylinder diesel engine'.

There was indeed renewed and strong interest in a diesel XJ during the 1990s and although the issue should strictly be dealt with in a later chapter, it is perhaps tidier to cover it here since the issue has been raised. VM returned to discussions with Jaguar in March 1994, bringing data on its enlarged in-line 6-cylinder indirect-injection engine with a 92mm bore and 94mm stroke (3,749cc) delivering 177bhp with turbocharging. This hefty engine did not have the technical credentials to impress Jaguar, at least by this time, and the project does not appear to have progressed to an actual installation.

Of more interest is the evidence that during this period (in other words, after the Ford takeover) Jaguar also spent some time talking to BMW, not only about 4-cylinder and 6-cylinder diesels, creating the XJ59 requirement, but also about 4-litre V8 petrol engines, of which 'up to 50,000 could have been supplied in 1995/96'. The latter suggestion was quickly dropped as it became clear Jaguar's own V8 (AJ26) was progressing well, but discussions continued regarding the possible supply of the BMW 2.5-litre indirect-injection 6-cylinder diesel engine (the BMW M51) complete with the ZF 5HP18 automatic transmission. Cars were certainly run in association with this project, which was cancelled when it was at an advanced stage, at the end of 1994. The trigger for cancellation seems to have been the discovery that BMW was well advanced with a new common-rail direct-injection 3-litre 6-cylinder engine which was finally announced in 1998. The archived Jaguar comment is that the company would have been 'entering into a 3-year contract with a limited-life engine … the project is not considered viable.'

One final project number firmly linked to the XJ6 is XJ60, allocated to road-running 'mules' powered by the AJ6 engine, for the XJ40 engineering programme. Among other things, the experience gained in installing the AJ6 engine in the 'old' body shell enabled this power unit as well as the V12 to be offered in the final XJ Majestic LWB. By that time, however, the history of the XJ6 had long been written so far as the engineers were concerned.

A racing XJ12C at Monza in 1977, the year the whole competitions programme was brought to an abrupt end. Broadspeed did its best to 'sort' the complex and overweight beast but the challenge was just too great. The car could be very fast, but never often enough or for long enough.
(Colin Taylor Productions)

10 The **V12 engine**, and a strange **V8**

Jaguar's celebrated V12 power unit had a chequered history, but one full of achievement. Its primary success was, of course, to be the only automotive V12 engine in genuine series production through the 1970s and most of the 1980s. There were other V12s at the time, from Ferrari and Lamborghini for example, but these were more or less hand-made and assembled, in hundreds rather than thousands, and certainly not to the tune of the all but 162,000 units produced by Jaguar. It was only towards the end of the Jaguar V12's career that true rivals appeared, from BMW and then from Mercedes.

There were times, especially during the politically inspired energy crises of the 1970s, when the V12 seemed to have been misconceived: too big, too thirsty, too complex. But when the engine first took shape, the idea of a V12 was entirely logical. First of all, one has to bear in mind that until the mid-1950s, Jaguar was essentially a manufacturer of large luxury saloons to which, almost by accident, a remarkable sports car line had been added. The XK, already well established, suited both products equally well but the logical view of the future was that the big saloons, the real money-earners, would become bigger and heavier still and would demand even more power and torque output to maintain and enhance Jaguar standards of performance.

Any substantially larger engine would need more cylinders. William Lyons and his engineering team did not want to venture too far down the 'big banger' path. The perspective of history is different now, but in the 1950s there were still plenty of people who had seen, heard and driven 1920s engines with capacities of more than 1 litre per cylinder – one firing stroke per telegraph pole, as the joke used to be – and they knew that was not the way to achieve the kind of operating refinement which was becoming an acknowledged Jaguar quality, every bit as much as its remarkable value for money. But more cylinders meant either eight or twelve, and already it seemed likely that the V8 would (as indeed it did) become commonplace in the USA; a vital Jaguar market. Being mechanical purists, the Jaguar team in those days did not favour the V8. As Walter Hassan put it to the Society of Automotive Engineers (SAE) many years later, 'a V8 configuration needs a two-plane crankshaft with wide outer crankshaft balance weights to eliminate its out-of-balance couple. The bank-to-bank firing sequence imposes severe limitations upon the achievement of an efficient induction system if carburettors are used.'

Thus at a very early stage, some Jaguar thoughts, notably those of Bill Heynes and Claude Baily (Walter Hassan had gone 'down the road' to Coventry Climax in 1950), were turning to a V12 of substantial capacity to power a new range of big saloons, the Mark X and its presumed successors. It is always important to remember that the V12, like the XK, was conceived not as a sports car engine but as a power unit for a large, fast and refined luxury car.

A protracted **birth**

The 'ideal' angle between the two cylinder banks of a V12 engine is 60° (or 120° or 180°, but not if you want the engine to be narrow enough to fit lengthwise into a bay between the front wheels). There is indeed the appeal, for a luxury-car designer, that a 60° V12 can be made narrower, although longer, than a 90° V8. A logical way of approaching the V12 requirement was to toy with the notion of two XK cylinder blocks and heads set in a 60° vee on a common crankcase and sharing a single crankshaft. In any such 'sharing' layout, including the pairing of two in-line 4-cylinder engines to form a V8, there is no need to retain the stroke of the original engine. The crankshaft, designed to provide twice as many big-end bearings, will be new in any case, so one might as well choose the most suitable stroke. The Jaguar engineers would have welcomed any opportunity to shorten the original over-long XK stroke (and thus also to reduce the overall height of the engine) while retaining the bore, but by how much?

Early experimental V12s consisted quite simply of two XK heads on a new V12 block, as seen here. The lack of space for an induction system 'in the vee' drove the team to the adoption of downdraught inlet ports from outboard-mounted SU carburettors, three per cylinder bank, allowing the exhaust to emerge from beneath. But the downdraught induction was found to inhibit efficiency and this was another factor in encouraging thoughts of an SOHC layout, especially for road-going engines where torque mattered as much as power. (JDHT)

As early as 1952, a list of Jaguar Works Order Numbers of experimental projects includes ZX/ZP505 for the 'XK 4.9-litre V12 engine'. Taking the original XK 3.4-litre bore of 83mm, then a 75mm stroke in a V12 engine rather conveniently yields a capacity of 4,870cc in a nicely proportioned engine, and this may have been the starting-point for the process when, as the evidence suggests, Bill Heynes encouraged Claude Baily to begin drawing-up V12

Above: Another view of the engine seen in the previous illustration, with carburettors and inlet manifolds removed and replaced by blanking-plates over the downdraught ports. In this form the engine looks undeniably handsome, but without the induction plumbing that was easy enough. The sheer DOHC

head-width of this engine seems to preclude even the 'cross-over' induction solutions adopted on later (German) DOHC V12 engines whose heads have much narrower included angles between inlet and exhaust valves – and much smaller valves, although four rather than two per cylinder. (JDHT)

schemes in the early 1950s. But why so much more capacity than the XK? One very good reason is that any V12 much smaller than 5-litre capacity begins to run into the opposite of 'big-banger' syndrome. The argument is that as individual cylinders are made smaller, thermal efficiency suffers because the ratio of surface area to volume of the swept cylinder quickly increases. However, the surface area through which heat can be rejected has an adverse effect on thermal efficiency, while the volume is the largest factor in power and torque-generating ability. This

relationship means that a small engine with lots of cylinders may provide plenty of piston area for high specific output, but (as some race engine designers of the 1950s discovered) it is no recipe for high thermal efficiency. The Jaguar engineers would have been well aware of this, and in any case, they wanted to be sure the new V12 engine would be substantially, indeed effortlessly capable of exceeding XK outputs. Hence the initial marker was 5-litre capacity, or something close to it, with an individual cylinder capacity of over 400cc.

A good deal of the background to the evolution of the V12 has been gleaned from a classic paper by Walter Hassan, originally presented to the SAE. The one drawback of this paper is that it is almost devoid of dates, but it is as well to recall that after serving as one of the 'founding fathers' of the XK, Walter Hassan left Jaguar in 1950 to work at Coventry Climax on what became a highly successful series of engines for Formula 1 and other racing applications. His eventual return to Jaguar in 1963 came about because that was the year in which Jaguar bought Coventry Climax to add to its then-growing empire. We know a V12 prototype was running in the XJ13 racing car by 1966, and it is scarcely credible that the whole programme was carried through, from initial concept to an engine capable of propelling the XJ13 to a record 160mph lap of the MIRA high-speed circuit, in less than three years. What Hassan (and Harry Mundy, who soon joined him) did was to carry forward the ideas which already existed, and which had been drawn up by Bill Heynes and Claude Baily, into a two-pronged V12 programme, one aimed at sports car racing, primarily Le Mans, through the 1960s and the other at evolving an engine for road cars 'which would deliver as much power (around 330bhp) as the most highly developed XK competition engines.' Administratively the picture is rather confused. The V12 race engine was accorded the first of a long series of Jaguar project numbers, XJ1, while a little later the designation XJ6 was allocated to the '12-cylinder and 8-cylinder engine range' although some time later, for reasons unclear, XJ6 was re-allocated to the '4/5-seater saloon' which began its works life as the XJ4. After that, it seems, new Jaguar engine series – not that there were many of them – were allocated project numbers from an AJ rather than an XJ range, the latter being reserved for vehicles.

Walter Hassan described in detail the long and ultimately fruitless development of the 4-cam, 5-litre (to comply with the then-current Le Mans prototype-class capacity limit) competition engine, with 87mm bore and 70mm stroke for a capacity of 4,991cc, which was fitted to the ill-fated XJ13 prototype and delivered 502bhp at 7,600rpm. This may not seem a very high specific power output these days but this was getting on for 40 years ago when 100bhp per litre from a naturally aspirated engine with two valves per cylinder was decidedly exotic. Even so, Hassan was not pleased to discover that the best brake mean effective pressure (BMEP) figure seen in the V12 was 'only' $191lb/in^2$, while the best of the 6-cylinder XK-derived competition engines had achieved $205lb/in^2$, or that its best specific fuel consumption was nearly 7 per cent worse than that of the 6-cylinder benchmark. There would have been scope for a great deal more work on the cylinder head design, but the lapsing of the competition requirement meant that work then concentrated on a road-going version. In retrospect, Hassan suggested the root of the problem lay in the downdraught inlet port arrangement which was adopted because the 60° angle between the cylinder banks, plus the twin-cam heads, meant there was no room within the vee for a proper inlet manifold, let alone the fuel delivery system, whether this was carburettors or injection. The later generation of V12s from BMW and Mercedes, now in production, overcomes this limitation – with the help of highly developed fuel injection – by 'crossing over' the manifolds so that the right-hand plenum chamber feeds the left-hand cylinder bank, and vice versa.

Admittedly, Walter Hassan took a slightly jaundiced view of the original V12 which, as already pointed out, was really the brainchild of Bill Heynes, assisted by Claude Baily who did most of the detail design. Heynes saw the engine as being equally capable of powering Jaguar's high-end road cars and of winning Le Mans, in exactly the same way as the XK but ten years on. When he returned from Coventry Climax, Walter Hassan was taken aback at the weight, complexity, bulk and general unsuitability of the Heynes/Baily 4-cam design. Paul Skilleter recalls being told by Hassan in 1975 that it wouldn't have fitted the car it was intended for, and its emissions were 'pretty hopeless' at a time when they were beginning to become a serious engineering constraint. Hassan's answer was in effect to work with Harry Mundy to design an alternative V12. Even then, Heynes remained wedded to the concept of 'his' 4-cam concept and towards the end of the 1960s it took a practical demonstration with two Mark Xs, one with the 4-cam engine, one with the new Hassan/Mundy single-cam unit, to prove the latter's superiority in terms of torque, and finally bring about the abandoning of the 4-cam design.

Hassan, aided and abetted by Mundy, was well aware that 502bhp was far more than the specification demanded for the road-going V12, but specifically he was worried that the chain drive to the four camshafts was complex, noisy, and a risk to long-term reliability. Consequently the two men, both ex-Coventry Climax, took a hard look at alternative cylinder head layouts and came down in favour of one which has served that engine specialist well – a 'Heron' head in which the valves sat upright and in line in a completely flat head, the combustion chamber being formed in the piston crown. The Heron head places a fairly severe restriction on valve diameter and consequently on gas flow, but in a road-going engine with the accent on mid-range torque this did not matter, in fact the high gas speed through a smaller valve curtain area was good for torque output where it mattered. The major advantage, though, was that the single-cam heads made the engine far more

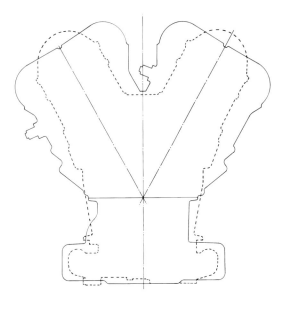

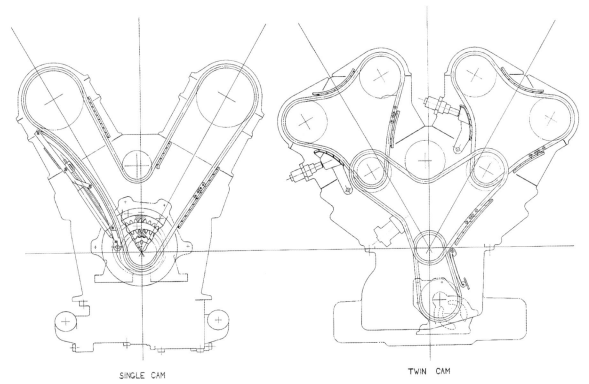

Left: One important reason for the selection of SOHC rather than DOHC design for the road-going V12 was the very significant reduction in engine bulk which resulted. The comparison, seen here, between the two layouts emphasises the saving, especially in installation width at cylinder head level. This made all the difference between being able to squeeze the V12 into engine compartments as a direct XK replacement, and having to indulge in substantial car redesign. (JDHT)

Below: Another advantage for the SOHC layout was a much simpler chain drive layout for the camshafts. The layout envisaged for the DOHC, as seen here, was in two stages with three chains of roughly equal length, and two intermediate pinions (the third, downward drive is to an oil pump). With SOHC, the designers were able to contemplate one single, although very long chain with a substantial blade tensioner (and a crescent-type oil pump built around the crankshaft). (JDHT)

SINGLE CAM

TWIN CAM

compact in cross-section (even though very slightly taller), that each head was 18lb lighter than its twin-cam equivalent, and that the chain drive to the camshafts was greatly simplified, to say nothing of the cost saving. On another tack altogether, at a time when – as already pointed out – emissions were first becoming a serious concern, the available evidence

suggested the Heron head would deliver better exhaust emissions performance, with lower hydro-carbon and NOx levels. These were strong argu-ments, especially when it was clear that the 330bhp 'headline' output target for the production V12 lay within easy reach, even more so given the decision (once free of the 5-litre racing sports car capacity

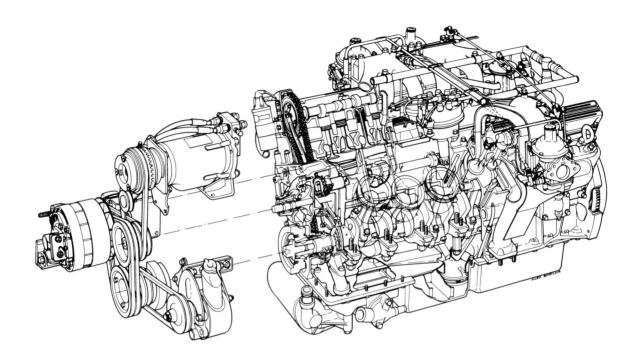

limit) to increase the bore to 90mm and thus the capacity to 5,343cc, the opportunity also being taken to make the big-end bearings wider.

Development of the V12 proceeded over an extremely long time – including the period in the late 1960s when the DOHC and SOHC engines were being developed in parallel prior to the definitive decision in favour of the latter – and was bedevilled by a number of problems, not least the question of fuel system design. As part of the high-tech modern image which the V12 was intended to foster, it was more or less assumed that it would have fuel injection – of some kind. The problem was that the British systems then under development were just that – under development. The minutes of a MPM dated 7 June 1966 noted that four systems were or had been studied from: AE Electronics ('slow development, problems with fuel temperature'); Marvel Schebler in the USA ('no commercial future'); Tecalemit ('little positive progress') and naturally from Lucas ('results awaited'). It should be no surprise not to find Robert Bosch on this list, because Bosch had close commercial ties with Daimler-Benz, and in the days of his full control William Lyons kept a bargepole to fend off anything that might connect Jaguar in any way, however indirectly, with Mercedes.

By 1968 the AE-Brico injection system had been further examined, and seems to have shown promise despite George Buck observing in one memo that 'the main Jaguar criticisms in the past have been poor driveability on manual cars due to part-throttle hunt, and inconsistent cold-start behaviour.' It seems that a decision was eventually taken, on the basis of some promising test results to adopt the Brico system for the V12. As Walter Hassan put it in his V12 engine paper, with the fully developed Brico system 'results were good, the driveaway from cold being outstanding … maximum power was appreciably better than that obtained from the carburettor set-up … moreover the installation was neater.' However, the process was doomed. The minutes of an MPM dated 5 February 1971 include the note that 'Mr England stated the XJ12 would go into production with carburettors as Brico had made the decision not to proceed with petrol injection.' Thus it was that the 5.4-litre V12 was first unveiled with a fuel system consisting of four Stromberg carburettors, and the rather disappointing peak power output of 276bhp at 5,850rpm. The torque output was 408Nm, somewhat more disappointing in being a 7 per cent improvement on the 4.2-litre XK for a capacity increase of around 26 per cent! But of course, apart from being hamstrung by the late decision on fuel system specification, the V12 had already gone some way down the road of meeting 1970s emissions requirements, even though at the time of its launch, requirements existed only in the USA, Canada and Sweden. On the credit side, the alloy V12 was only 80lb heavier than the 4.2-litre XK.

Road-going development of the V12 was conducted mainly in Mark X (XJ5) 'mules' under the designation XJ10. There was never any serious intention that the big car should enter production with V12 power, but they were less conspicuous than a V12 E-type would have been, and more readily available, with more room for instrumentation. The MPM of 7 June 1966 makes reference to these tests and in particular to the effort which had to be devoted to 'sorting' the complex accelerator linkage. There was also an amazing mechanical linkage which ensured automatic temperature control when starting the engine from cold.

A V8 diversion

The Jaguar archives also reveal an intriguing cul-de-sac leading off the V12 programme, in the form of an allied V8. As we have seen, in his SAE paper, Walter Hassan set out arguments in favour of the V12, and against the V8, which could be seen as disingenuous in view of the effort Jaguar was actually devoting to such a unit. This engine consisted quite literally of the middle two-thirds of the V12, with two cylinders lopped off either end. The result, inevitably, was a V8 with the 'wrong' included angle between banks of 60° rather than 90°, but also an engine which could potentially be machined on a common line with the V12 and which, with a swept volume of 3,563cc, might replace the XK with a lighter, higher revving and altogether more modern power unit suitable for a new sports car or a range of smaller saloons. Even the narrow cylinder angle was seen as not necessarily a disadvantage, since it made the engine more compact and easier to install in-line between front wheel arches – so long as the cylinder head design and manifolding could be sorted out. As a

serious engineering exercise, the programme ran from late 1965. Engine No.5 in the V12 development programme was actually a V8, and by mid-1966 it had been run initially with a fuel injection system and then with carburettors. Jaguar records show that in 1965, a 3.3-litre V8 with Lucas fuel injection and one throttle valve per cylinder was giving 235bhp at 6,500rpm on a compression ratio of 9:1, but with the miserable BMEP figure of only 147.4lb/in² at 5,500rpm. More representative of a production car unit was the 3,560cc unit tested in 1967 with twin SU carburettors and 10:1 compression ratio, yielding 204bhp at 5,750rpm but with only marginally better BMEP, 150.3lb/in2 at 4,500rpm. In short, it looks not only as though the mechanical balance of the V8 was problematic, but also that unless a decent inlet manifold arrangement could be devised, it would also be inefficient and consequently rather thirsty.

Even so, development of the V8 continued right up to 1971. In the minutes from the MPM of 5 February 1971 it was further noted that 'the double bulkhead in the XJ6 chassis has been completed and Mr Mundy has driven the car. He reports a noticeable improvement in noise suppression, but there is still some resonance confined to the floor panels, especially at 2,700-3,200rpm with wide-open throttle. Above this speed there are no further critical periods and in the higher range he considers the unit to be noticeably smoother than either the 4.2 or the 2.8 (XK).' By the MPM of 10 August 1971 'the V8 engine has been given twin balancer shafts, driven at twice engine speed by toothed belts. Mr England stated that a positive development programme for the V8 was to be drawn up by the next meeting.' In fact, it was the next-but-one meeting, on 10th November, which pulled the plug on the programme: 'Following the final assessment of the V8 engine it has been decided to stop further development work … the engine in its present state is thought to be just acceptable, but it is not considered to be an economical production proposition …' Thus ended a technically intriguing project which never saw the official light of day. Since then, a number of V8 engines have emerged with 'wrong' vee angles although not, so far as the author is aware, with a 60° angle. By contrast, there have been a good many V6s with a 90° angle, either because they began their lives as V8s which lost two cylinders, or simply to reduce installed engine height. And balancer shafts have become part of the engine designer's stock-in-trade …

Developing **the V12 – and** a matching **gearbox**

As observed in the chapter introduction, when the V12 was launched in the E-type in 1971, it gave Jaguar the only genuine series-production power unit of its kind in the world. The V12 engines in Italian specialist sports cars like Ferrari were not only hand-assembled but even hand-manufactured, with features such as crankshafts machined from the solid. It was a technical lead Jaguar was to maintain over its German rivals, BMW and Mercedes, for more than a decade, although when they entered the fray, it was with 4-cam engines and ultimately with 48 valves, something Jaguar never contemplated, at least for production.

What it did contemplate, even before the 5.4-litre unit had reached the market, was enlargement. It is interesting to note that when first announcing the Series 3 E-type and the V12, Jaguar stated in the press kit that 'In this engine we have provided ... a substantial reserve for capacity increases ... it is [also] relatively easy to derive a substantially smaller engine from the design.' As a statement, it was somewhat meretricious. The obvious way of increasing the engine capacity was to increase the stroke – there was hardly any scope for increasing the cylinder bore – and this had not only been tried but was destined to be put firmly on hold. As for the smaller engine, this was plainly a reference to the 60° V8 derivative whose career was about to be terminated before it had even begun.

What of that longer-stroke V12? This was a pet project of Harry Mundy's, and he tried as hard as he could to push it through. There was room for a crankshaft with a longer throw, but if the existing connecting rods were to be retained (and shorter ones would have degraded the engine's refinement by assuming greater angles and increasing sideways piston forces), then the block faces needed to be raised by the same distance as the extra stroke – and Mundy was proposing a stretch all the way from 70mm to 84mm, taking the engine's capacity to 6,413cc. This meant the deck height needed raising by more than half an inch (in 'old money'). At the MPM of 1 July 1971 it was noted that 'the costs of modification of the machining facility to accommodate the taller block are estimated at £40,000.' This, however, implied the use of a new, taller block casting which would call for much greater expenditure. The ingenious Harry Mundy had his answer ready: 'The use of a sandwich plate on the block (thus lifting the entire block relative to the crankshaft centre-line) could provide an easier alternative and is technically acceptable. The prototype engines have been manufactured in this way.' It was enough to sway the meeting, some of whose members' appetites had probably been whetted by driving the 6.4-litre XJ12 prototypes. Certainly the programme continued for another full year, with a further presentation to the MPM held on 2 June 1972 detailing the changes which would need to be made to a 'sandwich-plate' engine, including a slight lengthening of the heads and a small (0.1in) increase in the width of the valve seats. The response from the meeting was to tell Harry to go away and cost it for production. A week later, Harry was back with a figure of £238,100 needed for additional plant, mainly for the machining of the sandwich plate. Even that was apparently too much, and the project was shelved. More than two decades later, in 1993, the V12 would finally be enlarged by lengthening its stroke, but only to 78.5mm to create a nominal capacity of 6 litres (actually 5,993cc). Power output in this final form was 318PS (DIN) at 5,350rpm, while torque was 478Nm at 2,850rpm. Impressive figures indeed, and still from a 24-valve engine, but by that time Harry Mundy was not only retired, but dead ...

As a part-aside, still thinking of the man, his other pet project, closely linked to his big V12, was a 5-speed manual gearbox capable of handling the 6.4-litre's formidable torque output, which can hardly have been less than 500Nm. Harry, as good a gearbox man as he was an engine wizard, put a lot of effort into designing a gearbox which would be sweet to operate as well as having the torque capacity. His project reached the hardware stage, for at the MPM of 9 December 1971 it was noted that 'the five units (of the 5-speed box) fitted in vehicles have now completed over 100,000 miles – one alone over 50,000.' An outstanding question was whether the gearbox should have a cast-iron or an aluminium casing, the latter more expensive but 24lb lighter. As late as the MPM of 29 November 1972 estimates were being requested for the time and cost needed to take the 5-speed gearbox forward to production, but thereafter it seems to vanish from the visible record. Almost certainly, reality overtook the project with the

THE V12 ENGINE, AND A STRANGE V8

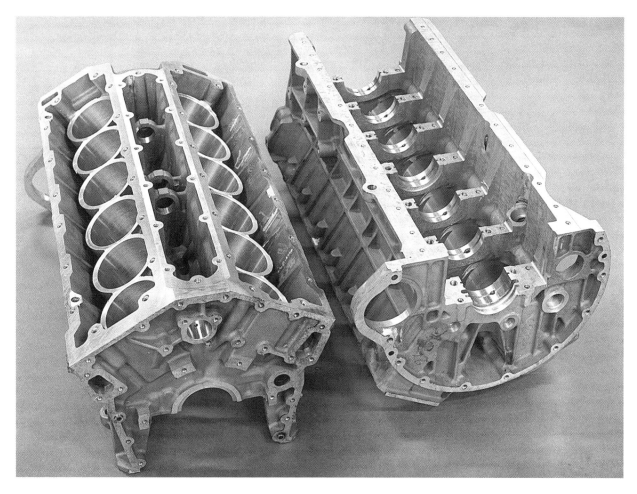

Left: Considerable facilities were installed at the Radford plant to manufacture the V12. The idea was that the 'slant-6' engine would in effect be half a V12 and would therefore be able to pass through the same production machinery, making it an economic proposition, but as described in Chapter 13 this simply did not happen. Ultimately, the V12 line produced a total getting on for 200,000 units, but it took over 20 years to do it. (JDHT)

Above: The quality of the V12 block was extremely high. Evident in this illustration is the 'open deck' design in which the cylinder head holds down the 'wet' cylinder liners against their locating spigots, and (looking from beneath) the way in which – unlike the venerable XK – the skirts of the V12 engine's cylinder block casting extend well below the crankshaft centre line, making the whole block stiffer and bearing alignment more reliable. (JDHT/Paul Skilleter)

realisation that automatic transmission was now becoming virtually standard for Jaguar's more powerful production cars, as a matter of customer choice rather than for any engineering reason. It is very unlikely that the Jaguar 5-speed gearbox would ever have covered its cost, and alternatives (from ZF or Getrag) would have been available if a small-volume niche had ever emerged.

To return to the V12: it saw two highly significant moves after it had been in production for a few years in the specially created facility in the former Daimler factory at Radford. The first was the adoption, at last, of electronically controlled fuel injection to replace the early carburettors. The change was essential partly as a move to improve the early XJ12's awful fuel consumption (the first *Autocar* road test figure was 11.4mpg) but mainly to anticipate the steady tightening of exhaust emission regulations which would eventually put the carburettor out of business altogether so far as cars for developed markets were concerned. The chosen system was Bosch's

D-Jetronic, but it needed to be adapted to suit the 12-cylinder engine and this work was carried out by Lucas, whose name gained at least equal billing when the development was announced. In retrospect it was a strange system in which the original Bosch electronic control unit ('which has all the complex transistorised circuitry of a modern FM radio', observed *Autocar*) was installed in the boot while the Lucas 12-cylinder adaptor unit was housed in the engine compartment. The injectors, fed with fuel from a gallery maintained at $28lb/in^2$, sprayed into the semi-downdraught inlet ports on the inside faces of the vee. As before, the incoming air passed above the cylinder heads from outboard plenum chambers, but the removal of the carburettors made the whole installation narrower and neater. With the aid of the new injection system, the power output of the V12 in a form which complied with exhaust emission regulations as they then existed, rose to 285bhp at 5,750rpm, with a torque figure of 399Nm at 3,500rpm.

Supply problems in the strike-ridden mid-1970s meant that the system was at first offered only in the XJ12C, the saloon continuing for the time being with the carburetted engine. Four months later, with the announcement of the V12-powered XJ-S (Chapter 11), the injected engine became the standard unit with a welcome, if small improvement in fuel economy. In 1980, this early-generation injection system was replaced by a Lucas system with fully digital control, which allowed the compression ratio to be raised from 9:1 to 10:1. This improved operating efficiency a little more but not, given the constraints of the time, anything like enough.

The **V12 HE** versions

The next great move in the V12 saga had everything to do with its fuel economy which, as the world lumbered from the first great energy crisis of the early 1970s into the second at the end of the decade, was becoming a major liability. Rapidly falling sales

Left: The author (left), on the way home from a Geneva Motor Show in the 1970s, talks to the Swiss engineer Michael May. It was May's concept of a high-compression, semi-stratified charge combustion chamber which proved the salvation of the V12 at a time when it might have been consigned to history for being hopelessly uneconomical. (Author)

Above: Comparison of the May 'Fireball' cylinder head (right) with the original V12 head (left). In the Jaguar HE (High Efficiency) engine with the May head, the original completely flat-faced head with in-line valve housings is replaced by one in which the valve housings are recessed, the inlet valve more notably so, forming a pocket in which initial rich-mixture combustion takes place before expanding into the main chamber as the piston descends. (JDHT)

indicated that the V12 would die unless something drastic was done to improve its efficiency. In fact, soon after the first introduction of fuel injection, the Jaguar engine development team under Harry Mundy had been seeking solutions. In 1981, after a five-year gestation period, the company announced a radically revised unit in which the original 'flat' Heron-type head was replaced by a new one in which complex combustion chambers were formed around recessed valves, with the exhaust valve withdrawn further than the inlet valve. The pistons now became flat-crowned rather than housing the combustion chamber as before.

The principle behind this combustion chamber configuration, was first devised by the Swiss engineer Michael May. This induced a very high swirl rate within the combustion chamber as the squish effect of the rising piston forced the mixture from the shallow recess around the inlet valve, via a carefully shaped channel into the much deeper recess around the exhaust valve in which the main fuel burn

V12 Engine Performance Torque Comparison
EUROPEAN SPECIFICATION DIN TEST

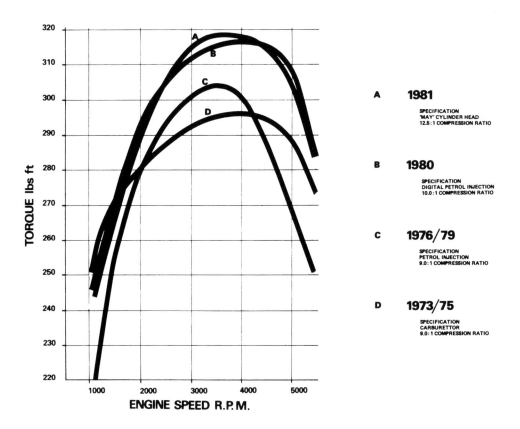

A **1981**
SPECIFICATION
'MAY' CYLINDER HEAD
12.5:1 COMPRESSION RATIO

B **1980**
SPECIFICATION
DIGITAL PETROL INJECTION
10.0:1 COMPRESSION RATIO

C **1976/79**
SPECIFICATION
PETROL INJECTION
9.0:1 COMPRESSION RATIO

D **1973/75**
SPECIFICATION
CARBURETTOR
9.0:1 COMPRESSION RATIO

actually took place. A high-energy sparking plug, energised by a twin-coil system, ignited the swirling mixture as it swept past, so that the flame front spread very quickly throughout the upper part of the chamber. The system had the further benefit of providing much more reliable combustion of weak mixtures, allowing the compression ratio to be increased to no less than 12.5:1. This was remarkable at that time, and avoided the twin dangers of detonation (knocking) and of misfiring which spelt trouble for the catalytic converters already required for the American market. The high compression ratio not only improved efficiency and thus fuel economy but also increased the BMEP and hence the engine's output, which rose to 299PS (DIN) at 5,500rpm, with 432Nm of torque at 3,000rpm. At that time, though, it was the economy that mattered, and Jaguar proudly proclaimed that the new V12, dubbed the HE (High Efficiency) engine, 'gives potential fuel consumption of better than 20mpg in out-of-town

motoring.' The new economy was assisted by a further rise in the final drive ratio which had begun life (in all V12-engined cars) at 3.31, then moved to 3.07 with the introduction of fuel injection, and now became 2.88:1.

It is worth pondering for a moment as to why the May 'Fireball' combustion chamber principle, so named because the bulk of combustion took place in the tightly swirling 'ball' of mixture in the small pocket beneath the exhaust valve, failed to gain wide acceptance elsewhere. To begin with, the May geometry was only applicable to engines with in-line, and preferably vertically installed valves – which was one reason why it appealed to Jaguar. That apart, you have to look at the five years it took to carry the idea from concept to production in the Jaguar engine. To achieve optimum results, the geometry of the chamber needed painstaking development which, at that time, involved huge amounts of 'cut and try' testing. Today it would be a different matter since

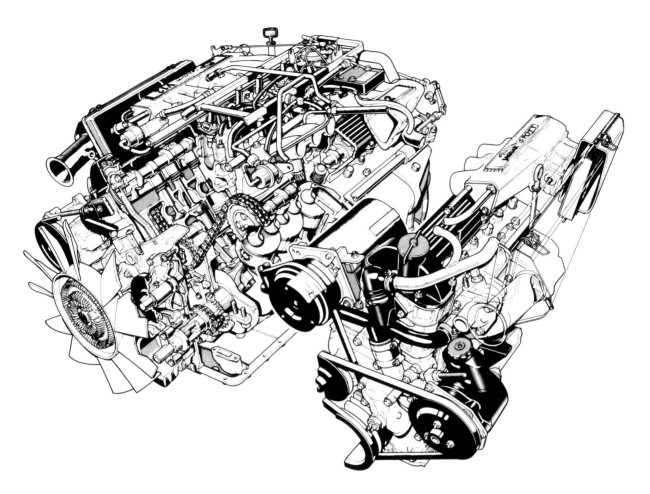

Left: Torque curves for four successive iterations of V12 development – curve D being the original specification, C showing the effect of switching to fuel injection, B (a very large gain) following the switch to injection with digital rather than analogue electronic control, and A the HE engine with the May 'Fireball' cylinder head. While this shows the HE engine achieved the highest peak torque of all, it fails to reveal that it was also more efficient and substantially more economical.
(JDHT/Paul Skilleter)

Above: The final evolution of the V12 as a production engine came in the 1990s when its capacity was stretched to a full 6 litres, through a lengthening of the stroke. This sectioned drawing, compared with that shown earlier, has few obvious changes to the engine's main structure, but of course the ancillaries and the induction, fuel delivery and ignition systems are completely different. Jaguar never did move to a crossover induction layout, however. (JDHT)

computer programs exist which would enable the whole system to be mathematically modelled and 'tweaked' without ever cutting metal, but Jaguar moved from long experiments with a single-cylinder test engine, to the running of a slant-6 engine in a car, to full clearance of the V12. It was a process that took so long that it saw Harry Mundy – who always had faith that the May head would rescue the V12 from its plight – into retirement and his place taken by Trevor Crisp, who oversaw its final stages. Just how crucial the matching process could be, was seen in what amounted to the carrying-over of the V12 HE head to the 2.9-litre 'economy' version of the 6-cylinder AJ6 engine, which might in many respects, be viewed as half a V12. It was not a success, although as explained in Chapter 13, that was not entirely the engine's fault.

From a production point of view, the HE engine was a minimum investment, which was part of its appeal. Clearly the cylinder head casting had to be new, incorporating the recessed combustion chambers. Otherwise, all that was needed were new facilities to finish-machine the combustion chambers, to machine the recesses for the repositioned valve seats, and to drill and tap the repositioned sparking plug housings (which were actually simpler than before, set at an angle to the vertical but perpendicular to the engine centre-line). The total cost was put at £500,000, almost insignificant compared with the investment needed to produce a completely new engine or one whose layout had been significantly changed.

Despite the success of the May HE head, speculation arose from time to time as to what might be achieved with a twin-cam, 4-valve head. In fact, two such engines had been prepared during the early 1970s as part of Harry Mundy's 'research programme'. The cylinder heads were distinctly 'modern' in the sense that the angle between the valves was much less than in the XK head – and in the end, this design led on to the 24-valve head for the AJ6 engine (Chapter 13). Of the two engines built, one was supposed to be in road-going form and was indeed installed in an XJ12 which Mundy drove for a time, complete with his 5-speed gearbox. The car's performance was electrifying, but most of the improvement came towards the top end of the rev range and the fuel consumption could only be described as frightening. The second engine was developed to a 'race' specification and delivered 630bhp on the test bed, but found no application. When, during the 1980s, Jaguar returned to racing 'by proxy' with the long XJR series, other means were used, culminating in a twin-turbo V6. The 48-valve racing V12 was at this time handed over to TWR, who are reputed to have stripped it and then scrapped it. What became of Harry Mundy's road car and its engine is not recorded.

It was not the end of 48-valve V12s, however, because two further versions were developed and run during the late 1980s. TWR developed 4-valve heads for its 7-litre racing engines, fielding such units from 1987[1], but these were never in any sense production units, nor was there any production engineering spin-off. Jaguar itself developed a new 4-valve head design which was fitted to the 6,222cc V12 assembled by TWR and installed in the sole XJ220 prototype of 1988, but again, matters progressed no further.

1 *Jaguar World*, January/February 1994, article by Michael Cotton

Possible applications for extremely large and powerful engines became very limited once the supercar fad of the late 1980s had evaporated, and Jaguar had other priorities claiming the attention of its limited budget.

All that was ever done to the production V12 HE by way of late-life development was to enlarge it to nominal 6-litre capacity (90mm bore by 78.5mm stroke, 5,994cc) for use initially in the final series V12 saloons launched early in 1993. In this form, DIN power output was given as 318PS at 5,400rpm and torque as 463Nm at 3,750rpm, these figures achieved despite a reduction in compression ratio to 'only' 11:1. Other changes included new cylinder liners, a new camshaft profile to overcome long-running complaints about noisy tappets if the production and assembly tolerances 'stacked up' in the wrong direction, and most important, a new forged-steel crankshaft similar – in principle – to that adopted for the 4-litre AJ6 engine. It all looked superficially promising but the signs were soon emerging that the V12 was reaching the end of its life. The real problem was ever-tightening emissions regulations which had lain behind the creation of the 6-litre version, teamed as it was with a low-loss catalytic converter system and 4-speed automatic transmission with overdrive. Anyone who kept an eye on such things was aware that the V12-engined Jaguars had been withdrawn from the US market at the end of the 1995 model-year, and the XJS V12s were even then available in the UK only, and to special order. In 1996 XJ-S production ceased altogether and towards the end of the year the V12 saloon was relegated to special-order status.

On 17 February the last V12 engine emerged from the Radford factory, which was subsequently de-activated and sold off. Future Jaguar engines would come from a special section of the Ford engine plant at Bridgend in Wales, or even from North America. On 17 April 1997 the final V12 saloon came off the line, to be taken – in accordance with tradition – directly into the Jaguar Daimler Heritage Trust Collection. It was the end of an era, but one in which the Jaguar V12 was no longer alone. Later V12s, better able to meet upcoming emissions requirements, had emerged from BMW, from Mercedes and even from Toyota. To an extent, they had all drawn inspiration from the Jaguar engine which was able, as it left the scene, to look back on 25 years of production. At times the build rate had been perilously small but it had survived, and eventually prospered to the tune of 161,996 engines off the line. Henceforth Jaguar would use other, more efficient ways of achieving similar results. Among its achievements, the V12 had long enabled Jaguar to remain pre-eminent in terms of operating refinement even during the darkest days of poor quality control, and it may indeed seem strange that Jaguar abandoned the configuration just when its German rivals had, at long last, embraced it. As we shall see, however, work carried out during the 1980s, and carried forward once Ford finance was available, led the company in a new direction.

Readily available at a relatively modest price, the Jaguar V12 had great appeal for the builders of scaled-down WW2 fighters like the two-thirds-scale Spitfire seen here. Compared with a real *Merlin engine the Jaguar was actually tiny, 5.4 instead of 27 litres, and 300 instead of well over 1,000bhp. But the configuration was right...* (Paul Skilleter)

11 XJ-S: a very different car from the E-type

By 1970 it was clear that the E-type had only limited production mileage ahead of it. It was still much admired but the V12 engine installation was something of a 'shoehorn job' and the implications of safety legislation were becoming a pressing concern. The nose structure of the E-type might have been strengthened to give it greater impact energy-absorbing capacity, but only at the cost of adding nose weight and, possibly, of spoiling that classic shape. And in any case, classic though it was, the design was coming up for ten years old. Given the time it would take to develop a replacement, it was already destined to remain in production longer than had the entire XK120/150 series. Beyond it, the situation called for a new car – but what kind of new car?

One strongly advocated possibility, then and for many years afterwards, was simply an updated E-type, an F-type, which would directly assume the mantle and continue the tradition of a technically advanced sports car with high performance, offering astonishing value for money. One problem with this approach was that Jaguar didn't have the right engine. The XK could no longer be regarded as technically advanced. It had been in production and continuous development for more than 20 years, and had reached the limit of its practical potential. The V12 was a splendid engine, but it was too big to power a 'classic' sports car and was larger than any V12 Ferrari had produced up to that time, for example. There were two engines which might have been more suitable, but one of them, the compact 60° V8 derived from the V12, had been discontinued without reaching production and the other, the 'slant-6' which had been conceived as a sort of half-V12 could not possibly be developed to production standard for several years. In the event, the latter finally emerged into public view in 1983.

However engineers may dislike them, there were also marketing and commercial considerations. The market for a car like the E-type was limited – the type had proved that itself. Many people might admire it and aspire to it, but for one reason or another they would or could not actually buy one. So, the argument ran (as it always does) if you are going to build a car in relatively small numbers, you might as well make it one which commands the largest possible margin – which achieves the highest 'value-added', in more modern jargon. This argued not for an elegantly minimalist sports car but for a luxury grand-tourer, the kind of car for which the V12 engine would be

well suited. It was the same argument which, within a year or two, saw Lotus abandon the Elan formula in favour of the heavier, faster and much more expensive Elite. Within Jaguar, the argument was accepted and the XJ-S duly appeared. Nobody ever saw it as an E-type replacement even though in 'the book' – the register of formally issued XJ project numbers – it was the XJ27, the 'XJ25 replacement'. As we have already seen, XJ25 was the final E-type, the 2+2 V12 Coupé.

The best benchmark by which to judge the XJ-S is not the E-type, even the 2+2 V12, but rather the XJ12C which as explained in Chapter 9, was announced two years earlier but through a process of production delay, actually went on sale within months of the new model. The XJ-S is 7in shorter in its wheelbase than the 2-door Coupé, with virtually the same track – a fraction wider at the front. In overall dimensions it is longer, but by less than 2in; wider, but by less than an inch; but lower, by more than 6in. It is also lighter, by 187lb. Except for the height and the wheelbase, these are not great differences. It makes it easier, perhaps, to understand why the Jaguar board eventually decided the two cars could not co-exist. But in that case, why create a brand-new body with less room inside rather than putting right the known, and not insuperable problems of the Coupé?

The XJ-S was never an E-type replacement, always a 2+2 Grand Touring model – and initially, with no alternative to the V12 engine, thus making it the first Jaguar model never to be powered by the XK engine since that power unit had been announced in the 1940s. Jaguar purists decried the styling, especially of the back end, although there are indications that its aerodynamics were substantially superior to those of the E-type. (Giles Chapman Library)

This was, as a politician would say, a good question. There seem to have been two plausible answers. One was purely engineering: the brand-new body – or rather, the all-new superstructure built on a shortened XJ platform – provided a much better chance to get everything right: the stressing of the shell, the compliance with the latest safety regulations, any lessons learned from seven years of XJ production. The second answer was marketing. The Coupé was not a new car, merely a derivative. Had it continued in preference to creation of the XJ-S, Jaguar would have been reduced in some important eyes to the status of a single-model company. At the time, that might have suited some in the British Leyland empire, which may in turn explain why the Jaguar board was so keen to do the XJ-S and to ditch the XJ12C. But there would

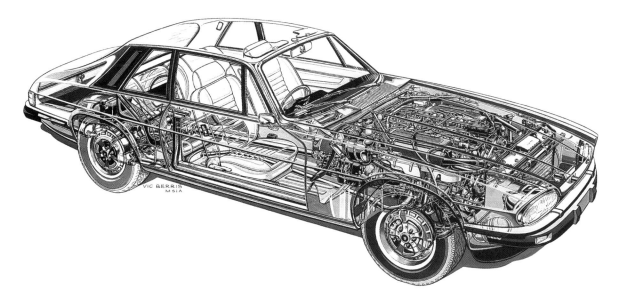

The XJS was structurally robust, certainly more so than the XJ Coupé which it effectively saw off. It was among other things the first new Jaguar model to be engineered with some knowledge of the extent to which future safety regulations would be imposed, and the result was a body shell which may not have been especially roomy, but which was stiff enough in torsion and bending to guarantee acceptable accuracy of suspension geometry, even under high loads. (LAT/Giles Chapman Library)

also have been a commercial argument. One has to assume that, aside from the question of amortising development costs, the two cars would cost much the same to make – the XJ-S probably slightly less, profiting from XJ experience. Yet in January 1976 the XJ-S was listed at £7,607 before tax, and the XJ12C – same engine, same automatic transmission – at £6,472, almost 15 per cent less, because how much more can you charge for a 2-door than for a bodily very similar but roomier 4-door, 4-seat saloon (which then listed at £6,039)? In other words, from the very start, there was little question as to which model was the more profitable.

Such arguments are cynical, perhaps. It is also true that the XJ-S might have assumed a different shape if, when serious design work began in 1970, it had not seemed that the American safety regulations were in effect going to outlaw convertibles. It was exactly the same situation which led Triumph to build the TR7 only as a hard-top, and which spelled the end of an older generation of sports cars, and it certainly

encouraged Jaguar to engineer the XJ-S purely as a top-of-the-market 2+2 GT Coupé (a full 4-seater the XJ-S never was), with the technical appeal of being powered by the only V12 engine in genuine series production. The engineers may not have needed much encouraging, since a closed body makes it much easier to achieve sufficient strength and stiffness without adding too much weight.

The actual design of the XJ-S has been questioned at length, yet it was the last Jaguar into which Sir William Lyons had any significant styling input, and also the last one to profit from Malcolm Sayers's aerodynamic expertise. And here lies an odd point. When the XJ-S was launched, Jaguar released figures for the aerodynamic drag coefficient of the new car, the E-type 2+2 Coupé and the XJ6, measured in the MIRA wind tunnel, together with frontal areas. The Cd figures were 0.48 for the XJ6, 0.455 for the E-type and 0.39 for the XJ-S; the frontal areas were 19.8, 17.8 and (again) 19.8 square feet respectively. Now, the Cd figures are something of a blow for those who regard the E-type as an object of aerodynamic purity. As a one-time aerospace industry wind tunnel engineer himself, the author is not going to take issue with the MIRA measurements except to observe that the E-type figure looks surprisingly bad. Why so, and how did the XJ-S, which looks aerodynamically so much worse around its nose section in particular, actually turn out so much better?

The answer, one suspects, is really quite simple. Like anyone coming from the aircraft industry to the motor industry, Malcolm Sayer would have found it a very different world. Techniques which work well on a shape flying in a homogenous gas can be confounded by the immediate presence of the ground, and of a wheel at each corner rotating at high speed. In particular, the way you design the back end of the car to achieve best results is not always obvious, although the trick is to leave behind a wake which is as stable and which contains as little energy as possible. It seems likely that Sayer learned a great deal from the competition cars and the E-type and thus came to terms with all this. That was what led him to the shape of the XJ-S, with its apparently high prow (but wide, shallow letter-box air intake and improved under-bonnet airflow) and its seemingly strange back end with the two 'sails' extending rearwards from the C-pillars along the rear wings. It was a shape which did a remarkably good aerodynamic job by the standards of the mid-1970s. A decade later, everyone was quoting drag coefficients, but it was not something the pundits worried about in 1975. As for the E-type Coupé, with the benefit of 20:20 hindsight, the smooth, uninterrupted curves of its back end now look like a recipe for unpredictable flow breakaway and a large trailing wake. The XJ-S 'wings' on the other hand, pulled two tight vortices onto that near-flat boot lid, to spill aft of the car in a much better organised manner. That did not stop them jarring in the eyes of the Jaguar traditionalists.

So far as the structure was concerned, the XJ-S started with a shortened, literally a 'cut and shut' XJ6 floorpan, complete with the XJ sub-frames carrying the suspension attachments, the front engine mountings and the final drive. One subtle change for the new car was an increase in castor angle, from 2.5° to 3.5°, to provide more positive self-centring. With Adwest power-assisted steering standard, there was no need to worry about steering effort. The chosen tyre size was 205/70VR15, extremely modest by the standards of today's often over-tyred high-performance cars but perfectly adequate for their task. Fitting an anti-roll bar to the rear suspension as well as at the front not only reduced roll angles but afforded the opportunity to tune the handling easily by varying the ratio of front to rear roll stiffness – although it has been suggested that the original XJ-S could have been made to behave perfectly satisfactorily with a front anti-roll bar alone.

From the floorpan upwards obviously the structure was new, strong and stiff. The lessons of the XJ6 2-door had been taken aboard. The wide C-pillars with their rear 'sails' might have been less than helpful for rearwards visibility but they fed loads into the roof – itself shorter and therefore stiffer than in the XJ – very efficiently. So did the windscreen pillars, rising from the extremely stiff structure in the scuttle area. Jaguar's body engineers had two big doors to hang, and they weren't going to risk structural deformation around the hinges. From the impact safety point of view the XJ-S structure looks crude today, but in 1975 it complied not only with existing but also with then-foreseen regulations. For the US market, the car came with 'Federal' front bumpers on collapsible, recuperating mounts. The back end owed as little to the XJ saloon in layout as it did in looks. The boot lid (a rear hatch would have been a very tricky structural undertaking) opened to reveal the spare wheel stowed vertically behind the back seat, rather than horizontally under the floor as in the XJ6, with the battery alongside. The single 20-gallon fuel tank was installed high, immediately behind the back seat. As a result, the entire rear overhang was little more than empty shell and crush-length – overkill, in some respects, in anticipation of rear-impact safety requirements which could be more conveniently met in other ways.

The new body was produced in what was soon destined to become – at last – Jaguar's own facility, although this came about by corporate accident rather than dedicated investment. In earlier and more prosperous times, BMC had sought to boost its capacity by taking control of the huge Birmingham facility of Fisher and Ludlow (installed in the former Castle Bromwich factory which, during the Second World War, had been responsible for building almost half of all the Spitfire fighters ever made). That was in 1953, and was one of the factors which drove Jaguar towards Pressed Steel with all its apparent limitations. Then, in 1965, BMC also swallowed Pressed Steel (a year before the 'autonomous merger' with Jaguar itself) and formed the unified Pressed Steel-Fisher. Thus both the XJ6 and the XJ-S bodies were sourced from the Castle Bromwich plant which was at least usefully close to Browns Lane. Then in 1980, when British Leyland was in process of unravelling, direct control of Castle Bromwich passed to Jaguar and the plant continued exclusively with body assembly and painting of both saloons and coupés. The actual pressed panels were still mainly supplied from Swindon by what had become Austin Rover, but at least Jaguar was running its own body assembly. Towards the end of the 1980s plans were made to switch panel pressing to a facility in Telford, to be run by a company (Venture Pressings) 50:50 owned by Jaguar and GKN.

Engine aspects

The XJ-S naturally began life with the latest fuel-injected V12 engine as its power unit, and thus with 285bhp (DIN) at 5,500rpm, and 399Nm of torque at 3,500rpm. It was offered, at least initially, with either the Borg-Warner Model 12 3-speed automatic or (perhaps as a final gesture towards the retiring E-type) Jaguar's 4-speed manual gearbox. In either case, the ratio of the Salisbury Powr-Lok limited-slip differential was 3.07. With the standard tyre size and no overdrive available, this meant that peak power was reached in top gear well before maximum speed. *Autocar*'s 1975 road test achieved an actual mean maximum speed of 153mph – achieved on German autobahns in a well-documented excursion – corresponding to an engine speed of 6,180rpm, quite enough to wreck an XK engine in a short time. The short-stroke V12 was made of sterner stuff, but the result did suggest that with a 2.88 final drive, that manual-transmission car might easily have exceeded 155mph which would then have corresponded to just short of 5,900rpm. The acceleration time to 60mph was 6.9sec, and the overall test fuel consumption, including long periods of high-speed driving in Germany, was 15.4mpg. The two lessons which appear to emerge from these figures are that the XJ-S was indeed aerodynamically superior to the XJ5.3C tested earlier in the same year, and that the Borg-Warner automatic with which the latter was fitted was doing no favours to acceleration or to fuel efficiency – which did not stop 80 per cent of early customers specifying it.

In any case, the Borg-Warner transmission was quickly supplanted by the General Motors THM400. As *Autocar*'s road test (written, it can now be confessed, by the author) of an automatic transmission XJ-S in 1977 explained, 'it was (always) Jaguar's intention to replace the Model 12 with the GM THM400, which they regarded as a superior transmission in many ways. For the first year or so of production, therefore, tests of automatic XJ-Ss were conspicuous by their absence.' Aside from the change of transmission, and minor details, the 1977 test car was identical with that of 1975. The automatic transmission took its toll of performance – inevitably so with only three speeds – and delivered a maximum speed of 142mph (the final drive was still 3.07, so the engine speed at maximum was 5,740rpm, still over its power peak) while the 0-60mph time was 7.5sec and the overall test fuel consumption 14mpg, both of

these figures extremely respectable when taken in context. The test noted that with the air conditioning switched on, the maximum fell to 138mph.

The test also mentions Jaguar's late conversion to the concept of slightly less power assistance with much better 'feel'. And in a comment which surely stands to this day, the test asserts that '… the handling is sufficiently good-natured that even a moderately skilled driver can use most of it. There is no feeling in the XJ-S, as in some of its contemporaries, that one needs to have been to racing school to drive it anything but gently.' That summary – even if it was the author's own, a rather horrifying 26 years ago – underlines the spirit of the XJ-S design specification. It was a car in which it was always possible to make extremely rapid progress without imposing demands beyond those of concentration and anticipation which must always go with such driving.

The XJ-S settled down to a long period of minimum change, surviving the traumas of the British Leyland times and emerging into the greater promise of the 'Egan era' in tandem with the XJ6 Series III. Then, in 1981, came the announcement of the HE (High Efficiency) version of the V12 engine which was still its only power unit. As in the XJ12, the new high-compression V12 produced 299PS (DIN) at 5,500rpm compared with the former 287PS, while its maximum torque rose from 383Nm to 432Nm, an increase of nearly 13 per cent. This not only increased the engine's efficiency but also allowed the final drive to be raised to 2.88:1, improving steady-speed fuel consumption still further. The official fuel consumption figures for the XJ-S HE were 27.1mpg at 56mph, 22.5mpg at 75mph, and 15.6mpg in the urban test cycle, compared with the previous 21.9mpg, 18.6mpg and 12.7mpg respectively. Complementary chassis changes included slightly wider tyres – the new Dunlop D7 – now 215/70VR15, on 6.5in rims replacing the former 6in size.

Oddly enough, no XJ project number seems ever to have been allocated to the development of the HE V12 or its fitting either to the XJ12 or the XJ-S. But new XJ numbers had been allocated for other purposes, first XJ57 for a new version of the XJ-S to be powered by the new 3.6-litre 24-valve slant-6 engine, followed by XJ58 for a companion version with a completely new cabriolet roof structure. Both of these cars appeared late in 1983, as 1984 model-year products, to run in parallel with the V12 HE. A further and rather pointless-seeming number in the series was XJ63, 'XJ57 with Getrag manual gearbox',

Beneath the bonnet, the new-series XJS was something else, since it provided the launch platform for the AJ6 'slant-6' engine in its original 3.6-litre form, as seen installed. Points to note in this view include not only the 15° slant of the engine to *the right, as viewed by the driver, but also the bulky fuel-injection system and the substantial bracing bars running from the bulkhead to the front wings, to discourage 'lozenging' of the nose structure under side loads.* (Author's archive)

the Getrag being standard issue by the time the AJ6 engined version emerged, so perhaps it is XJ57 which should be regarded as redundant.

The history of the slant-6 engine series has Chapter 13 to itself, but the XJ-S provided its launch platform. By 1983 standards it was a thoroughly modern engine, virtually 'square' in its dimensions (91mm bore, 92mm stroke) with a capacity of 3,590cc and an output of 225bhp (DIN) at 5,300rpm, with a peak torque of 325Nm at 4,000rpm. It is interesting that in the first eight years of its existence the XJ-S was never offered with the 4.2-litre XK engine, which would obviously have fitted because the engine compartment was in essence that of the XJ6. This

remained the case even through those energy-crisis days which saw demand for the thirsty pre-HE V12 dwindle to little more than 1,000 units a year. It was 'V12 or nothing' until the AJ6 appeared, with an output only slightly greater than that of the 4.2 XK in its final fuel-injected and emissions-compliant form: 225bhp rather than 205bhp, 325Nm rather than 314Nm. It achieved this advantage, despite its 15 per cent smaller capacity, by virtue of its more modern dimensions, valve layout and combustion chamber design. It was able to run a substantially higher compression ratio, set at 9.6:1, and to breathe better. It was also substantially more economical, and of course much lighter, in fact reckoned to weigh nearly 30 per cent less than the XK.

The advent of this new, eager and lightweight engine in Jaguar's sporting (if not sports) car was a signal for the return of a manual gearbox, an option which had been deleted with the arrival of the V12 HE with its higher torque. The new box was a 5-speed unit bought-in from Getrag. In this form the final drive was dropped to 3.54:1, but with the overdrive fifth of the Getrag box (0.76:1) the overall gearing was still higher than that of the automatic-

only V12 HE, which continued to use the 3-speed GM transmission, at 28.9 compared with 27.0mph/ 1,000rpm. This meant that at the claimed maximum speed of 145mph – compared with 150mph for the V12 – the AJ6 engine was turning at almost exactly 5,000rpm, somewhat below its power peak and inevitably leading some to speculate on the possible effects of switching to a 3.7 final drive. Undoubtedly, though, the chosen ratio was better for fuel economy and for noise levels, and gave usefully higher maximum speeds in the intermediate gears. Calculations based on squeezing out another 2-3mph maximum speed are fairly pointless. Jaguar also claimed the 3.6-litre car with manual gearbox would reach 60mph from rest as quickly as the V12 HE with automatic (in 7.6sec) although the bigger-engined car drew away at higher speeds. One significant

Above: The XJ-S had been in production for seven years with few apparent changes (although steadily upgraded beneath the bonnet, not least with the arrival of the HE V12 engine) when the XJSC appeared. This version had been developed at a time when US regulations seemed effectively to forbid full convertibles. The result was the strange open-framework roof seen here, the gaps filled by two 'targa' panels and the vestigial rear hood. (Author's archive)

Right: Alongside the XJSC, the standard 2+2 continued, still with few visible changes to its distinctive if not universally admired shape. The aerodynamics are subtle – note the 'chin' spoiler beneath the front bumper – and figures indicate that the bluff-looking nose with forward-leaning radiator grille was not as bad as it looked. Heavy bumpers were the result of US no-damage requirements in minor impacts. (Author's archive)

performance factor was that the lighter engine and follow-through savings (such as the use of a 2-row rather than a 3-row radiator) and of course the difference between the manual gearbox and the automatic transmission, meant the 3.6 was lighter by a useful 210lb.

The official fuel consumption figures for the XJS 3.6 did not look all that impressive when set against the V12, especially in the urban cycle where a specified test method allowed the automatic to shift for itself while the manual was confined to its three lowest gears. Consequently the figures (with those for the V12 HE in brackets) were 36.2mpg (27.1mpg) at 56mph, 29.4mpg (22.5mpg) at 75mph, but only 14.9mpg (15.6mpg) in the urban cycle. Most road tests indicated the 3.6 was actually 10–15 per cent more economical than the V12 HE but

it still wasn't a 20mpg car, at least not in enthusiastic hands. In 1987, after the launch of the XJ40 saloon which also used the AJ6 power unit, the engine was switched to a fully integrated (injection plus ignition) solid-state engine management system which for the XJ-S produced a substantial economy improvement, especially in the urban cycle, the new figures being 37.1mpg, 32.0mpg and 18.6mpg (urban) respectively. At the same point, the 3.6 became available with automatic transmission for the first time, being teamed with the 4-speed ZF 4HP22 with 'new generation' automatic features. According to Jaguar, the performance penalty with this automatic was only 2mph in maximum speed, and 0.7sec added to the 0–60mph time (8.1 instead of 7.4sec). Things were improving, but the car's considerable weight still exerted a malign influence.

That **cabriolet** body

Back in 1983, the other point of major interest besides the all-new engine was the appearance of the XJ-SC, the Cabriolet with its radically revised body. Not everyone approved, because the decision had been taken to make the Cabriolet a strict 2-seater in which the small back seat was replaced by twin lockable stowage bins hidden beneath an internal luggage platform. The Cabriolet was still far from being a full convertible – that would come later – but the roof and rear quarter panels (thus including the 'sails') were removed and replaced by a skeleton structure consisting of two very strong cantrails – built around internal tubes – joined by an equally strong cross-rail above and behind the occupants' heads. Additional stiffening for the body was provided within the transmission tunnel and above the final drive. The space between the roof cross-member and the windscreen arch was filled by a mirror-image pair of removable 'targa' panels neatly latching into place, while the enclosure of the cabin was completed, for Coupé-type motoring, by a vestigial fabric hood which lifted to attach to the rear of the cross-member. This could be replaced, for greater security or winter driving, by a fabric-trimmed 'half-hardtop' formed from a double skin of GRP and complete with a bonded-in heated rear window. Remarkably, the complete Cabriolet weighed no more than the Coupé.

The beast was certainly strong: in 1985 the author, driving an XJ-SC and paying too much attention to road test instrumentation – waiting, waiting, waiting for 120mph to flash up on the digital speed display in a top-gear run – left himself with too little braking distance at the 'tight' end of the acceleration straight at the Millbrook proving ground and understeered up the steeply-banked turn, seriously bending both the front and then the rear wing of the car in contact with the Armco. Afterwards, the car was still as straight as a die, the (undamaged) door still opened and closed normally and the poor thing could still be driven as though nothing had happened …

The manufacturing process for the cabriolet body was a tortuous one. Shells from the Castle Bromwich plant, minus roof, were taken to the specialists Park Sheet Metal in Coventry for the building-up of the cabriolet framework – a considerable task – before returning to Castle Bromwich to be put through the paint line. Then they were taken to Browns Lane for final assembly, except that in this case it was not final: yet another journey was involved, to Aston Martin

Tickford at Bedworth for installation of the 'targa' panels and the rear hood; four transfers to complete the vehicle! To begin with, the XJ-SC was a 3.6-litre car only, but in July 1985 it was also made available with the V12 engine. At that point Jaguar gave a figure of 31,818 XJ-S of all types sold since introduction, 6,028 of them having been sold in 1984 alone. This was a huge advance from the nadir of 1981 when sales dropped to only 1,199 units, and the production rate was said still to be picking up.

Despite this clear success and the fanfare of new introductions, behind the scenes all was not well with the XJ-S. In its press kit text for the 1983 launch, Jaguar actually admits, speaking of the end of the 1970s, that XJ-S sales were reduced to a trickle by 'a reputation for high fuel consumption, indifferent quality and poor residual value.' They had tackled the question of fuel consumption – as far as was reasonably possible – but the quality problems remained obstinately on the agenda, despite the introduction of various quality improvement schemes and the heroic achievements of John Egan himself in 'talking up' Jaguar's reputation through sheer force of personality. Yet one finds in the archive notes such as the minutes of the Model Progress Meeting of 9 July 1986, in which it is reported that 'the XJ-S suffers many known service problems.' It goes on to list no less than 18 of them including 'transmission noisy and subject to failure of linkage; leather trim doesn't last; specifications for trim screws inadequate; fuel smells in trunk; door hinges seize …' It was also noted that the XJ-S was 'near the bottom of the JD Power customer satisfaction index with a score of 88; at least this is better than the Porsche 928 (81) but is nothing like as good as the BMW 633 CSi (113).' To cap it all, 'there is a long history of stalling in the US market from 1983 onwards.' Even without this last comment, the reference to 'trunk' reveals that this all springs from a tirade from Jaguar in the USA, weathering a mass of customer complaints and pointing out that it and its dealers were spending money to make arriving cars saleable. Clearly there was more

work to be done on this front, and urgently. In fact, it was already under way, and involved investment on a scale Jaguar could once only have dreamed about: for example, £13.5 million simply to refurbish and modernise the Castle Bromwich paint shop, a project completed in mid-1986, while in 1988, the company officially opened its highly integrated Engineering Centre at Whitley, on the site of a former Rootes Group/Chrysler/Peugeot-Talbot factory – another £55 million invested. In mid-1987 it was noted that

two production milestones had been passed: the 50,000th XJ-S, and the 100,000th V12 engine.

Meanwhile there were further plans afoot to extend the XJ-S range, although not all came to fruition or were even intended to. Project number XJ71 was allocated to the XJ-S 'mules' running components – most notably powertrains – for the ill-fated XJ41 sports coupé programme (Chapter 12) while XJ79 covered 'XJ-S 4WD for development only – cancelled February 1989'. The 4WD system is

also discussed in some detail in Chapter 12. Much more to the point, a product planning paper from Trevor Crisp dated 18 March 1986 mentions that 'the V12 XJ-S Convertible is planned for the 1988 model year ... Model year 89 for V12 digital ignition, new headlamps, 4-litre AJ6, steering and suspension modifications ... facelift introduction delayed by six months to avoid XJ40 clash.'

The 1988 model year saw the deletion of the XJ-SC 3.6, leaving only the V12, but substantial changes were made to the suspension and steering of the 3.6 Coupé to give it a more sporting feel. Both front and rear spring rates were increased – at the front by 39 per cent, at the rear by 34 per cent –

and both anti-roll bars were stiffened. These changes were complemented by wider tyres, Jaguar choosing to switch to Pirelli with the fitting of the 235/60–15 P600. The steering rack was more firmly mounted, the column and linkage modified to make the system 17 per cent more torsionally stiff, and the degree of power assistance was reduced. The result was a far 'stiffer' car with less roll and more ultimate cornering power. Seats with more sideways support were added as though to emphasise the fact. None of these changes was duplicated in the V12 versions which thus became relatively softer and more comfortable, especially on mediocre road surfaces.

A genuine **convertible**

The fully open XJ-S Convertible (with allocated project numbers XJ77 for the V12, XJ78 with the AJ6 engine) was previewed at the 1988 Geneva Motor Show although it did not become available until April of that year. Geneva did, however, also see the rather overdue announcement that a Teves anti-lock braking system would henceforth be standard on all XJ-Ss. When the Convertible was officially announced, it was in V12-powered (XJ77) form only, although a 6-cylinder counterpart would eventually emerge. Jaguar pointed out in their release that this was the fourth series-production convertible design from the stable, following on from the SS100, the XK series and the E-type. It was however (and understandably) the first to be fitted with a fully power-operated hood, the whole installation developed in collaboration with Karmann. Among other things, the launch of the Convertible meant the end of the road for the Cabriolet with its Byzantine production logistics.

The engineering challenge in any convertible is to achieve sufficient torsional and beam stiffness in the absence of a roof through which to carry loads. There is only one way to do this, and that is to make the floor area sufficiently stiff. In torsion, this in turn means making the sill sections as large and stiff as possible – the transmission tunnel, if there is one, adds usefully to beam stiffness but you can't make a flat panel, even with a channel running along its centre-line, torsionally stiff. The task is then completed by creating stiff front and rear bulkhead assemblies and tying them very firmly to the critical floorpan section and especially to the sills. There is a further challenge at the front, in any modern convertible, because the windscreen arch must be strong enough to resist crushing loads in the rollover accident case.

Thus, as Jaguar itself put it in the XJ-S Convertible press release: 'The shell has been strengthened around the transmission tunnel, the front and rear bulkheads and rear floor area. Steel tubes in the inner sills and A-posts further optimise torsional rigidity.' This is a three-line throw-away of what was actually a substantial engineering exercise. The exterior shape was radically altered as well, naturally, with Jaguar claiming that in all, 150 body panels, a third of all the pressings in the vehicle, were either new or modified. No figures were actually quoted for torsional stiffness but on the road, the results of the exercise certainly seemed satisfactory. The finished Convertible weighed an additional 220lb by comparison with the Coupé, part of the extra being accounted for by the hood and its operating mechanism.

The XJ-S Convertible – especially as a V12 – was unashamedly aimed very high in the market, and was better able to do so because Jaguar's quality improvement drive, stung by the company's American experience in particular, was beginning to pay off. Another thing which would clearly be appreciated by this stratospheric segment was even more power, and this eventually arrived (see Chapter 10) in the form of a 6-litre derivative of the V12, delivering 318bhp (DIN) at 5,250rpm with nearly 500Nm of torque. This version of the engine was destined to see wider service but to begin with it was offered in a specialised XJ-S derivative, the XJR-S, from 1989. The XJR-S 6.0 was one of several high-performance derivatives developed and prepared by JaguarSport, a company jointly created by Jaguar and TWR, the engineering company founded by the Scottish former racing driver Tom Walkinshaw. TWR had been responsible for most of the engineering of the long series of (mainly) Jaguar-powered XJR sports-racing cars campaigned with considerable success – including two more Le Mans wins – through the late 1980s.

Final fling

Even at this stage, nearly 15 years after the XJ-S's introduction and with Jaguar about to come under Ford's management, there remained three more iterations of the theme before the story finally ended. The first of these was the facelift mentioned by Trevor Crisp in 1986, which finally came to fruition in 1991. This involved, to quote the Jaguar briefing text, 'body styling changes, a redesigned interior, improved feature and equipment levels and the adoption of the AJ6 4.0 engine in place of the 3.6' and was covered by a whole clutch of very late XJ project numbers: XJ87 for the V12 Coupé with XJ88 for its AJ6 (4.0) counterpart; XJ89 allocated to a facelifted Cabriolet (but the Cabriolet actually died with the appearance of the Convertible in 1988), and XJ97 and XJ98 for the facelifted Convertibles, V12 and AJ6. In fact, the XJ98 did not form part of the facelift launch but was 'revealed' at the 1992 Geneva Show before going on sale in May of that year. By that time the XJR-S had had its 6-litre engine further developed to deliver 333bhp, perhaps in anticipation of the fact that the 6-litre capacity would become the standard V12 size during the engine's run-out period.

The enlarged, longer-stroke AJ6 had already been launched in the revised XJ40 range and provided 223bhp (DIN) at 4,750rpm with a catalytic converter fitted. This was at a time when European regulations were about to insist on the fitting of converters to all new cars; when fitted with the same system, the output of the 3.6-litre engine was reduced to 199bhp (DIN). The bigger engine delivered no less than 23 per cent more torque (377Nm). In consequence, both manual and automatic transmissions needed up-rating, the manual version now using the Getrag 290 5-speed gearbox in place of the 265, and the automatic moving up to the electronically controlled ZF 4HP24 transmission with 30 per cent higher torque capacity and two-mode (Sport or Normal) shift timing. The body was substantially revised, not least to take advantage of the move from Austin Rover to Venture Pressings, jointly owned, as already pointed out, by Jaguar and GKN, as the pressed panel source. Panel sizes were increased and the number of separate pressings therefore reduced (for example, the rear wings were now single-piece instead of being fabricated from five separate pressings).

The facelift also saw the culmination of the quality improvement programme which had been triggered in 1986, which involved over 1,200 new or revised parts and the investment of £50 million. Outwardly, perhaps there was less to show of this in the facelift car than one might have expected. Jaguar called the exterior changes 'significant in scope yet subtle in character' which is certainly one way of saying 'it doesn't look very different unless you closely examine old and new side-by-side'. Yet 40 per cent of the external panels were in fact new, including the boot, rear wings, doors, sills, and the roof panel in the Coupé. The May 1992 package also saw the addition of a stainless steel tubular 'X' brace on the 4.0 and 5.3 Convertibles, its rear legs mounted on the jacking points under the footwells while its front legs picked up on the cross-member beneath the radiator. Although it made no contribution to the stiffness of the crucial centre-section, the brace markedly reduced front end shudder.

Now there were but two significant changes remaining. In May 1993 Jaguar announced yet another 'New XJS range' whose two key points were the replacement of the 5.3-litre V12 engine by the 6-litre recently introduced in the XJ40 saloon, and a 2+2 version of the Convertible. Just as important in some ways, the V12 engine gained a 4-speed automatic transmission to replace the long-running 3-speed. The new unit came from the same source, General Motors (and this despite the fact that Jaguar was now Ford-owned). Indeed, the GM4L80-E was mechanically the same unit with an additional gear train to provide the overdrive fourth ratio, although electronically it was much improved. The 2+2

involved no stretching of the body shell, merely the insertion of a sub-assembly to provide a seat back and pan in place of the interior luggage lockers and platform. Jaguar dubbed these seats 'occasional' and that certainly summed them up from the point of view of anyone more than ten years old. As a final part of this 1993 package, the XJS Coupé (4.0 and 6.0) received the stiffer 'sports' suspension described earlier, although the Convertibles remained softer and more comfortable. The sports suspension package now also included wider and larger wheels and tyres, the standard fit being the Pirelli P600, size 225/55ZR16; the 'comfort' tyre was the P4000E, 225/60 ZR16. After an interval of more than 30 years, the most sporting Jaguar again sat on 16in wheels! Interestingly, Jaguar claimed a maximum speed of no less than 161mph – 3mph more than for the low-volume XJR-S. The increase could only have been due to the change to the 4-speed transmission and the difference in overall gearing, but this very high maximum seems never to have been verified in any authoritative press test.

Virtually the final stage of the story was written in June 1994 when the press release headline was: 'Jaguar improves record-breaking XJS range'. While most of the changes, interior and exterior, were cosmetic the 4-litre engine was upgraded from AJ6 to AJ16, the much improved slant-6 engine which was about to be launched also in the final X300 iteration of the XJ40. Catalytic converters were now mandatory in every market that mattered, and this final straight-6 Jaguar sports car ended its days with 241bhp at a modest 4,700rpm, and 382Nm of torque at a high-seeming 4,000rpm. A year later still, in May 1995, another press release proclaimed: 'New XJS models celebrate 60 years of Jaguar marque', but closer inspection suggested the XJS Celebration Coupé and Convertible were 'special editions' to maintain interest during the model's run-out period. It was said even then that sales were booming, most of all in the USA which had taken nearly 4,300 XJSs in 1994, a year-on-year increase of 45 per cent. What it did not say was that the XJS V12s had already been reduced to special-order-only status, and that tightening exhaust emission regulations would force the V12's withdrawal from the USA at the end of the 1995 model year.

The end was not long coming. In March 1996 the new XK8 was unveiled at the Geneva Motor Show, some play being made of the fact that it was then exactly 35 years since the E-type had made its debut at the same show. In April the XK8 made its first North American appearance in New York, and it was announced that the new car would go on sale in October. As the press statement of the day said: 'The introduction of the XK8 marks the beginning of a new era in Jaguar sports car history and the departure of its predecessor, the XJS. Having earned the distinction of being Jaguar's best-selling sports car ever (approximately 112,000 will have been sold) and its longest in production (21 years), XJS build will cease in April.' And that, with a whimper rather than a bang, was that. The XJS had indeed sold substantially more copies than the E-type, had been in production many years longer, had been the launching pad for the AJ6 engine, had accounted for a large share of all Jaguar V12 chassis (the last V12 off the Radford line, in February 1997, was number 161,996) and weathered a number of storms which might have killed off lesser models. Importantly, as stated at the outset, it maintained Jaguar's status as producer of a two-model range for the whole if its production life. In accordance with Jaguar policy, the very last XJS off the line was retained for the Jaguar Heritage Collection.

The US market was a significant contributor to the sales success of the XJS, and the Convertible, *seen here its final 1996 form, sold particularly well to women drivers.* (Jaguar)

12 XJ41: The **F-type** that never was

lthough the XJ-S had been thought of within Jaguar, at least during its conception, as an 'E-type replacement' it quickly became clear that the market did not regard it in that light. There was constant pressure, fuelled to some extent by wishful speculation in the enthusiast motoring press, that a 'proper' F-type, a smaller, lighter and more nimble 2-seater with the emphasis on performance and handling, would at some stage emerge. And there were plenty of people within Jaguar who thought the same, except that they could see the difficulties.

Remember we are talking here of the late 1970s – the E-type having ceased production in 1974, the XJ-S having been launched in 1975 – when the company was in dire straits. Sir William Lyons had retired in 1972 and although his distant hand sometimes reached out to touch the helm, the only fair way to describe Jaguar in the later 1970s is as a mess. It had already suffered the trauma of seeing Geoffrey Robinson installed as a British Leyland appointee Managing Director, becoming sufficiently enthused to draw up an ambitious expansion plan, and having the whole concept dashed to pieces in 1975 with the publication of the horribly misconceived Ryder Report. (Robinson departed to become a Labour MP, rising to become Paymaster General in the early days of the Blair government.) Lord Ryder had been asked in effect to prepare a 'rescue plan' for the heavily indebted and steadily weakening British Leyland, but among his conclusions, few of which stood the test of time, he cast grave doubt on the need for, or the desirability of, Jaguar surviving as a separate entity. Add to all this the political situation in the Middle East and the creation of the first 'energy crisis' of 1972/73 (and the second one, at the end of the decade) which threw the market for thirsty engines like Jaguar's V12 into reverse, and it is small wonder that, to quote Andrew Whyte: 'Lofty England, who believed in continuity and therefore in "overlapping succession" was trying to line up possible candidates (to be the next Chairman of Jaguar) who were already running car companies themselves. Not unnaturally, they told him they were happy where they were.'

A prime example of British Leyland-inspired mismanagement was that through the mid-1970s, for a short while and despite the corporation's financial condition, money had been thrown at an ill-starred campaign in the European Touring Car Championship using the overweight, floppy and generally unsuitable XJ12 2-door – the programme being carried through by Broadspeed to avoid committing manpower Browns Lane didn't have. The programme was abruptly terminated before the 1977 season come to an end. The XJ12s were often fastest in practice but were always slowed or stopped by technical problems during the races. Being regularly beaten by the big BMW coupés had done little to help maintain the Jaguar image and the programme had swallowed a great deal of funds (an estimated £500,000 per year, equivalent to several millions today) which would – with the benefit of hindsight, admittedly – have been better spent on recruiting a couple of dozen good engineers and technicians and providing them with a prototype shop and a couple of engine test-benches.

One outcome of the Ryder Report was that the rump of British Leyland separated out into Austin-Morris, the 'volume car division' and Jaguar-Rover-Triumph, the 'specialised cars division'. It was an arrangement which lasted only two years – although that was quite a long time for the British Leyland of the 1970s to move consistently in one direction. Eventually and inevitably, in 1977, the Government appointed a Managing Director (Michael Edwardes, later Sir Michael) whose primary task was to break the workshop power of the trades unions and sweep away the arcane practices of generations, demarcation disputes and the rest, which were very close to bringing British Leyland (including Jaguar) to its knees. Just in time, Edwardes succeeded in convincing the bulk of his workforce that going on strike once a week, not for reasons it understood but because it was told to by a handful of people with a political agenda, could only end in the dole queue.

There is nothing of engineering in all that, but it paints the backdrop to the engineering position. Jaguar hardly had enough technical staff to cope with the flood of safety and emissions homologation work on existing models, and even if it had, there was no money to spend on anything completely new. Getting the XJ-S established, maintaining some kind of momentum in the XJ6 programme (including the 2-door versions, and culminating in the 1979

The XJ41 and XJ42 (convertible) family lined up in a studio during the 1980s. Facing the camera is one of the road-running prototypes. The programme eventually included both fixed-head coupé and hatchback with removable 'targa' panels, and the more conventional soft-top. Intended power unit was always the 'slant-6', and no V12 version was even proposed – at least, not seriously. High power was instead to be achieved with a turbocharged version. (JDHT)

announcement of the Series 3) and preparing the AJ6 engine eventually to take over from the XK was as much as could be managed, and that only just. Without the sterling efforts of Bob Knight, who eventually became for a short time the caretaker Managing Director, it is doubtful whether even that would have been achieved. Even as it was, this was a period in which Jaguar product quality was seriously degraded as skilled craftsmen began to retire and the awful industrial relations of the period, already referred to and from which for a time, Jaguar suffered almost as badly, took their toll. From an engineering point of view, in fact, the late 1970s was a time to address current and urgent problems simply in order to survive, without thinking too much about the future.

Yet, of course, they did think about the future, even if they did it in their spare moments and the work never progressed beyond the drawing board. The realists knew than a completely new car was out of the question, and a completely new engine even more so. The best that could be foreseen was a car based on a shortened XJ6 platform and powered by the new AJ6 engine. Why not the V12? Although the V12 had been 'shoehorned' into the E-type, and eventually to the XJ6 from which the new sports car would be derived, it seems generally to have been felt that the V12 was simply too big and too thirsty for the market at a time when even the US government was showing concern about 'gas-guzzlers'. Also, confining the programme to a single engine – with the added appeal of being an all-new unit – would yield

XJ41: THE F-TYPE THAT NEVER WAS

Left: An unusual view from above of an XJ41 Coupé prototype (note the tax disc!) with the split of the 'targa' roof panels clearly visible, along with the shut-line of the very short boot lid, which was provided with a special mechanism to allow it to open sufficiently wide. Pop-up headlamps were practically an obligatory feature of high-performance cars designed during the 1980s. (JDHT)

Above: A mock-up of the XJ42 Convertible. Neat features of the XJ41/42 design include the incorporation of bumpers into the overall nose and tail design, a great move forward compared with the XJS, although it does lead to apparently substantial front overhang. But could this ever have been thought of as an 'F-type'? (JDHT)

great cost, time and weight savings. It was not that the V12 could not have been made to fit, for it had after all been developed specifically to take up little more space than the XK; but if the 'F-type' was to succeed at all, it would need to be cheap and quick both to develop and to produce, and that ruled out the big engine, however sadly.

At least there was no shortage of ideas when the happy day came, in 1980, that Jaguar once again achieved some degree of operating independence and gained a new Chairman, John Egan, who had a clear idea of the direction in which the company should head, and a strategy for taking it there. Before too long Sir John Egan, as he deservedly became, headed Jaguar's return to full business independence in 1984. Having been swallowed and nearly destroyed

by one government's belief in nationalisation, the company was freed by another's enthusiasm for privatisation. From his beginning, though, Egan properly appreciated that one way to court trouble was to spread his engineering staff too thinly over too many projects, and the first priority was to bring the AJ6 into production and pension-off the venerable XK, while the second was to bring the staple product, the XJ, thoroughly up to date with the announcement of the largely new XJ40 in 1986. Only when these projects were well underway could any serious energy be devoted to an 'F-type'.

Thus a small team undertook initial studies for the new car, under the allocated project numbers XJ41 (fixed-head coupé) and XJ42 (equivalent convertible), using the AJ6 engine only, from 1982 onwards. Although mid-engined sports cars were then the vogue and the XJ13 had been mid-engined, there was never any question that the XJ41 would have anything other than a conventional front engine and rear-wheel drive. The author, talking to Jim Randle during the XJ40 launch and 'fishing' for details of the car, elicited the comment that 'I think God made that space between the front wheel arches for an in-line engine …'

Above: The back ends of two XJ41 mock-ups, with a conventional fixed-head coupé on the left and a hatchback on the right. The engineering divergence of these two body types, as the programme progressed, was one of the factors in its eventual demise in 1990. Evident here also is the rather ugly lower back-end treatment built around the twin tailpipes. (JDHT)

Above right: Seen from the side, the XJ41 Coupé open boot lid, shows the complex mechanism which raised it high enough to be out of the way of anyone loading items into the car – not that the boot was especially roomy by

class standards. Ploys like this all added to the expense of a programme which began as an essentially simple concept. (JDHT)

Right: The back end of the XJ41 hatchback, seen during an internal presentation, with on the right, Mike Beasley, who went on to become Jaguar's Managing Director until he retired in 2003. One has to wonder what the point was of engineering a 'hatchback' for a car in which the fuel tank was installed immediately behind the back seat, thus allowing only 'conventional' luggage space. The split luggage shelf arrangement is just as odd. (JDHT)

The first task was to 'freeze' the general concept and the XJ41 is notable as being the last Jaguar over which Sir William Lyons exerted styling influence. The Porter and Skilleter biography[1] tells the story, relayed by designer Keith Helfet, of how Sir William '… made the decision of which theme to pick for the XJ41 … he just said: 'You must do this one. That's the Jaguar.' The proposal on which he alighted had smooth, flowing lines, quite unlike the flat-surfaced, sharp-edged shapes which were then in fashion. This, remember, was in the early 1980s when Sir William was in declining health (he died early in 1985, at the age of 83).

The original launch date for the XJ41 was 1986, but by 1984 it was realised that this was wildly optimistic, and the launch target was relaxed to October 1988. Because potential rival products were becoming more powerful and faster, a twin-turbo 4.0-litre variant was now added for post-launch availability. In 1985, the New Vehicle Concepts (NVC) department was formed, and because XJ41 was a 'new vehicle' it fell within the NVC area of responsi-

Above: Structurally, the XJ41 was conventional – seen here as a body-in-white for the Coupé, with 'targa' roof panels still to be fitted. As in any car with a non-continuous roofline, the bulk of the strength had to be engineered into the floor and sills. (JDHT)

bility. However, NVC decided wholesale revisions were needed and effectively the project was recommenced almost from scratch, this time using new technologies including CAD/CAM. Because the twin-turbo 4-litre power unit promised at least 330bhp, the decision was taken to add a 4WD transmission to the programme, while the car was also made 50mm wider, thus making it wider than the XJ-S! Karmann completed three running cars during 1989; these were not true engineering prototypes, but rather functioning 'lookalikes'.

Throughout the programme, the engineering manpower constraints remained. In March 1986 Trevor Crisp prepared a product planning paper which, alongside more detailed proposals for the XJ-S and the XJ40, noted that the XJ41 'would require additional headcount'. To counter this he proposed that the timing plan might be reviewed 'to address

1   *Sir William Lyons, the official biography*, pp.263–264

the possibility of the phased introduction of models.' At that time the medium-term schedule foresaw the launch of XJ41 for the 1991 model year – in other words, in October 1990 – with the higher performance 4-litre turbo following a year later. What Trevor was saying was that sheer lack of engineering capacity was forcing the programme backwards; this was a time not only when safety and emissions legislation was biting particularly hard, but when the XJ40 saloon was in the final pre-stages before production.

The recommendation was clearly accepted, because the MPM on 8 April 1986 noted that the launch timing for the naturally aspirated XJ41 in the USA (its principal target market, into which it would be launched first) was October 1991, with the turbocharged version to follow a year later. By this time the requirement for a 4WD version of the turbocharged car had been mooted, and product planning input from the USA was calling for a foot-operated parking brake! Still the constraints bit, especially when it came to preparing prototypes, and in the MPM a month later it was noted that 'Karmann and Chausson had advised their inability to support concept vehicle build', although as we have seen, in 1989 Karmann did eventually deliver three 'lookalike' cars for assessment purposes. Thus was a programme whose first thoughts had come in the 1970s, pushed further into the 1990s.

According to the MPM record, things then went quiet on the XJ41 front except for a note in the September meeting that 'JNR [Jim Randle} stated that the XJ41 would adopt a similar electrical system to the XJ40'. A great deal of effort had been devoted in the XJ40 programme to developing a far more reliable electrical system (see Chapter 14) and it was clearly desirable that this work should be carried over.

Then the programme came back to MPM prominence in the February 1987 meeting when 'CQC advised the following XJ41 product concerns:

a) Suspension (all-new or carryover XJ40? One prototype with each solution).
b) Torque tube for Turbo/4WD derivatives.
c) Wiper motor/screen packaging.
d) Interior design.
e) Crash performance.'

This indicates that even at this stage, fundamental engineering decisions had still not been frozen and it is hard to see, from an early 1987 starting date, how an October 1991 launch could be achieved in the days when computer-aided design was still in its infancy. Even worse was apparently to come, since Trevor Crisp's XJ41 file contains a later note that the naturally aspirated engine had been 'reinstated', having apparently been dropped through fear that it would not achieve sufficient performance to satisfy the market.

In January 1989 it was noted that 'several development vehicles [at least eight] are running.' These were modified XJ-S with the allocated project number XJ71, with XJ41 running gear. The fleet quickly grew, and in February the MPM was told that car numbers (XJ)71/2 to 71/23 included 14 4-litre cars and one 3.6. These included eight turbocharged cars, including two with 4WD. Figures taken with car 71/15, a naturally aspirated 4-litre running a 3.58 final drive, showed standing-start acceleration times of 2.3sec to 30mph and 6.4sec to 60mph. Sadly, no performance figures for a turbocharged car are recorded, but the 0-60mph figure would surely have been close to 5sec. In the late 1980s, performance figures of this order, and the risk of excessive wheel-spin, seemed automatically to prompt consideration of a 4WD system. It was, in fact, a time when very high-performance 4WD cars were coming strongly into fashion.

The 4WD concept for the XJ41 Turbo was reasonably advanced. The running gear had first been installed in an XJ27 (XJ-S), with an electro-magnetically operated clutch (EMC) in the centre differential. Installations were prepared not only for the XJ41 but also for the XJ-S itself, in V12 and AJ6 forms, under the project number XJ79, although the latter was discontinued early in 1989. The front differential was integral with, but did not share its oil supply with the sump, and drop-gears were provided on each side of the sump to enable a cross-shaft to clear the low skirt of the cylinder block, while also keeping equal-length front drive-shafts. The centre differential was a viscous coupling, with an epicyclic drive splitter dividing the torque 36 per cent front and 64 per cent rear. Considerable engineering changes were needed to accommodate this driveline. Of necessity, the front suspension was new, and considerable changes were needed to the longitudinal side members and to the transmission tunnel. Initial reported driving impressions were favourable, with 'much better acceleration on low-grip surfaces', which is hardly a surprise. The key question was, of course, whether the complication, cost and weight of

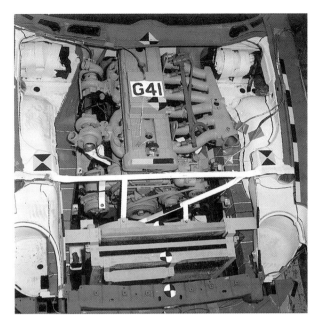

Above: An exceptionally interesting series of photographs showing an XJ41 momentarily before and after impact at MIRA's crash-test facility. Details visible beneath the bonnet include two turbochargers 'in tandem', each driven by the exhaust from three cylinders. The intake ducts are extremely long. There is no indication, however, of how the pressure output from the turbochargers was supposed to reach the other side of the engine. In terms of safety performance, the result looks impressive, although there is no indication of impact speed. (JDHT)

Right: An intriguing pair of photographs showing a road-going XJ41 Coupé in the MIRA wind tunnel, with and without the 'camouflage' panels applied for testing on public roads. The idea, it seems, was to establish the effect of the camouflage in aerodynamic drag so that results achieved with the disguise in place could be read back to the definitive car. One hopes the latter achieved a better drag coefficient than the former! (Both JDHT)

the system justified its adoption in a car not designed for it in the first place? Neither BMW nor Mercedes can claim any great success with their own approaches to the same challenge, even though they were made to work from the purely technical point of view. The XJ41 was neither a Porsche 959 nor an Audi Quattro, and the challenge of handling the high torque of its turbocharged engine would today unhesitatingly be tackled with a combination of traction control and ESP, or something even more advanced but basically electronic rather than mechanical.

Running a prototype fleet as large as the XJ71 'stable' had become was a heavy engineering load, and representations to that effect would certainly have been made. In any event, by August 1989 it was being recorded that 'Discussions are currently being held over the future product plan [for the XJ41]. This may include either a reduction in the number of specifications available and/or an extension to the overall timing plan.' The discussions seem to have been conclusive, because seven weeks later (MPM of 26th September 1989) it was noted that 'The engineering requirement to meet the [XJ41] programme, as laid down in PDL 365, is too large to handle. It is suggested that the programme will be revised to consist of a single compression ratio, turbo, 2-wheel-drive specification, manual or automatic, to be launched into the UK/Europe for the 1994 model year and the USA six months later. The naturally aspirated version will be deleted and the 4WD will be given to JaguarSport.' In other words, the programme had slipped by three years (in about three years!) and had been drastically curtailed into the bargain. Even then, a note from November 1989 shows that the revised programme still called for 60 development engines, including 23 for the XJ71 'mules', 20 for representative XJ41 prototypes, ten for test bed work and seven spares, all needed for June 1990.

Then, towards the end of the year everything seemed to change again. The final MPM of 1989, on 11 December, was told that 'A ride and drive has taken place which indicates that the naturally aspirated engine can meet the objectives defined by marketing.' So it was back almost to square one, with a programme now scheduled to include:

- 2 bodies: 2+2 hatch coupé, 2-door convertible 2-seater
- 2 engines: 4-litre AJ6 naturally aspirated, 10:1 compression, or turbocharged, 9:1

- 2 transmissions: Getrag 5-speed manual, GM 4L80 4-speed auto
- Rear-wheel drive
- Final drive 3.51 (naturally aspirated), 3.31 (turbo).

The proposed launch dates were: 1994 model year for the naturally aspirated coupé, manual and automatic; 1994½ (thus early 1994) for the turbo coupé, manual, and finally the 1995 model year for the turbo coupé auto, and the convertible.

Sadly, the December proposals were a false dawn. In March 1990 – and as background to all this one should bear in mind that following Ford's purchase of Jaguar, the formidably hard-headed Bill Hayden arrived to take over as Managing Director at the end of March 1990, with Sir John Egan heading off to the British Airports Authority – Trevor Crisp presented a paper to the product planning committee whose main points ran as follows:

'A 1994 model year introduction is not possible. The 1995 model year is the last opportunity for major project change before XJ90 [the 'Series 5' XJ6 which actually emerged as the internally redesignated X300]. The potential for 1995 model year introduction is not yet confirmed … the XJ41 product fails to meet Jaguar customer expectation in critical areas of design … and is not commercially viable [not capable of sufficient return on capital invested]. Apart from this, it is improbable that volume build could be achieved even by the 1995 model year. This would bring it into direct conflict with the strategically more important XJ90.

'Therefore it is recommended that the XJ41 project be terminated. Whilst it is recognised that there remains a strategic requirement to reinforce the Jaguar brand image, the various means by which this is achieved … should be re-appraised at a future date.'

This damning indictment wrote the effective end to the project, but the recommendation was further supported by some notes which bear close study as a lesson for all product planners and vehicle programme engineers. Trevor Crisp noted that the XJ41 had been 'conceived in the early 1980s, to complete a three-model lineup (XJ6, XJ-S, XJ41 F-type) and to make optimum use of existing components and facilities.' In fact, the original concept had been little more than a cut-and-shut XJ40 platform and running gear, powered by the most powerful existing AJ6 engine variant and clothed in a suitably lithe 'Jaguar' body. The problem was, he suggested, that the programme had quickly diverged from this simple objective. Among other moves he cited:

* 'Proportion of carry-over components reduced'
* 'Addition of turbocharged and 4WD versions'
* 'Original volume aspirations of 20,000 per year steadily declined as more details of product compromises have become known …'
* 'Lack of engineering resources to resolve concept problems.'

On the question of weight, Crisp pointed out that the original naturally aspirated European-specification target of 1,500kg set in May 1986 had grown to 1,597kg by September 1988, and no less than 1,807kg by March 1990. Among the concept changes inflicted on the development team, mostly during 1987, were the replacement of the coupé boot by a rear hatch, new interior styling, the adoption of twin 'targa' roof panels to allow stowage in the boot, and the adoption of a tilt, rather than an axially adjustable steering column (to permit the safe installation of an airbag). The rear-hatch decision meant the development of two largely different bodies, from the B-pillar aft, whereas in the old XK120/150 tradition, the originally proposed fixed-head coupé with boot would have been much more of a derivative. As we have already seen, other 'suggestions' included an all-new suspension, and the US-market foot-operated parking brake…

In other words, from simple beginnings, the XJ41/42 had become too heavy and too complicated – mainly, Trevor Crisp implies, because the marketing departments piled every possible requirement into it when they thought they had the chance, with scant regard for the effect on weight and cost, and because of cost, ultimately on production volume. More than anything, it was the steady erosion in the proportion of XJ40 parts used in the XJ41 that made it uneconomic. Quite apart from the programme slippage, the car was locked in a disastrous downward spiral which meant that smaller numbers meant a higher price which meant even smaller numbers … What it needed was a stern decision, in the mid 1980s, to 'lock out' everything which was not faithful to the original concept. Every decision to discard a standard XJ40 component in favour of one which had been specially developed should have been subject to the severest scrutiny. It simply did not happen, until it was much too late.

In some ways, of course, the lessons were not wasted – they were merely applied to the XK8 ('X100') which it might be argued was to the XJ90/X300 what the XJ41 was to the XJ40. And when one considers that the XK8 (Chapter 16) was on sale for the 1997 model year, barely two years after the ultimately slipped announcement date for the XJ41, it seems as though the lessons were extremely well learned.

The Jaguar archives, and especially the XJ project number ledger, throw up a few more tantalising project numbers with a sporting flavour. There was for example, the XJ47, listed as a 'flagship' V12 sports coupé and thus, in effect, an XJ-S successor. This had a cabriolet counterpart to which XJ48 was allotted, although this had vanished from the (internally) published list by early 1989. At some point, still on the drawing-board, the XJ47 appears to have evolved into the XJ99, likewise identified in 'the book' as a 'flagship sports coupé' with the suggestion that it was now more directly related to the XJ90. But the XJ47 concept clearly dates from the early 1980s and stood no chance of proceeding, given the fact that the demise of the XJ41 was due in large part to sheer lack of engineering manpower for essential work. In addition, its future as a project clearly depended on the continuation of the V12 engine and in practice, of course, it didn't, giving way to the V8 by 1997.

The project number ledger at one point also refers to the XJ64 'sports car' but the archives throw no further light on it. Since in the sequence it comes well after XJ41, one likes to think the idea may have existed to take the project 'back to basics' with something lighter and cheaper…

13 AJ6: the 'slant-6' engine

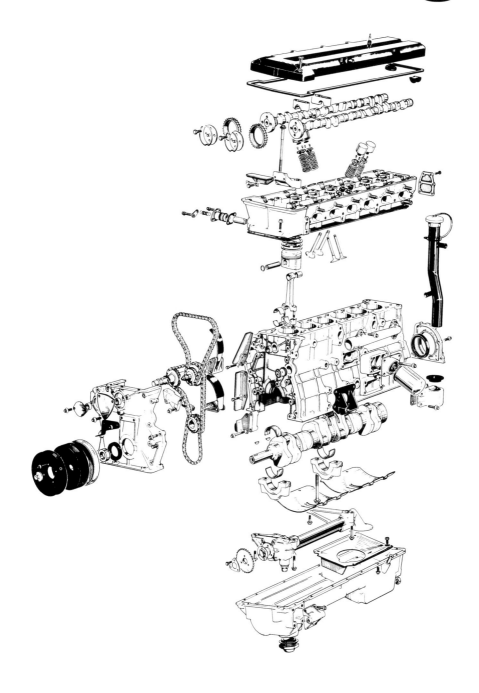

The thought, always at the back of Jaguar minds during the 1960s, that one day the company should and would produce a proper 'F-type' and a smaller saloon than the XJ6, prompted a further step in the chain of logic. Such cars would need a lighter, more compact and more modern engine than the redoubtable XK whose age was beginning to show, and whose under-square dimensions and long stroke set limits on its development potential. As early as 1966, an archived memorandum from Bob Knight links the project number XJ18 to a '3-litre production engine' which might have been either a 3-litre XK or a reference to the need for a new, lighter and more advanced unit. Even at that stage, it seems to have been accepted that any new engine would in effect need to be a long-term replacement for the XK. Lighter, more modern and more compact it would inevitably be, but it would have to be just as powerful. The question was how to set about the task. A completely new engine was always a possibility, although an expensive one. An alternative was to derive an engine from the then-new V12. As described in Chapter 10, the first option to be studied in depth was a V8 which consisted of the V12 shorn of a pair of cylinders at either end.

The superficial attraction of this engine was that it would fit anywhere the V12 would (and by implication, almost anywhere the XK would) while allowing the engine compartment and the car nose to be made shorter – good news for a smaller, lighter car. Being exactly two-thirds of the V12 it was also an attractive size, at 3,563cc, with the promise of delivering substantially more power and torque than the 3.8-litre XK. It could also, as pointed out in Chapter 10, be passed through the V12 machining process, greatly reducing the need for new investment. The attraction was superficial because this was also a slightly odd-seeming unit with its 'wrong' 60° angle between banks creating an inherent mechanical imbalance. Even so, it progressed a surprisingly long way, with prototypes running on the bench and in cars, but the eventual conclusion was that the imbalance could only be overcome, and the engine made sufficiently refined, with the aid of twin balancer shafts – 'Lanchester shafts', first proposed by one of Coventry's foremost engineers of an earlier era – running at twice crankshaft speed. This feature was duly fitted to the V8's last iteration with generally satisfactory results, but by now the engine looked complicated and the chances of running it through

any significant part of the V12 production line were receding. Consequently (Chapter 10) the whole project was discontinued towards the end of 1971, long before engine designers began to use balancer shafts almost as a matter of course, even to smooth the balance diagrams of straightforward in-line 4-cylinder 2-litre power units.

This decision left two 6-cylinder alternatives, both of them in effect half of the V12. One possibility was a V6 formed by halving the V12 crosswise, as it were, while the other was an in-line 6-cylinder formed by splitting it lengthwise. The choice, it might be said, lay between a short, fat engine and a long, thin one. Either way, the capacity would be 2,672cc, smaller than Jaguar really needed, at least if the engine was to serve as an XK replacement. The V6, unlike the V8, would have had the 'right' included angle but at that time, V6s were thin on the ground and those which existed were not, if one excepts Lancia's pioneering masterpiece for the Aurelia, particularly inspiring. The in-line 6-cylinder on the other hand was very much a known quantity. There is no evidence that the V6 was ever taken seriously, but the straight-6 plant took root and continued to grow, though at varying rates through its chequered history.

Within Jaguar, the engine was long known as the 'slant-6' because a lengthwise half of the V12 was, evidently, an in-line 6-cylinder engine leaning over at 30°. There were good reasons for retaining this layout rather than sitting the engine bolt-upright. First, it would ease the task of handling the 6-cylinder on the same engine machining lines as the V12: one could easily envisage half the tools making a 'blind pass' while the other half performed as normal on the 6-cylinder block. Second, an in-line engine leaning over at a substantial angle reduced the overall height and allowed a lower bonnet line, something which had already occurred to manufacturers like Peugeot (in the 404) and Mercedes.

By the end of the 1960s, a fair amount of work had been done on the slant-6. For a time it laboured in the shadow of the V8 and there is a note in the minutes

Features of the AJ6 evident in this exploded view include the two-stage chain drive to the twin camshafts, and the deep side skirts of the cylinder block. These gave a degree of additional stiffness without carrying loads into the main bearing caps, which may have seemed a good idea at the time. With the benefit of hindsight, a 'baseplate' solution tying the caps together would have been better, and might have avoided the poor refinement for which early AJ6s were noted. (Jaguar)

of the MPM of 4 May 1971 that 'no further work is being undertaken on this unit' (the slant-6). But as related in Chapter 10, the meeting of 10 November 1971 was told that the V8 was to be abandoned, and that meant the 6-cylinder was firmly back in the frame. Now the problem of the half-V12 capacity being too small for Jaguar's purposes had to be addressed. There was no room in the V12 cylinder bank for more than a minimal boring-out, so the stroke had to be lengthened. Here there was scope, because the V12 was substantially over-square (90mm bore, 70mm stroke) and could be enlarged by making it 90mm 'square' for a capacity of 3,435cc.

The problem with substantially lengthening the stroke was that with suitably lengthened connecting rods (there being limits on the ratio of connecting rod length to stroke to avoid excessive side-loads on the piston and poor refinement) the block would have to be made taller and the 6-cylinder engine would no longer be compatible with the V12 machining arrangements. To accept this as an argument might have been to put the cart before the horse, since a successful 6-cylinder engine would inevitably be made at a higher rate than the V12. On the other hand, the V12 transfer line had been commissioned on the basis that it would also handle the slant-6, and the change of plan meant the V12 facility was doomed to under-utilisation and a failure ever to pay for itself. At the same time, had this been appreciated at an earlier stage, the slant-6 might have begun life as a cleaner sheet of paper and emerged with a shorter, stiffer cylinder block than was imposed by the lengthwise splitting of the V12. By now it was too late to take any action on either front...

In any case, it seems the 3.4-litre capacity was regarded as not quite sufficient and so a little space was found, by increasing the bore by 1mm and the stroke by 2mm to arrive at the nominal 3.6-litre capacity (3,590cc) with which the definitive AJ6 (Advanced Jaguar 6-cylinder) would be launched, more than a decade into the future. It is also, it should be noted, virtually the same capacity as the aborted 90mm x 70mm V8. In the minutes of the MPM of 6 January 1972 it is noted that 'slant-6 engines are being converted to the larger 3.6-litre capacity'. Even at that stage some thought was also

being given to the question of a suitable transmission and the MPM of 3 October 1972 recorded a suggestion that the Rover '77mm' gearbox – being developed initially for the Rover SD1/3500 – might be a suitable candidate (by this time, remember, Jaguar was completely within the orbit of the British Leyland group). On 29 November 1972 it was reported to an MPM that a slant-6 engine with high-lift cams had been run in a vehicle and produced 150bhp at 4,500rpm, and 171bhp at 5,500rpm.

Thereafter the story becomes impossible to track through the archives but it is clear that by the end of 1972, what one might call the bottom end of the engine existed, that it had been extensively run, and that – if that 171bhp is any guide – it wasn't powerful enough. Potentially the bottom end was immensely strong, because a guiding principle of the slant-6 design was that the V12 bore centres had to be retained, if only in the hope that this would be bound to lead to savings somewhere in the production system. Hence the slant-6 always had seven main bearings spaced as they were in the V12, but subject only to a fraction of the load. The factors that limited output were those of cylinder head design.

What happened after that is more difficult to track through the archive, but other published material, notably a short technical history and description issued at the time of the first AJ6 release in 1983, links the subsequent development of the AJ6 top end to a programme conducted from 1972, to return the V12 to its origins by adapting it for racing. The original 5-litre V12 of course had four camshafts but only two valves per cylinder; the aim now was to adapt the design to four valves per cylinder, in line with the latest racing practice. This would have been an attractive idea to Walter Hassan, harking back to his experience with Coventry Climax before Jaguar acquired it in 1963, and to his 'partner in crime' Harry Mundy. Hassan retired in 1972, so would have had time to prepare the ground, while Mundy was thereafter responsible for engine development until he in turn retired in 1980, making him the prime mover in the key years of the 6-cylinder development programme. This also ties in with a quoted reminiscence in a Jaguar internal communications publication that 'Harry Mundy and Ron Burr designed the AJ6 engine.'

What is said to have happened is that at least one 4-cam, 48-valve V12 prototype was prepared, using the stock 5.3-litre block and crankshaft, and run successfully to produce no less than 630bhp, substantially more than the original V12. It is said that this engine was handed over to TWR who also ran it, stripped it for examination and then apparently scrapped it. The racing requirement was subsequently abandoned, but the 4-valve concept lingered. An obvious possibility was to adapt the XK to 4-valve operation for, as Walter Hassan had long since pointed out, several British designers – including Bentley – had used such a cylinder head layout in the period 1919-39 as a means of packing as much valve area as possible into the small cylinder bores dictated by the old RAC rating system, from which, in its dimensions, the XK was a hangover. Adapting one of the 24-valve V12 heads to the XK ought to have been fairly easy since the two cylinder bores differed by only 2mm.

In a broader context, the appeal of this approach was that if it was not possible to create an engine which could share the V12 production facilities, perhaps it would be possible to develop one which would pass down the long-established XK line. The official Jaguar history states that three prototypes were built using a simplified and lightened XK block, with the bore reduced to a V12-matching 90mm and stroke of 100mm for a capacity of 3,817cc. To this was bolted the 24-valve head laid out by Harry Mundy, whose credentials already included the design of the Lotus Twin Cam cylinder head conversion of the Ford OHV 'Kent' engine, a task carried out in his spare time while he was still Technical Editor of *Autocar*. These engines ran with considerable success from 1975 onwards but Harry Mundy had reservations about some aspects of the XK design that were still retained, especially the crankshaft oil sealing arrangements which included a front lip seal housed half in the timing cover and half in the sump, and an old-fashioned rear rope seal. He had less admiration for the XK than some, since he did not, unlike Walter Hassan and the rest of the 'gang of four', personally look back to the 1940s and the story of its original development. Ideally, especially given the emerging trend in engine design, Mundy was looking to a deep-

A possible alternative to the 'slant-6' project was to engineer a deep-skirted, 24-valve, fuel-injected version of the venerable XK. Prototypes were built and tested, including the one seen here. In the end, it was found that a comprehensive 'new XK' programme would cost almost as much as one which started with a clean sheet of paper and fewer engineering constraints. (Trevor Crisp)

skirted block which would extend below the crank-shaft centre line for greater stiffness, better bearing alignment and better oil sealing.

Into this equation was then thrown the May high-compression head which proved so successful in improving the thermal efficiency and thus the fuel economy of the V12 engine in its production form from 1981 onwards. The attractive idea – possibly encouraged by Harry Mundy, who respected Michael May and admired the concept he brought to the V12 – grew within Jaguar's management that a single engine design might be developed which used a 24-valve head for a high performance version and the May 'Fireball' head – carefully adapted as it was to the V12 head layout with two in-line valves per cylinder – in an economy-optimised version. It was a good idea in principle but it put paid to any prospect of resur-recting the XK engine and meant that a new engine would have to be designed from scratch – or rather, on the basis of the work which had been devoted to creating the 3.6-litre slant-6 engine in 1972.

In 1976, Harry Mundy set to work with a will, making a number of changes he thought highly desirable and which, with the production-machinery link to the V12 effectively cut, he could now incor-porate. First, although the engine remained slanted, it was now set at 15° from the vertical rather than the 30° which would have been dictated by quasi-com-monality with the V12. The new angle gave sufficient under-bonnet clearance (oddly enough, Mercedes chose the same angle for their new-generation medium-range engines at about the same time) with-out creating problems of access to the 'underside' or making the engine package as installed unduly wide. Next, the actual block construction was changed. While it was still cast in light alloy, Mundy made it a closed-deck casting with shrink-fitted 'dry' liners, in contrast with the V12 which was of open-deck construction with the cylinder heads squeezing 'wet' liners into place. At some cost in ease of casting, this saved a little weight and made the block substantially stiffer, an important consideration for the in-line 6-cylinder engine, unable to profit from the inherent stiffness of a vee. This stiffness might have been even more important if, as was proposed at one stage following the second great energy crisis, a diesel version of the engine had been developed (something which would have been anathema to Harry Mundy). Stiffness, especially lengthwise but also in torsion, was also increased by the extension of the crankcase skirt to well below the crankshaft centre-line.

The third change was from toothed belt to chain drive for the twin overhead camshafts. In truth, the slant-6 prototypes had only used toothed belts because they made prototyping easier, and Mundy had always preferred chains which meant smaller diameter sprockets on each crankshaft nose. This was an important consideration in a cylinder head in which the included valve angle was much narrower than in the XK (46.5° instead of 70°, or even 75° in the '35/40' head) meaning that in turn the camshafts were closer together, as had been decided to retain the system of direct-acting bucket tappets used by Jaguar ever since the birth of the XK. A chain drive also meant some saving in engine length, and in Mundy's opinion, more accurate timing of valve operation. Engine length was in fact critical. Although the AJ6 as it shaped-up was slimmer than the XK it was no shorter, in fact it hardly could be with 91mm bores and the obligatory 7-bearing crankshaft. Further length was therefore saved by deleting the crescent-type oil pump on the crankshaft nose and reverting to a chain-driven pump in the engine sump. Close attention to oil-tightness led to the adoption not only of a modern PTFE rear oil seal, but to the use of a mould-in-place RTV (room temperature vulcanising) sealant bead to replace conventional gaskets in most of the engine's 'cool' joint faces.

A fully representative 3.6-litre AJ6 ran for the first time in 1979, and quickly produced outputs in line with specification, so Harry Mundy's last major task was complete and he retired from Jaguar, like Bob Knight, in 1980, three years before the engine was revealed in its first production application, the XJ-S 3.6. Its detail development and readying for produc-tion were overseen by the 'new boys' in charge, in the form of Jim Randle as Engineering Director, and Trevor Crisp as Chief Engineer (Power Units). In fact, even they were already Jaguar men of long standing, although their new boss, John Egan, had come from elsewhere.

Apart from the actual cost of development, the AJ6 called for major investment by Jaguar at a critical financial period, just as the 'Leyland Days' were coming to an end and John Egan led the company back to independence. Somehow the then massive total of £21 million was pulled together to fund the production facility, with £6 million spent on a single transfer line for machining the cylinder block. The 24-valve XK would have been cheaper, but the AJ6 family, as it then seemed, had the more long-term potential. The AJ6 production line was built

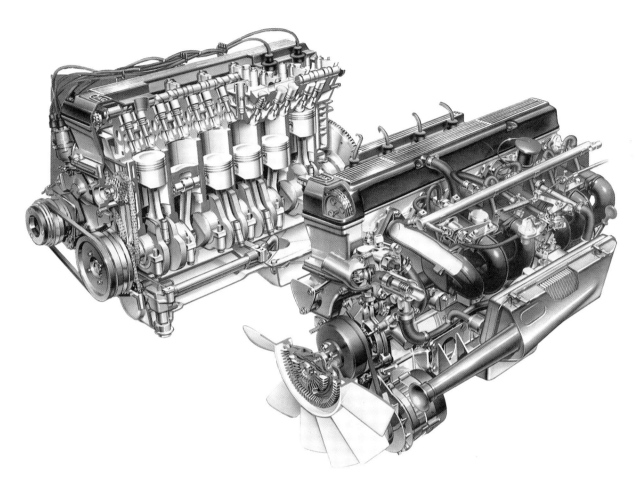

Above: When it entered production many years later, the 3.6-litre AJ6 engine was a far cry from being 'half the V12' which had been the starting point for the exercise. The angle of inclination was now 15° rather than 30°, which gave plenty of clearance

for the bulky induction system to the left of the unit as installed. This detailed view of a 24-valve cylinder head is interesting, as is Harry Mundy's choice of a dry-lined block rather than the open-deck, wet-lined design of the V12. (Jaguar)

within 'the Daimler' at Radford, in 60 Shop which had once housed Daimler bus assembly. The planned production rate was over 1,000 engines a week in addition to the V12 and the (now reducing) volume of 4.2-litre XKs.

The XJ-S 3.6 was very much the performance-orientated face of the AJ6, but it had to establish the engine's reputation before the time came for the next stage – the all important installation in the new XJ40 saloon, successor to the XJ6 Series III. Partly for this reason, the 3.6 engine in its original 1983 form was

deliberately conservative in its approach to engine management. At a time when unified engine management, initially in the form of Bosch's Motronic, controlling both fuel injection and ignition response to signals from a single set of sensors, was beginning to make an impact the AJ6 retained two separate systems, the Lucas (out of Bosch) electronic fuel injection system and a Lucas constant-energy contactless ignition system. It satisfied the needs of the time but left scope for improvement.

Also much in need of improvement at the time of the engine's first appearance in the XJ-S was its operating refinement. For all the work that had gone into it, the relative lack of stiffness in the long, narrow cylinder block led to noise and vibration levels which might be laughed off in a car with sporting pre-tensions, but which would certainly doom any luxury saloon. Accordingly, the three-year period between the XJ-S launch and that of the XJ40 in 1986 saw some fairly desperate remedial work being carried out. Some indication of this is provided, in suitably guarded terms, by the 1986 product press release.

This points out that 'Combining power and refinement in a 4-valve combustion chamber, all-aluminium alloy engine is a significant challenge for design engineers. Overcoming these problems has involved a great deal of development work by Jaguar's engineering team.' Among the changes made since 1983 the release cites modified cam profiles for reduced valve acceleration and quieter valve drive, stiffer camshafts and lighter bucket tappets, redesigned tensioners 'to ensure that the chain drives stay quiet under all operating conditions', and a widespread reduction of tolerances and clearances together with improved balancing. This included the balancing of crankshaft damper, timing ring and pulley as an assembly rather than as individual parts.

With these changes, the AJ6 revealed its 'economy' face in 1986 when it was introduced as the entry-level power unit for the new XJ40 saloon – in marketing terms, the fourth-series XJ6. The new version featured reduced capacity, retaining the same 91mm bore but with the stroke reduced all the way to 74.8mm, making the engine extremely over-square and with a capacity of 2,919cc, nominally 2.9 litres. Despite this, the block height remained the same – changing the closed-deck casting would have been a wearisome business – so the connecting rods had to be lengthened by half as much (8.6mm) as the stroke was shortened. This significantly increased the ratio of rod length to stroke, reducing the angle through which the rod swung and consequently making the engine noticeably smoother. It is indeed worth noting, in passing, that the block height remained the same in all four capacity versions of the AJ6, all of which therefore have different connecting rod lengths to achieve the same piston height at top dead centre.

The cylinder head of the 2.9 was completely different, virtually lifted direct from the V12 – not quite identical, but with the same in-line valves, porting, valves and camshaft, and well able to be machined on the V12 head line. The May Fireball combustion chambers meant the AJ6 2.9 could run a compression ratio as high as 12.6:1 without risk of detonation, and consequently with high efficiency as in the V12 HE engine which had by then already accumulated five years of in-service experience. It was noteworthy even then that the two versions of the engine used different management systems. The 3.6 now had an integrated engine management unit developed by Lucas, with then-sophisticated functions such as idling speed control and fuel cut-off on

the overrun, and a limp-home reversion mode. The 2.9 by contrast used separate injection and ignition systems, both directly sourced from Bosch, the injection being LH-Jetronic. Despite its high compression ratio the engine had no knock sensor but depended entirely on accurate pre-programming of the ignition timing control to stay clear of trouble.

The power output of the 2.9 was a relatively modest 165bhp (DIN) at 5,700rpm, with peak torque of 239Nm at 4,000rpm, both figures well down on the 24-valve 3.6, but this was the economy version, after all. One problem was that the economy did not show all that clearly. At the XJ40 launch exercise, journalists were encouraged to compare the AJ3.6 with the 4.2-litre XK which it effectively replaced, and the 2.9 with the 3.4XK, and in both cases the economy improvement implied by the 'official' consumption figures was considerable, both at steady speeds and in the urban cycle. But there was no escaping the fact that when the 2.9 was compared back-to-back with the 3.6, the differences were less impressive. With the 3.6 figures in brackets, and for manual-transmission cars, they were 19.5mpg (18.6) urban, 38.7mpg (35.6) at 56mph, and 31.0mpg (29.7) at 75mph. *Autocar*'s first road-test 2.9, an automatic, achieved only 19.3mpg overall, which was bad; their first 3.6, with manual gearbox admittedly, managed 20.7mpg.

This is really a discussion for the chapter on the XJ40 (Chapter 14) but it rather points to the fact that the 2.9 was not up to its task. In a lighter, smaller car it might have proved excellent, but in the XJ40, scaling over 1,700kg (nearly 3,800lb) even in 'entry-level' form, it spent too much of its time far away from that area on the speed/load chart where the May combustion system helped the engine to realise its best specific fuel consumption. Were this not enough, there were mutterings that the AJ6 3.6 still did not deliver operating refinement to match that of the ultimately developed XK, certainly not of the V12, nor yet – Heaven forbid – of the latest-generation of 6-cylinder BMW engines which were among its closest competitors. A considerable amount of further development seemed to be called for, and here lay a problem, the thorny but familiar one of engineering manpower. In a product planning paper dated 18 March 1986, in other words six months prior to the XJ40 launch, Trevor Crisp wrote: 'Only two engine programmes are supportable. One must be the 4.0-litre 4-valve engine with forged-steel 8-counterweight crankshaft for the 1989 model year [first approved for the 1988 model year]; and the other, the 2.9-litre 4-valve – first approved for the 1989 model year – with consideration given to a stretch to 3.3-litres. Therefore no major changes to the 5.3 V12 can be contemplated.'

It is therefore clear that even before the 2.9 was exposed in the XJ40, plans were afoot to increase its output by standardising the 4-valve head and by increasing its capacity. Plans moved ahead rapidly it seems, for the minutes of an MPM on 12 November 1986 record a strong argument in favour of the 2.9 being replaced by a 24-valve 3.2 'which would be capable of clearing 200km/h in catalyst form', by 1991. An acknowledged counter-argument was that this would raise the smaller-engined XJ40's fiscal power rating in the French market from 15CV to 18CV, which would increase its annual tax liability from 1,812 to 2,716 francs. The fiscal anomalies of some overseas markets continued to weigh, but no longer as heavily. With catalytic converters looming and the need to maintain performance standards, the 2.9 was doomed.

As Trevor Crisp's paper suggested, the first major move affected not the 2.9, but the 3.6-litre. For the 1990 model year (thus in September 1989) the XJ40 was substantially revised – only three years after its launch – and a major feature was the enlargement of the 3.6-litre engine to nominal 4-litre capacity. There was only one way to achieve this, and that was by lengthening the stroke from the original 92mm to 102mm, in some ways bringing its dimensions uncannily close to those of the 4.2-litre XK and increasing the capacity to 3,980cc. To support the longer stroke, and not only maintain but actually to improve refinement, the forged-steel crankshaft with eight counterweights, referred to by Trevor Crisp in 1986, replaced the former cast-iron component. The integrated engine management system was further improved, with extra computer memory allowing a comprehensive diagnostic function to be incorporated for the first time.

Even by 1989, considerable test bed and running experience had been accumulated with 4-litre versions of the AJ6 since, as related in Chapter 10, it had been proposed that the XJ41 'F-type' should be powered by the this engine in both naturally aspirated and turbocharged forms. The XJ41 never came to pass and neither did the AJ6 turbo, but by the time the 4-litre engine finally appeared in the XJ40 it had certainly been around for some time, and with a forged-steel crankshaft, for nothing less would have

been acceptable in a turbocharged version with its much higher big-end loads. So why did it not appear earlier, perhaps even at the time of the XJ40 launch in 1986? The answer appears to be that 1986 was a little too early; at that time the XJ41 was still a current project and it might have seemed unwise to pre-empt the new sports car by announcing it with an engine that had already appeared in the saloon.

There was also the vexed question of engineering to comply with the rapidly evolving requirements of exhaust emission control, not only in the USA but also in Europe. The press material issued for the XJ40 launch emphasises – perhaps more in retrospect than at the time – the upheaval which was being created by the coming of universal catalytic converters for spark-ignition engines, something then firmly on the European agenda although still a couple of years away. Consequently, full sets of output figures were given for engines in both catalytic and non-catalytic form (and we can appreciate why Trevor Crisp was so exercised about manpower commitments). From our perspective it is more relevant to compare the 4.0 with the former 3.6 in catalytic form, the power outputs being 223bhp at 4,750rpm (199bhp at 5,250rpm) and the torque outputs 377Nm at 3,650rpm (302Nm at 4,000rpm). It is also worth noting that in terms of output, the catalyst penalty for the 4.0 was 12bhp and 10Nm.

The direction of development is clear. From 3.6 to 4.0, the torque benefit was much greater than the power increase – a virtually 25 per cent improvement compared with a more modest 12 per cent, for an actual 11 per cent increase in capacity. What was more, the peaks came at lower speed, indicating the tuning of the new engine for mid-range torque and superior driveability. For the first time, Jaguar even made the point in its press material that the new engine's torque output was as much as 340Nm even at 1,400rpm (it had also been modified as necessary to enable it to run on unleaded petrol).

It only took another year – but a year which saw Ford assume control – to see the end of the 2.9-litre engine and its replacement by the 3.2-litre version. It was not so much a case of evolution as of devolution, since the Jaguar press pack made it clear that this new version was to be regarded simply as a shorter-stroke (83mm, thus 3,239cc capacity) version of the 4.0 engine. Everything but the crankshaft was carried over, including the latest engine management system, suitably recalibrated. Because the cylinder bore was 91mm in both cases, the 4-valve head could be carried across directly – no problems there. The point was explicitly made that this was the first Jaguar engine variant to be developed in catalytic converter form only. Power output was given as 200bhp at 5,250rpm compared with the wretched 148bhp at 5,500rpm for the catalyst-equipped 2.9, and torque as 298Nm at 4,000rpm compared with 225Nm at 4,300Nm. The fuel economy was actually improved, not least because the overall gearing could be substantially raised, while the performance deficit had been overcome.

After this there was one, but only one salvo left in the 'slant-6' locker, but at least it was a salvo rather than a single shot. The Jaguar engineering team had never given up on the engine even though powers within Ford were pushing for a different and more rational approach to engine design and sourcing. But for the first entirely Ford-managed vehicle programme, the X300 saloon (Chapter 16) which had actually begun its project life as the XJ90 successor to the XJ40, the in-line 6-cylinder engine in both sizes, 3.2 and 4.0, was perforce retained. It had however been substantially improved, so much so that the project management team redesignated it AJ16 rather than AJ6. The new car was announced in September 1994, for the 1995 model year.

Because the main dimensions were not touched, the improvements in performance seen in the AJ16 were less than sensational, but they were certainly useful. The 4.0 version delivered 249PS (DIN) at 4,800rpm and 392Nm of torque at 4,000rpm, increases of 10 per cent and 4 per cent respectively over the AJ6. The 3.2 now managed 219PS at 5,100rpm and 315Nm at 4,500rpm, representing increases of 8 per cent and 6 per cent respectively. In each case there was an overall fuel economy benefit of around 3 per cent. Those were the raw figures but they did not convey the amount of work which had gone into overcoming those early criticisms of the AJ6 as being less refined than it ought to have been. The extra output came from increased compression ratio (to 10:1), revised inlet and exhaust ports, and new cam profiles with higher lift, but that was only the beginning. In all, changes had been made to more than 100 engine and ancillary components. Among the most notable were an entirely new engine management system, GEMS (Generic Engine Management System), a cylinder block modified to increase its stiffness, lighter pistons, coil-on-plug 'direct ignition', and valves which had been lightened by slimming the stems from 8mm to 7mm diameter, for a 20 per cent weight saving. Still more changes had been made to

improve durability, while GEMS allowed fully sequential fuel injection and benefited from knock sensing, allowing it to run the engine as efficiently as possible right up to the knock threshold. Even more to the point, perhaps, was the fact that the AJ16 felt extremely refined, in contrast to the first AJ6 of a decade previously which had been notably lacking in this department.

There was also an exciting finale, a supercharged version of the engine designated XJR6 and fitted to the high-performance XJR 4.0 saloon. Jaguar engineers said they had chosen mechanical supercharging rather than turbocharging to avoid any possibility of turbo lag. To ensure strong boost pressure at low to medium speeds they ran the Eaton M90 Roots-type supercharger at 2.5 times crankshaft speed, by way of a polyvee belt. Even though the compression ratio was reduced to 8.5:1, driving the supercharger this fast inevitably meant some wasteful spillage of pressure via a bypass valve at high speeds if detonation was to be avoided (the maximum permitted boost pressure was 10psi). The air-to-coolant-to-air intercooler also served as the induction plenum chamber. Very few changes were needed to enable the AJ16 to accept the much higher BMEP and output. The lower-compression pistons were of necessity new, together with the induction system. As is customary, the valve timing was 'unwound' with greatly reduced overlap to exploit the natural scavenging effect of positive induction pressure. Some other changes first introduced for the supercharged version, including an improved head gasket design, higher head clamping loads and local stiffening of the cylinder head around the combustion chambers, were made standard, to the benefit of the naturally aspirated engine's durability. Output of the supercharged XJR6 was 326PS at 5,000rpm, but as with all pressure-induction systems the real benefit was seen in the torque output which rose to 512Nm at 3.050rpm, better than a 30 per cent increase over that of the naturally aspirated 4-litre and allowing the XJR 4.0 to accelerate from rest to 60mph in 5.9sec, performance to put any E-type, even the V12, in the shade.

A similarly supercharged version of the 3.2-litre AJ16 was also developed, but not for Jaguar's own use. Instead, it went in the new Aston Martin DB7, the Newport Pagnell company having become a stablemate of sorts, also under Ford ownership.

That high note remarkably signalled the end of the 'slant-6' story. Within a few years it was to be supplanted by a new generation of V8 and then V6

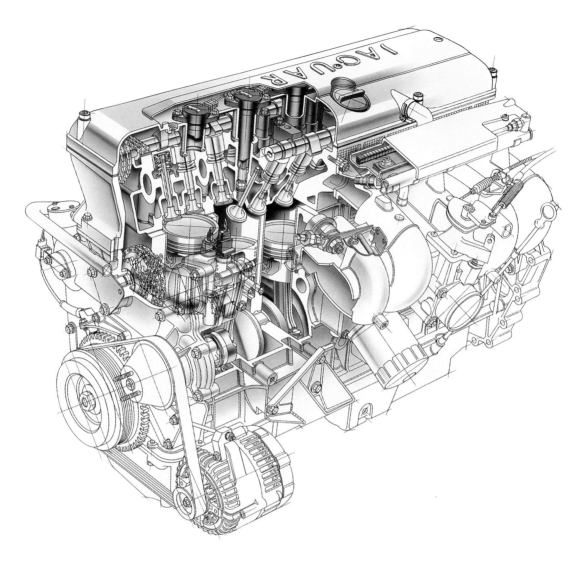

By the time the career of the slant-6 engine came to an end, the original 3.6-litre AJ6 had evolved into the AJ16, offered in two sizes, 3.2-litre and 4-litre (there had been a 12-valve 2.9-litre as well). In this final form the AJ16 proved to be an outstanding engine with hundreds of modifications

which overcame the drawbacks of the original (compare, for example, the AJ6 and AJ16 crankshafts). Sadly, it was not sufficient to ensure the engine's survival, and it was shortly to be replaced by V8 and V6 power units, bringing the Jaguar straight-6 story to an end. (Jaguar)

engines, and the AJ16 was the last in-line 6-cylinder Jaguar engine. It might be argued that it was no more than a qualified success and may not have deserved to survive. As it was, it enjoyed a production life of only 14 years between the first XJ-S 3.6 and the last of the X300 saloons, in contrast to the XK which ran from 1948 well into the 1980s. It is interesting to speculate what might have happened if the other fork in the road had been taken and the 24-valve XK had been pursued. But it wasn't, and we have to acknowledge the key role played by the 'slant-6' in Jaguar's product range through the later 1980s and into the early days of the Ford takeover. It might equally be argued that if Jaguar had somehow managed to continue independently – not that it was ever really an option – the true worth of the ultimate AJ16 might have won more recognition. But that was not to be, either.

14 XJ40: a real XJ6 replacement

As we saw in Chapter 9, when the XJ6 was launched in 1968 it was expected it to last for 'at least seven years'. In the event, it had to survive for 16 years, through three evolving series and many minor changes, seeing Jaguar through the darkest days of the 1970s as its principal product, supported only by the XJ-S which, until the mid-1980s, was hampered through being powered only by the thirsty V12 engine.

The true successor to the XJ6 was therefore not launched until 1986 and was in no sense a carry-over; as the text of Jaguar's press material put it: 'Only the names – XJ6, Sovereign and Daimler – have been retained from the Series III saloons. Everything else is completely new. Body styling has changed, but the line is familiar and uniquely Jaguar. A new all-aluminium six-cylinder engine had been designed specifically for the car and will be available in 2.9-litre and 3.6-litre versions.'

This was a slightly odd way of referring to the AJ6 power unit which, by the time the new saloon appeared, had been used in 3.6-litre form in the XJ-S for three years. However, the point is really that throughout its long gestation period, as described in Chapter 13, the 'slant-6' programme, which culminated in the AJ6, had always been primarily intended for the saloon. It was merely that around 1980, when it was becoming clear that the AJ6 could be in production by 1983, while the definitive saloon had barely been signed off for development, it seemed a doubly good idea to put the engine in the XJ-S as a more economical alternative to the V12, and also to gain valuable running experience.

The Jaguar press statement also said the new saloon was 'the culmination of a seven-year, £200 million development programme', but there was a lot more to it than that. Seven years took the story back to 1979 and the launch of the XJ6 Series III, but the immediate giveaway is the XJ project number allocated to the new saloon: XJ40. Numerically this precedes almost all the XJ numbers allocated to the Series III, which with one strange and inexplicable exception (XJ39 'XJ6 Series 3 special bodies') ran from XJ50 onwards. Intriguingly, some early entries in the XJ number ledger refer to the XJ40 as the 'Series 4'. What seems to have happened is that during the 1970s it was acknowledged within Jaguar engineering and product planning, that the original XJ6 needed replacing with an all-new design, and the XJ40 number was duly allocated. But during that decade there was insufficient money or manpower available to carry through such an ambitious programme, and the Series III was quickly developed as a stop-gap, hence XJ50 onwards. Once it was clear that the Series III would appear first, it was logical to refer to the more radical and more distant XJ40 as 'Series 4' even if it was not eventually announced as such.

Certainly, work on what became the XJ40 had been going on long before 1979. Two notes in MPM minutes from as early as 1972 reveal that thought was being given to an XJ6 successor – by no means at odds with the need for a 1975 launch in line with Sir William's target seven-year model life. On 3 October it was recorded that an XJ40 concept had been prepared and submitted to Jaguar's then masters at BLMC Berkeley Square. On 29 November it was noted that an XJ40 clay model was in preparation. By the time the first XJ6 was ten years old, in 1978, it had already exceeded the target life set for it by Sir William Lyons and any good product team would have been deep into looking at the size, shape and feature content of a replacement, even if in some respects – although only some – the old car set standards which would be hard to improve on.

If the XJ40 was going to proceed at all, however, then at the end of the 1970s it still needed approval from the powers that were in British Leyland. On 14 February 1979 the Jaguar team made a major presentation on the XJ40 to BL management, and in many respects did not spare themselves. Among the points made was the painful one that 'There is no doubt that the quality and reliability of the current vehicle (the XJ6 Series II) is well below the standard set by the competition.' It also pointed out that 'current Jaguar engines are heavy, the XK due to age, the V12 due to size.' This was important because better fuel consumption was becoming a marketing priority and weight saving was one of the keys to economy. The point was strongly made that the CAFE (Corporate Average Fleet Economy) legislation then taking shape in the USA was seen as a real threat to Jaguar's

The long-running project XJ40 was finally launched in 1986 as the definitive replacement for the XJ6 Series 3. To confuse matters, the new car was similarly known as XJ6 – and the old XJ12 Series 3 remained in production because the XJ40 had not been engineered to accept the larger power unit. Thus as launched, the new saloon offered only the slant-6 engine – plus a completely new body (however familiar it may have looked) and chassis design, with heavily revised rear suspension. (Giles Chapman Library)

continued existence in this key market unless the economy of its mainstream product could be significantly improved.

It must be said that the Jaguar team making this presentation would have been aware of an earlier BL corporate plan covering the period 1975-85, clearly showing an intention to launch the XJ40 in 1982 (and indeed for XJ-S production to cease towards the end of 1984!). This may have encouraged a certain playing

During the gestation of the XJ40 project, which lasted through most of the 1970s and half the 1980s, specialist designers were invited to try their hands at creating a fresh image while retaining the Jaguar hallmarks. Bertone and Italdesign interpretations are seen lined up here. Ultimately, and thankfully, the definitive design remained in-house. (JDHT)

of Devil's advocate, as though inviting the BL board to jump in the wrong direction. Having admitted to dreadful product quality – the result, be it said, of under-investment in decent development or production facilities, plus the insidious effects of hardly a week going by without a strike of some kind at Browns Lane – the document suggested that perhaps this didn't matter! 'Attractive styling is a very important part of the Jaguar appeal especially in the USA and contributes significantly to the prestige image of the XJ6 … the combination of comfort and performance in addition to style give Jaguar a uniqueness not matched by any competitive vehicle.' How many owners, one wonders, decided not to return for a second dose after being confronted by the day-to-day consequences of that philosophy?

The essence of the XJ40 proposal was simple enough, however. It was to be a car very much the same size as the existing one, but with an estimated 485lb of weight-saving achieved through more modern body design and a new powertrain. Durability targets would be greatly increased compared with the standard set by the XJ6. The powertrain would centre on the AJ6 engine in a range of three versions, a 12-valve 2.9, a 12-valve 3.8 (rather than the 3.6 which eventually emerged), and a 24-valve 3.8. It was proposed to offer the Rover 5-speed '77mm' gearbox but predictions were that the demand would be 95 per cent automatic, and the 3-speed Borg-Warner Model 66 would be standard. The plainly stated alternatives to the XJ40 proposal were either to proceed with a reskin of the Series III, at that time about to enter production – or to do nothing.

The engine was clearly a key factor and the Jaguar team emphasised not only the weight saving which would be made with this all-aluminium unit, but also the promise that it would achieve much better utilisation of the V12 production machinery at Radford and the 12-valve versions would also be able to exploit the 'new, high compression technology' (the May Fireball cylinder head) already well through its development process for application to the V12.

Alternative engine strategies were discussed however. One was simply to carry on with the existing XK engine range and hope the CAFE requirements could still be met somehow. A second and more interesting possibility lay in further developing the XK, a cause which had been eagerly espoused by Geoffrey Robinson during his brief tenure as Jaguar's Managing Director in the earlier 1970s. This programme would have involved two main steps, the

evolution of a 24-valve head at least for the top-range version of the car, and a complete redesign of the cylinder block into a simpler, lighter, thin-walled cast iron unit with a deeper skirt (for stiffness and better oil sealing), but still capable of being machined for the most part on the existing XK line. Certainly, during the 1970s XJ6s were running with prototypes of such an 'ultimate XK', sometimes in back-to-back comparison with 'slant-6' powered cars. It would have made an interesting final chapter to the XK story had it come to pass, but the XJ40 presentation made three further points. One was that even the new, improved XK would be 100lb heavier than the AJ6, another that the new car's bonnet line would need modifying to enable the XK to fit – proving that XJ40 body design work had already progressed to the stage where such things could be a worry. Finally and apparently conclusively, it was argued that 'extensive re-equipment, at a cost of £11.5 million, is needed to both repair the worn-out XK plant and to expand capacity to 1,000 engines per week.' In other words, the apparently cheap option of retaining the XK would not, in fact, have been cheap at all.

There was one further option, which was to scrap the idea of a unique Jaguar engine and to adopt the Rover 3.5-litre V8, already admired both for its light weight – it too being of linered all-alloy construction – and for the efficiency with which it powered the Rover 3500 (SD1) and Range Rover. It was already known that the V8 would stretch at least to 4-litre capacity and, with fuel injection, ought to deliver enough power to enable the high-range XJ40 to meet its performance targets. There is a story that the Jaguar body designers deliberately ensured the V8 would be very difficult to fit beneath the XJ40 bonnet but the truth is more mundane. The Jaguar argument in this case was four-fold. One: however good the Rover engine might be, 'Jaguar owners expect a unique Jaguar engine in their cars.' Two: 'the Rover V8 is basically of US design and this would not be good for the US market in which the Jaguar would be seen as having an 'ordinary' engine.' (It is interesting that this consideration did not stop the Range Rover from enjoying considerable later success in the USA). Three: an estimated '£11,870,000 investment would be needed to duplicate the Rover engine plant to provide sufficient capacity.' In other words the Rover alternative would be at least as expensive as the updated XK one. Four: the adoption of a Rover engine with the implication that engine production would be moved away from Radford would be likely to cause 'industrial relations problems' there; and everybody in the conference room in which the case was presented would have devoted a lot of their time to worrying about industrial relations problems. It is odd now to look back with the knowledge of hindsight, and note that in 1997 the Radford plant pushed out the last V12 engine and then shut its doors; but in 1979 that seems to have been a conclusive argument. Not only the XJ40, but also the AJ6 would go ahead, Jaguar would get its unique (and lightweight) engine and production would take place at Radford.

To some extent the XJ40 programme still had to work within limitations. The old model had sprawled into a number of versions, not only the XJ12 but also two different wheelbases and of course the 2-door coupé body. When working towards the 1986 launch of the new car, the engineering team concentrated entirely on one wheelbase (113in), one 4-door body shell, and on the AJ6 powertrain, to the exclusion of the V12. As the 1986 press release stated, 'the V12-powered versions of the Series III will … continue to be produced for markets such as the United Kingdom and Germany where there is still strong demand for the V12 engine.' More specifically, in the body of the text, was the comment that 'The initial design concept did not call for the new car to have a V12 engine. In 1980 the company, in common with many others, felt that large-capacity engines would have a limited future. Falling petrol prices (through the early 1980s) together with fuel economy developments to the engine have, however, resulted in renewed demand for the V12 unit. For this reason Jaguar will continue to manufacture the Series III saloon in V12 form until the new car can be re-engineered to accept the V12 power unit.' Thereafter, a long guessing-game ensued as to when, or even whether, a V12 version of the XJ40 would ever emerge. The question was not answered until the 1993 model year.

As it emerged, the XJ40 was extremely close in size to the XJ6 Series III. To be more precise, its wheelbase was one inch longer, its front and rear tracks fractions of an inch wider, its overall length just over an inch more (and still just inside the crucial 5 metres), its overall width and height almost identical. Jaguar claimed an inch more front legroom, 'maintained' headroom, and up to 3in more shoulder room because of the reduced tumblehome of the 'glasshouse'. Despite all the pious hopes of saving 465lb in weight, the 3.6-litre XJ40 scaled a modest though useful 132lb less than the 4.2 XJ6, and this

despite its undeniably lighter powertrain. The increasing demands of safety legislation, Jaguar's understandable concerns about durability, and the need to enhance the standard specification to keep up with the opposition, had eaten into the margin once envisaged. More specifically, Jaguar stated that the XJ40 body-in-white weighed 18lb less than the XJ6, with more savings coming through the use of thinner glass – a trend everyone was pursuing in the 1980s. Thus most of the weight saving was indeed due to the lighter powertrain. Certainly there was nothing structurally unusual about the body, and Jaguar engineers were much keener to talk about its lower noise and vibration levels, its improved aerodynamics – the drag coefficient had been held down to 0.37 through careful attention to detail, especially the radiusing of edges and corners – and its improved corrosion resistance and paint quality. However, the XJ6 was the first Jaguar to derive serious benefit from computer-aided design (CAD) and one result of this work was a 25 per cent reduction in the number of separate panels needed to form the body, 136 pieces fewer than the Series III.

Because the body was new, the suspension had to be new but it remained the same in principle with double wishbones at the front and an adaptation of the earlier system with the fixed-length drive shaft forming the upper member of a double-wishbone geometry. Here, though, there were some radical differences. Most noticeably to a casual glance, the disc brakes had been moved from their inboard position to a more conventional outboard one integral with the wheels. This, as Engineering Director Jim Randle observed, meant 'no more cooking of final drives' in hard driving with red-hot discs a few inches away on either side. Moving the discs had two dis-advantages: first, of increasing the unsprung weight and second, of requiring the lower wishbone to react to all the braking torque as well as the drive torque and cornering forces. Randle argued that the unsprung weight increase was barely significant, and he had an elegant answer for the other problem in the form of what he called a 'pendulum' mounting arrangement for the lower wishbone which allowed it some freedom to move fore and aft – compliance, in fact – while locating it very firmly against lateral forces, for the sake of good and consistent handling.

Another obvious change in the XJ40 was that the earlier twin coil spring and damper units, one either side of the drive shaft, had been replaced by a single one; not only cheaper, but presenting one less pathway for noise and vibration trying to enter the body. More to the point, Randle had used this arrangement to ensure that the front mountings of the rear sub-frame took all the static load, and the rear ones most of the important dynamic loads, which made it easier to design suitable bushes for each location. With the new arrangement being self-levelling, an idea so firmly rejected in an earlier era for the XJ6, it now became standard on the high-line versions of the XJ40 (Sovereign and Daimler) and an option across the range.

As to other elements of the chassis, Jaguar had moved with the times in providing anti-lock braking, again optionally on the cheaper versions. Otherwise the steering – power-assisted rack-and-pinion – and the brakes, especially now with the outboard rear discs, looked state of the art. For the XJ40 launch, Jaguar decided – unwisely with the benefit of hindsight – to go with the jointly developed Michelin/Dunlop TD tyre system which used non-standard millimetric rims of special design, incompatible with anything but specially manufactured tyres. The TD rim was specially shaped to retain a punctured tyre in position while slowing down; the tyres also contained a sealant gel which was claimed capable of sealing 65 to 70 per cent of all punctures.

The AJ6 engine has the previous chapter to itself and it suffices here to note that by 1986 the 24-valve 3.6-litre version had become familiar in the XJ-S in which it appeared during 1983, while the smaller capacity 12-valve 2.9-litre complete with a cylinder head which could (almost) be swapped for one of the heads on a V12 engine was new. Although Jaguar claimed the 2.9 AJ6 engine matched the old 3.4 XK in output, it really didn't feel like it when driven, and this version was destined for a short life.

By the time the XJ40 appeared, all thoughts of a 3-speed automatic transmission for a luxury-class European car were fast disappearing – and Borg-Warner had withdrawn from its former British facilities in Letchworth and Kenfig – and Jaguar went to ZF for the excellent 4-speed 4HP22 transmission which, like most units of that generation, was in effect a basic 3-speed geartrain with an additional stage to give an overdrive fourth gear. With this transmission there appeared a pet idea of Jim Randle's, the 'J-gate' selector in which P-R-N-D were in-line to the right, while moving the lever to the left while in D placed it in a parallel D-3-2 gate. 'Randle's Handle' as it became known within Jaguar engineering, was one of those things which seemed like a

good idea at the time but did not survive the test of long-term opinion. Meanwhile, for the small minority of customers who still wanted manual transmission, Jaguar offered the 5-speed Getrag 265, all former supply links with Rover having been broken.

As pointed out in Chapter 13, the power output of the 2.9 was substantially less than that of the 24-valve 3.6, 165bhp compared with 221bhp (DIN), while its peak torque of 239Nm was woefully down on the 337Nm of the bigger engine. This was supposed to be the 'economy' version of the car (and engine) but it only worked out like that for a driver who treated the car in a particular way, rarely approaching maximum load or high speed but instead keeping the engine close to the fairly confined part of the speed/load chart within which the high compression and high-speed burn characteristics of the May head really paid dividends. For many drivers the output of the V12 was so great that it was quite easy to remain close to this 'economy peak' but with the 2.9 AJ6, far more drivers spent most of their time at a considerable distance, so to speak. The effect was magnified by the lower gearing required to achieve acceptable mid-range acceleration in the 2.9: 3.77:1 compared with 3.54:1 in the 3.6 with the manual gearbox, and 4.09:1 compared with 3.54:1 (again) with automatic. Thus the official fuel consumption figures – then coming into fashion – showed the 2.9 to be only 5 per cent more economical in urban driving, 9 per cent better at a steady 56mph, and a meagre 4 per cent better at a steady 75mph. True, it was more economical than its predecessor the 3.4 XK in the Series III, but that was not really the issue. Most customers probably thought that the entry-level car would give them less performance but better economy in exchange for less money; in practice all most of them saw was the inferior performance.

This was doubly worrying because Jaguar continued to suffer concerns about the XJ40 being hit with a 'gas-guzzler' tax under the American Federal CAFE regulations. Changes which were seriously considered, according to the record, included weight reduction by every possible means, lower-drag tyres, a programme to reduce engine internal friction, and the introduction of a final drive ratio as high as 2.55:1, which would certainly have done nothing to help performance. In the event, the US domestic 'big three' car manufacturers lobbied hard enough to prevent the CAFE limitations ever becoming sufficiently severe to cause real concern.

Comparisons of the XJ40 with the XJ6 Series III

suggest that, in terms of power output, weight, frontal area and drag coefficient, the new car should have shown no more than a modest margin in acceleration, and a slightly higher maximum speed, as the old one. *Autocar*, testing the manual-transmission 3.6 and looking back to its last 4.2-litre (fuel injected) Series III, actually saw 137mph maximum (compared with 131mph for the older car) and 7.4sec to 60mph (8.6sec formerly). Over-all fuel consumption for the 3.6 was 20.7mpg as against 20.1mpg – not much improvement there. *Autocar*'s figures were fairly well in line with those claimed by Jaguar, but it is interesting to note that overtones of the 'Bob Berry Special' still lingered: the minutes of an MPM on 22 September 1986 note that 'JNR [Jim Randle] confirmed that the press cars would be specially prepared to ensure the best possible performance, in view of the launch venue being 2,500 feet above sea level.' The same meeting seems also to have decided that the 'J-gate' was not a terribly good idea and that attention should be given to engineering a conventional

Above: Once it had been announced, facelifts and range changes for the XJ40 kept on coming. For the 1990 model year, the main news was the increase in size for the AJ6 engine, from 3.6 to 4-litre capacity and the introduction of the JaguarSport XJR-4.0 Litre. (Jaguar)

Right: For the 1990 model year, it was still felt worth maintaining a distinction

between the plain Jaguar XJ6 (above) and the Daimler-flavoured Jaguar Sovereign (below), although the principal difference to the casual observer was confined to headlamp configuration. Inside, the Sovereign was more obviously up-market, but it seems strange that Jaguar's PR department should have photographed two nominally different cars with the same registration number! (Both Jaguar)

linear gate for the automatic transmission selector.

Clearly, the 2.9 situation could not be allowed to linger for very long and as noted in Chapter 13, the minutes of the MPM of 12 November 1986 show that the decision had already been taken to replace it with a 24-valve 3.2-litre AJ6 by 1991. The same

meeting also intriguingly mentions consideration being given to a replacement limousine based on the XJ40 but with a wheelbase and body stretch of no less than 40in. Submissions were to be sought from Coleman Milne and Bob Jankel (Panther Westwinds) but nothing came of the idea in the end and as we have already seen, the old limousine soldiered on until it ceased to be in any way economic.

Some XJ40 improvements could not (and did not have to) await the development of the 3.2 version, and in September 1989 Jaguar launched a minor facelift centred on the replacement of the 3.6-litre AJ6 with the new, longer-stroke 4.0-litre with its

Above and right: For the 1991 model year, the big news was that the under-powered 2.9-litre 12-valve engine had made way for the much more satisfactory 3.2-litre (above), creating the fourth mechanically different version of the AJ6 engine (the bore and indeed the cylinder block was always the same, always the stroke changed, and with it the length of the connecting rod). Externally, the XJ40 was barely changed, but the introduction of an optional 'sports pack', seen here on the 3.2-litre, gave the car a more purposeful air. (Both Jaguar)

forged-steel crankshaft (see Chapter 13). The timing was still just sufficiently early for Jaguar to discuss both catalyst-equipped and non-catalyst versions of the revised engine, the catalyst version gaining no less than 12 per cent in power (from 199bhp to 223bhp) and a remarkable 25 per cent in torque (from 302Nm to 377Nm), all for an 11 per cent increase in capacity. For the catalyst-equipped car with automatic transmission, Jaguar claimed a 0–60mph time of 8.6sec compared with 9.4sec for the 3.6, and a maximum speed no less than 6mph higher, at 136mph. Fuel economy was improved too, helped by a more advanced engine management system.

To match the torque output of the new engine, the transmissions – still from the same suppliers – were uprated: the manual 5-speed gearbox was now the Getrag 290, and the automatic the ZF 4HP24E with fully electronic control, providing 'normal' and 'sport' shift timing modes. Teves anti-lock braking replaced the former Girling/Bosch system. Actual styling

changes were minor and mainly confined to the car's interior, especially the instrument panel. Much more important from Jaguar's point of view had been the investment of £40 million in a decent body line at the Castle Bromwich plant where an army of Comau robots took over most of the welding.

Two years later, in September 1991 and following the upheaval brought about by the Ford takeover in 1990, there came a second minor facelift, this time centred around the replacement of the 12-valve 2.9-litre AJ6 with the slightly longer-stroke, 24-valve 3.2-litre. In fact, the cylinder heads of the 3.2 and 4.0 versions were identical, the crankshaft being the only substantially different component. Now the entry-level XJ40 had an engine of reasonable output – 200bhp instead of 148bhp (DIN), 298Nm instead of 225Nm torque. Catalytic converters were standard; from January 1992 they would in any case be legally required anywhere within the European Community. The performance improvement was of course

substantial. With automatic transmission (demand for cars with manual transmission having dwindled to a die-hard trickle) Jaguar's figures showed the 3.2 was 2.4sec quicker to 60mph (9.5sec from 11.9sec) while the maximum speed had risen from 114mph to 131mph. According to the official test figures, fuel economy had also usefully improved. Along with the new engine, Jaguar now also offered a carefully developed 'Sports Handling Pack' as an optional extra. This provided substantially stiffer spring rates

During the early 1990s, there was at least the remote prospect that a version of the XJ40 might emerge with a two-stroke engine. Chief Powertrain Engineer Trevor Crisp was sufficiently impressed by the idea's potential to create the supercharged 2-stroke V6

seen here. Although smooth and powerful, the engine (like others of its kind) fell foul of ever-tightening exhaust emission regulations, especially those relating to oxides of nitrogen. It was decided that diesels were a more realistic line of study. (JDHT)

(and a stiffer anti-roll bar) at the front, and more mildly stiffened springs at the rear, with recalibrated dampers, reduced power steering assistance for better 'feel', and 225/55ZR16 Pirelli P600 tyres on new wheels, replacing the standard 225/65VR15s.

All this, however, seemed almost incidental to the enthusiasts who had now been waiting six years for an XJ40 with a V12 engine. It might have been even worse had they known that in his comprehensive product planning review of March 1986, Trevor Crisp had targeted the 1990 model year for the 'long-wheelbase V12' with a 'ZF 4-speed auto for V12' to follow for model year 1991. In fact the plans were bedevilled by indecision resulting from external pressures, including the gas-guzzler fears already referred to – and far more serious in the case of the V12 – the Ford takeover of 1990 which involved the stern review of any project not actually committed to production.

Actually, the V12 was given the go-ahead but the enthusiasts were 'teased' until October 1992, and even then had to be content with Jaguar's bald announcement, coincident with the British Motor Show, that longer-wheelbase Majestic versions of the XJ40 would now be available, with a 125mm stretch after of the B-pillar (so, as with the long-ago creation of the LWB XJ6, the extra length went into back seat space and rear door length) – and that 'the Majestic saloons will initially be available with either the 3.2 or 4.0 litre AJ6 engine. The intro-duction of V12 engined variants will follow in Autumn 1993.' Just a year still to wait, and meanwhile the very last Series III V12 emerged from its production line.

The wait was actually only until February 1993 when the new V12 saloons were announced. These were not the promised (and still-to-come) LWB Majestics but the standard 113in-wheelbase body with the V12 inserted. It was revealed that the best part of a year previously, the XJ40 body shell had been extensively, although invisibly revised, with 140 new or modified panels, to enable either the AJ6 or the V12 to be fitted to the same shell, the V12 requiring only the addition of a new front cross-member. In its final form the V12 had been stretched to 6-litre capacity with a longer stroke – calling for investment to manufacture a new crankshaft, the engine having been around since 1989 when it

appeared in the highly specialised XJR-S derivative of the XJ-S (Chapter 10). Now the new XJ12, with automatic transmission (the GM 4L80-E, one of the few units with sufficient torque capacity) only, and with 318bhp and 463Nm of torque available, could surge to 60mph from rest in 6.8sec and go on to 155mph. It came in two forms, Jaguar with stiff 'sports' suspension and 225/55ZR16 Dunlop SP2000 tyres, and the softer Daimler Double Six with 225/65ZR15 Pirelli P4000s. A new ZF steering rack completed the chassis work.

Very little else seems ever to have been said about the long- wheelbase XJ40s although they were clearly never intended for volume production, even though no less than three LWB project numbers were allocated, XJ82 for the V12, XJ83 for the AJ6 version, and XJ84 for a stillborn version with a 6.4-litre V12. Prior to this, XJ81 was allocated to the 'standard' XJ12 with 113in wheelbase, while XJ85 and XJ86 covered the project, likewise not proceeded with, for an XJ40 2-door coupé with V12 and AJ6 power units respectively. Rounding off the list come XJ95 and XJ96, reserved for convertible derivatives of XJ85 and XJ86 which, likewise, never left the drawing board and styling studio.

Just how limited production of the long-wheelbase (118in) cars had to be is seen in their manufacturing process. To produce them, bodies were taken from the Castle Bromwich line, sent to Project Aerospace in Coventry to be chopped in half, extended and rewelded before return whence they came for painting, followed by transportation to Browns Lane for final trimming and assembly in a newly created Special Vehicle Operations Department with a hand-picked 40-strong workforce.

There was now little more to come for the last of the 'pre-Ford' Jaguar saloons. There were a few marketing-inspired retrimmings, the XJ3.2S of 1993, a 'tax threshold special' with the firmer sports suspension settings; the matching XJ4.0S later in the year, replacing the formerly standard 4.0 for the 1994 model year; and early in 1994, the XJ6 Gold, a fairly unashamed 'special edition' for a model which had only a few months left to run. In September 1994, the XJ40 series was replaced by a new design, carrying the new-series internal designation X300, outwardly the product of the first all-Ford managed programme, although still with Jaguar power units.

15 XK8: a 'proper' sports car again

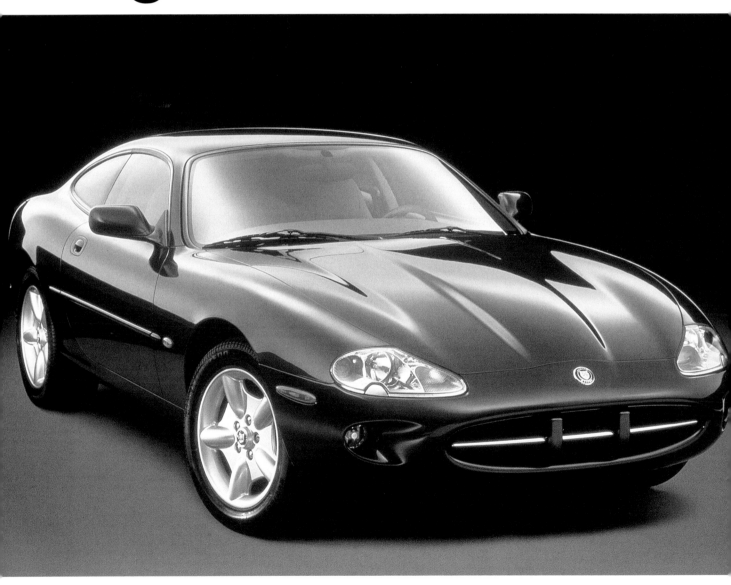

When Ford took over Jaguar in 1990, one of its urgent tasks was to consider the shape of a replacement for the XJS, then approaching its 20th birthday and clearly incapable of sustaining its career for very much longer. The Ford market specialists were well aware that the XJS had always been poorly regarded by a substantial part of its target market which had never forgiven it for being a large, heavy and expensive GT car rather than a replacement for the E-type. As soon as they had access to Jaguar's records they became equally aware of the trials and tribulations which had led to the demise of the XJ41, which would have been much closer in spirit to the old sports car, but which had been dragged down by over-ambitious and poorly directed marketing considerations too far in the direction of the XJS. Before examining what happened, however, it is worth looking at a preface to the story of Jaguar's reviving sports car fortunes, in the shape of the XJ220.

There was a time, in the boom years of the late 1980s, when it seemed that one easy way to gain notoriety and make some quick money was to design and build a 'supercar' – an extremely powerful, brutal-looking sports/GT car capable not only of being driven on, but of achieving 200mph on the road. This was the only figure which seemed to matter. If it could be achieved, then the theory went that there were enough seriously rich enthusiasts in the world that you could build a run of 50 or 100 examples of your car, more or less name your own price, and dispose of them in the knowledge that very few would ever be extended even to half their performance, while most would pass their lives in heated motor-houses awaiting the time when they would become 'classics' worth even more than they had cost. This doubtful philosophy, founded in part on the ridiculous prices then being paid for classic Ferraris, became so pervasive that one widely read enthusiast magazine was able to pull together a story that included details of no fewer than 20 such projects; and one of them was a Jaguar, the XK220.

The car began life in 1985 as a 'doodle' by Engineering Director Jim Randle and a small group of engineers who in effect wanted to see if it was possible to take the old XJ13 racing car and re-interpret the concept with modern materials, using modern knowledge (especially of ground-effect aerodynamics), and in line with current racing regulations. Possibly because the team consisted entirely of engineers, with no economist or accountant to exert a

calming influence, the XJ220 became an extremely large, complicated and heavy beast. In the end, about the only things it had in common with the XJ13 were a V12 engine, mid-mounted in-line, four wheels, and a body which managed to retain many of the Jaguar styling hallmarks despite its latter-day aerodynamic sophistication, mostly out of sight beneath its floor.

The V12 really was a throwback to the XJ13 in many respects, a 4-cam unit which was both bored-out to 92mm – a slightly nail-biting experience given the limited space between the bores – and stroked to 78mm for a capacity of 6,222cc. The stroke was still much shorter than the 84mm Harry Mundy had been proposing in the 1970s but this promised a higher rev limit for racing – if it ever came to that (and it did, although not in the XJ220). What it also had that the XJ13 did not, was a pair of 24-valve cylinder heads. When the car – the only example ever built, although at least it was a genuine 'runner' – was revealed at the 1988 British Motor Show, the engine's stated output of 500bhp (373kW) at 7,000rpm seemed almost a disappointment, a mere 80bhp per litre from an advanced multivalve engine with few of the normal constraints of driveability. Nor did its 544Nm of torque seem high, especially in relation to valve timing which set the torque peak as high as 5,000rpm. But it was supposed to be capable of 220mph, hence its designation.

The XK8 sports car programme was carried through swiftly and with great success – but the result was still a significantly bigger and heavier car than the dear old E-type. Among other things, the XK8 was the launch platform for Jaguar's new 4-cam, 32-valve, 4-litre V8 engine which proved equally successful in most respects. (Jaguar)

Probably unwisely, the engineering team opted for 4-wheel drive, so the XJ220 had an extremely complicated transmission with an epicyclic centre differential giving a front-to-rear drive split of 31:69. Some rival teams had done the same thing, witness the Porsche 959 and Bugatti EB110. Ferrari in the F40 very wisely did not; even a small proportion of front-drive in such cars seems to encourage massive understeer in some circumstances. Porsche found an answer in some extremely sophisticated control technology, but then the 959 was always more of a technology demonstrator than a simple supercar.

Despite having an aluminium body and only two seats, the XJ220 weighed a reported 3,450lb which was only around 500lb less than a fully equipped V12-engined XJ-S Coupé. In part this was because the car covered a lot more road area than the XJ40 saloon: its

overall length was 202.4in and its width a staggering 86.7in. By sensible road car standards its ground clearance was negligible because of the underbody venturi, created by splitter plates clearly visible from the rear, which were said to induce up to 2,500lb of downforce at high speed.

Although the XJ220 created a mild sensation when it was shown and every rich enthusiast wanted one, Jaguar was in no way able to produce it. To have done so would have been a monumental distraction from the business of survival. To quieten the mob and maintain the interest, the company instead turned to JaguarSport, its joint venture with TWR, which through the mid-1980s, had been campaigning a series of Jaguar-sponsored, sometimes even Jaguar-powered sports-racing prototypes in appropriate champion-ships, with considerable success including two Le

Mans wins, in 1988 and 1990, with Jaguar V12-engined cars. TWR was better able to undertake the small-volume production being contemplated, but first of all it needed to modify the car considerably in order to make it at least moderately practical.

The result, when it emerged in 1989, was a car which looked not dissimilar but was actually a good deal smaller. The wheelbase had shrunk from 112in to 104in; the overall length had come down to 191in – almost a foot shorter – and the sides had been pulled in to a more rational width of 79in. The biggest changes, however, had been made in the powertrain. Gone was the mighty, but bulky and heavy V12 and in its place sat a 3.5-litre V6 (94mm by 84mm, 3,498cc) with twin turbochargers. This 500bhp, 640Nm engine was said to be a 'race-developed' Jaguar unit yet it was not even half the V12, having a

Left: Jaguar's first step along the 'modern' sports car road was the XJ13, conceived during the 1960s as a Le Mans winner, but was consigned to history when it was realised it stood no serious chance. Written-off in a major accident it has since been lovingly

re-created. Smoothly aerodynamic, with mid-mounted 4-cam V12 engine, it became something of an icon for Jaguar engineering staff who always wanted to use it as a starting point for something faster. (Author's collection)

90° angle between its cylinder blocks, and it sported some extremely un-Jaguar features such as toothed-belt drive to its four camshafts. In fact, it came more or less directly from the engine developed for the TWR racing cars (XJR-10, XJR-11 and XJR-14) which in turn had its ancestry in, of all things, the engine originally developed to power the Group B rallying Metro 6R4. This was not necessarily a bad thing, but it did mean the Jaguar links had become tenuous. The 4-wheel drive transmission had gone too, as being far too heavy, complicated and expensive to compensate for any advantage it might have conferred. In its place was a simple 5-speed manual gearbox and a 2.88:1 rear final drive. Its suspension was 'Group C race derived' double wishbone all round; the rack-and-pinion steering had no power assistance, it being thought unnecessary in a rear-heavy, mid-engined car. To emphasise the nonsense aspect of it all, tyre sizes were 245/45-17 front but 345/35-18 rear. Drag coefficient was stated as 0.32 and Cz (the vertical force coefficient, counterpart to the lengthwise drag) was -0.25, in other words, the aerodynamic downforce was still positive. The large-format brochure, slim on hard information, promised 0–60mph in 4sec, 0-100mph in 8sec and a maximum speed 'over 200mph' (of course, otherwise there would have been no point).

JaguarSport proudly proclaimed that a maximum of 350 such cars would be made, each one individually numbered, to be sold at £290,000. Sadly, harder economic times were afoot, Ferrari prices at auction fell through the floor, the vast majority of the supercar projects were stillborn and JaguarSport had great difficulty disposing of the 280-odd units it actually made before it bowed to the inevitable. It was a sad end to a project which might have had an impact on Jaguar's image but which had nothing to do with the business of building and selling cars by the thousand.

Powering **the XK8**

Nobody would have been more aware of this than Jaguar's product planners, now ultimately answerable to Ford management, drawing up their proposals for something to fill that line on the time-chart beyond the point at which the XJS stopped. They quickly decided the original XJ41 concept had been not-too-far from the mark and that a fresh start should be made on the concept of a beautiful 2-seat sports car body sitting on an adapted XJS platform. This time there would be a fixed-head coupé and a convertible having the greater part of their structure in common. This represented a return to the original E-type concept, prior to the arrival of the 2+2. For the new car, there would be no repeat of the process which led to the XJ41 Coupé with its rear hatch and radically different body aft of the B-pillar. There would be one other change too. An early Ford decision was to approve the new engine programme upon which Jaguar had embarked during the latter years of the 1980s.

The basic idea behind the engine concept was that of a family of 'modular' V-configuration power units, V6, V8 and V12, using the latest technology, more powerful and more efficient than the AJ6/16 but still cheaper to produce. The new programme was given the designation AJ26, derived – so it is said – from the fact that 26 is the sum of the numbers 6, 8 and 12. At an early stage the programme began to focus on the V8, which took shape as a DOHC 90° unit of 4-litre capacity, with an extremely stiff and nicely compact alloy crankcase. This was the engine to which Ford management gave rapid approval in 1990, with the accompanying decision to produce it in a special 'cell' within the massive Ford engine factory at Bridgend, which otherwise churned out 4-cylinder Zetec engines by the hundreds of thousands a year. One outcome of this decision was that engine production at the Radford factory would cease and the premises would become redundant.

One reason for the speed of the Ford decision was that the company was entirely familiar, and therefore comfortable with 90° V8s. It had after all built millions of them in North America, although never one like this, all-alloy and DOHC. The basic design decisions had been easy enough for the Jaguar team which included Trevor Crisp and Dave Szczupak, the latter destined soon to be spirited away from Whitley and put in charge of overall corporate powertrain engineering in Detroit. The target engine capacity

Previous spread: XJ220 (because it was theoretically capable of 220mph) was a one-off concept car of similar general layout to XJ13, but much larger and with 4WD transmission. Interest from punters during the 'supercar silly season' around 1990 led to the small-volume production of a similar-looking but smaller car by JaguarSport. (Jaguar)

Below: The 'production' XJ220 reverted to rear-drive and was powered by this 90° V6 Turbo engine with twin belt-driven overhead camshafts per bank. This was never a Jaguar engine in anything but name, owing more to the power unit in the Metro 6R4 Group B rally car of the early 1980s. No production Jaguar engine has ever used toothed-belt camshaft drive. (JDHT)

was the 4 litres of the larger AJ6, and for this capacity there was plenty of evidence that eight cylinders were better than six. A V8 block could be made compact and extremely stiff in relation to its weight. The 90° inter-bank angle is the correct one for optimum V8 balance – unlike the 60° V8 which Jaguar contemplated using during the 1970s – and its only drawback is that the engine becomes relatively wide (but also usefully lower, hence a number of 90° V6s). Yet again, the 90° angle opens up sufficient space between the banks to enable induction and fuel system equipment to be installed there.

One great advantage of the V8 was that it could readily be installed – given a little allowance for its

width – in a short, compact engine bay. This made it extremely suitable for the new sports car, internally designated X100. Detailed development work began immediately within the steadily expanding Whitley Technical Centre, using all the advanced techniques already applied to the X300 saloon that preceded it through the system. The X100 platform was derived from that of the 102in-wheelbase XJS, and on this foundation Geoff Lawson and Keith Helfet created a shape that was both modern and 'Jaguar'. The X100 was unveiled in coupé form at the 1996 Geneva Motor Show as the XK8, and shortly afterwards the convertible version went on the stand at the New York Motor Show, with the promise of production

Below: The V8 engine was all-alloy, to keep weight as low as possible. Because the included angle was 90° (the V8 ideal) there was plenty of room within the vee to accommodate a complex induction system featuring inlet tracts of carefully calculated length, while inlet valves were provided with continuously variable valve timing. The engine's bottom end was immensely strong, helped by a massive aluminium bedplate closing off the lower face of the block. (Jaguar)

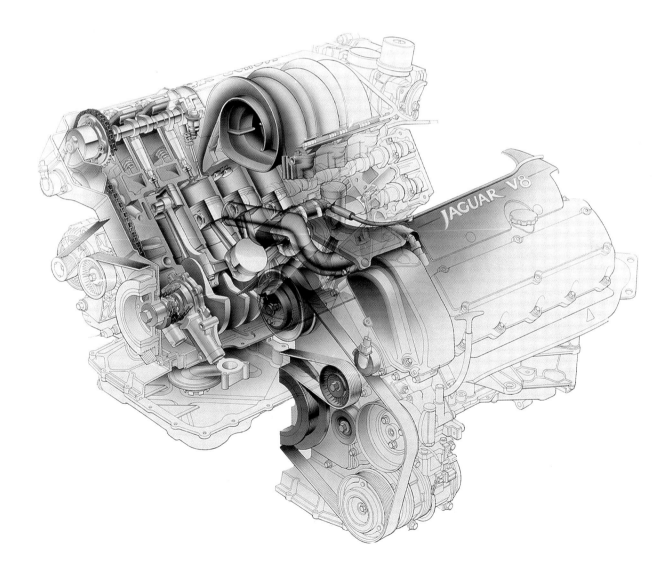

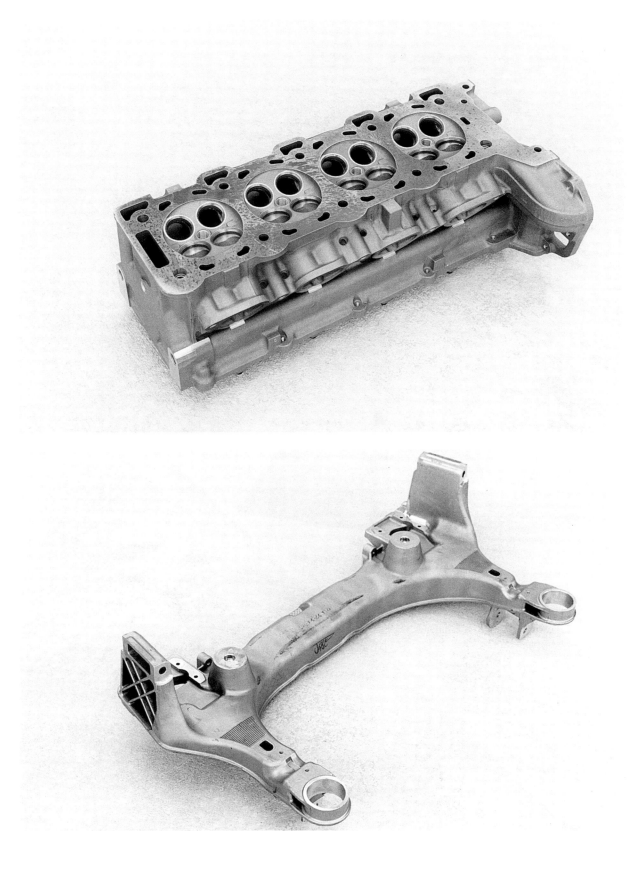

XK8: A 'PROPER' SPORTS CAR AGAIN

beginning almost immediately to build stocks for an October sales launch. The car was immediately admired for its looks (one group of Italian opinion-formers quickly voted it 'the world's most beautiful car') and only a few cynics wondered aloud how much artistic cross-fertilisation there might have been between the new Jaguar and the already-extant Aston Martin DB7 (in engineering rather than styling terms they were very different, the XK8 having a new rear suspension and V8 power unit in contrast to the DB7 which was essentially a reskinned XJS complete with original suspension and an adapted AJ6 engine). One thing which quickly became clear was that even this attractive newcomer, however obviously a sports car, was a bigger, heavier propos-ition than the E-type. It is well worth comparing the XK8 with the 4.2-litre E-type Coupé, and to ponder the reasons for the differences. The XK8 wheelbase was 6in longer and the front and rear tracks no less than 9in wider than those of the E-type; its body was just over a foot (12.4in) longer, 7in wider and 3in higher. Rather more startling perhaps is the difference in weight, the XK8 scaling 3,560lb compared with the E-type's 2,811lb, a massive 27 per cent heavier (and the convertible, with its stiffness-restoring add-ons and its fully power operated hood, was heavier still).

To some extent the increased size acknowledged that people had become larger. The E-type had been reckoned a tight fit by anyone bigger than average in the early 1960s. The XK8 provided comfortable space for larger-than-average 1990s people – and demographic data shows that 1990s people are significantly taller and heavier than their counterparts a generation previously. The extended dimensions account almost entirely for the new car's greater weight. On a simplified reckoning the XK8 body encloses around 26 per cent more space than the E-type's. When one considers the new car meets all

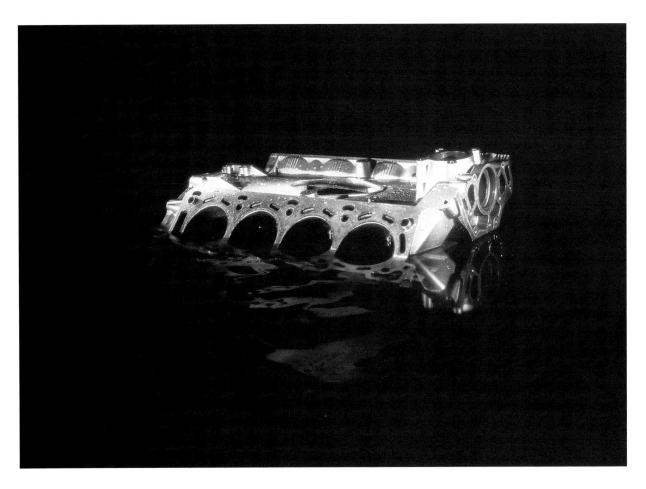

Above: The least-fortunate aspect of the V8 engine was the choice of plated rather than lined cylinder bores (the block seen here emerging from the plating process). Eventually, it became clear that the plating was being attacked by compounds formed by some very high-sulphur petrols, and with little fanfare, the plating was replaced by thin-walled steel liners which were satisfactorily resistant. (Jaguar)

those safety regulations which were still somewhere in the distant future when the E-type was on the drawing-board, and that it provides a range of features of which the E-type buyer would scarcely have dreamed, the efficiency of modern computer-aided structural design becomes more obvious. However, the extra weight was more than enough to offset the higher power and torque of the new V8 engine compared with that of the (pre-emissions) 4.2-litre in the E-type, which opened the car to some criticism that performance had not advanced very much, if at all, in the intervening period – although actually, Jaguar claimed a 155mph maximum for the

XK8 and a 0–60mph time of 6.4sec. For those seeking something substantially quicker, Jaguar had an answer in the works.

Although the XK8 platform was in essence a modified XJS item, the running gear came from the XJ saloon branch of the Jaguar family. The suspension, brakes and steering looked familiar to anyone who knew the X300 XJ6, although in fact the front wishbone geometry was revised and one of the changes associated with the new engine was a light but extremely strong cast-alloy cross-member – in effect the front sub-frame – which accepted the suspension loads and the front engine mounts. Otherwise the biggest novelty was the introduction, as a European-market option for the coupé only, of CATS (Computer Active Technology Suspension) which was a computer-controlled adaptive damping system, switching damper rates between two settings according to driving condition as deduced from the signals sent by lateral and vertical accelerometers and other sensors. Traction control and automatic stability enhancement were standard. As a point of

interest however, it is worth noting the contrast between the 4.2 E-type and XK8 wheel and tyre sizes, the former on 'first generation' 185–15 radials and the latter on 245/50ZR17 radials of the latest generation.

One of the main points of interest in the new Jaguar, however, was its V8 engine. Very little was said about the power unit when the car was unveiled, but Jaguar made up for this in the autumn of 1996 with a full-scale powertrain presentation rather in advance of the XK8's arrival in the showrooms. What the audience found was rather more than many of them had expected. For a start, this was a Jaguar engine, not an adapted Ford V8. It had been developed in 36

months and at a cost of £200 million. Production, as already mentioned, was to take place in a 'plant within a plant' at Ford's Bridgend works in Wales.

The V8 was 'square', with both bore and stroke set at 86mm for a capacity of 3,996cc. It was a 32-valve unit with twin overhead camshafts per bank. There was considerable interest, given the popularity of hydraulic tappets, that Jaguar had elected to stay with the valve operating system it knew best – direct operation with 'bucket' tappets beneath the cams, and clearance adjustment by shims, yielding a substantially lower-inertia valve train than would have been possible with zero-lash tappets. The camshafts were, naturally, chain-driven but for the first time in a Jaguar engine, variable timing actuators were fitted to the inlet camshaft sprockets.

Of equal interest, the engine was virtually all-alloy, the cylinder bores being protected by the Nicasil plating process rather than being linered. This turned out to be a questionable decision in that the high sulphur content of low-grade fuels in some markets attacked the plating and caused bore-wear problems.

(Jaguar was not the only manufacturer to suffer in this respect.) The problems were addressed under warranty, and to overcome the danger the engine was eventually modified to incorporate conventional cast-in-place iron liners.

The crankcase itself was only crankshaft centre-line deep but beneath it was bolted a massive cast-alloy bedplate, in turn carrying the cast sump. Perhaps surprising to some, the crankshaft was made of SG cast iron rather than steel as the V12 and AJ16 cranks had been. This was one of the advantages of the V8 configuration which enabled the crankshaft to be made amply stiff and strong without resorting to expensive materials and machining. Within the heads, the 4-valve combustion chambers, the narrow angle (just over 28°) between inlet and exhaust valves enabling the compression ratio to be as high as 10.75:1 with flat-crowned (therefore lighter) pistons. The powerful, all-new engine

management system came from Nippondenso, another break with tradition. All accessory drives were entrusted to a single very long poly-vee belt. And so on, and so on … the engine positively bristling with innovation and neat touches wherever one looked – in lubrication, in cooling, in emission control. Thus Jaguar could make a whole series of 'best in class' claims ranging from lightest-in-class (200kg/441lb), highest specific power and torque, lowest friction levels and even best-in-class service costs. To complement the engine, Jaguar took the then-new 5-speed ZF 5HP24 automatic transmission. Eyebrows were raised at the news that this transmission was to be standard: there would be no manual alternative.

There was a degree of logic to this decision. When the XK8 Convertible was unveiled in New York, Jaguar's production plans for the car were discussed. There was a forecast of 12,000 units in 1997 (when the sales figures were in, the actual figure was over 14,600) of which no less than 60 per cent would be earmarked for the USA. It was anticipated that 70 per cent of these, in other words 42 per cent of all production, would be convertibles. Clearly, the US market would be predominantly automatic and in

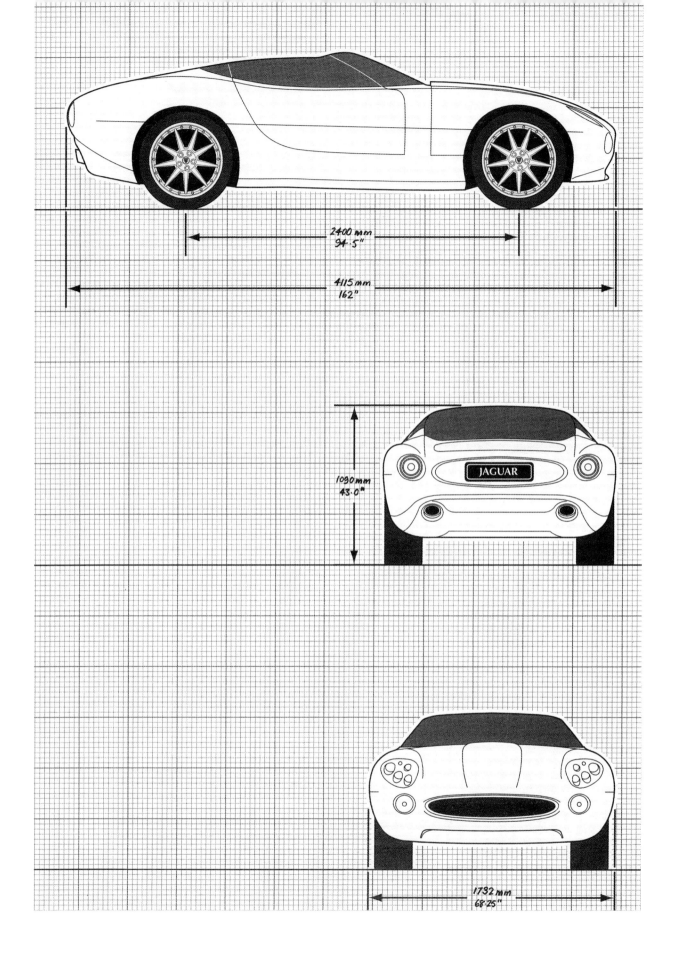

2400 mm
94·5"

4115 mm
162"

1090 mm
43·0"

JAGUAR

1732 mm
68·25"

Left: A three-view drawing of the XK180 emphasises compactness and short overhangs in side view – but it was still significantly wider than the E-type, and the tyres were getting on for

twice the width. The XK180, which was a fully driveable demonstrator, was only a further step on the road leading to what may one day be christened 'F-type'.
(Jaguar)

view of the excellence of the ZF transmission and the degree of manual control which could be exerted over it, the time, cost and engineering manpower needed to develop a manual alternative must have looked unlikely ever to pay for itself.

Any doubts about performance potential were removed in May 1998 with the appearance of the XKR, which had been anticipated ever since the latest-series XJ6 (X308) saloon had been announced in a range which included a supercharged 4-litre V8 engine, with pressure induction via an Eaton M112 Roots-type blower. Now the XK could deploy 370PS and a massive 525Nm of torque. Yet again there was no manual option, the 5-speed automatic being retained. It wasn't much of a handicap; the XKR accelerated to 60mph in 5.2sec, bringing performance into that range where the skill of the driver in getting off the line in a manual transmission car, and the speed of the first manual gearshift, are so variable (and so wearing) compared with the effortless delivery of an automatic, that there is very little point in persisting. Similarly, it was pointless to ask about maximum speed, as it was governed to 155mph (250km/hour) like most of the highest-performance cars in Europe, in the interests both of road safety and tyre limitations. Without the governor, the XKR with its extra 70PS would probably have been good for at least 170mph (274km/hour).

The XKR was always going to be a minority interest but Jaguar forecast 1,500 sales a year, mainly in Europe and particularly, for obvious reasons, in Germany. It would have taken a long time to recoup any major engineering investment at that rate, but taking the engine from the XJR saloon simply created incremental volume. Chassis changes were restricted to the standard fitting of the CATS system, Pirelli P-Zero tyres on different sized rims (245/45ZR18 on 8in front rims, 255/45ZR-18 on 9in rims at the rear) in order to reduce slightly the natural understeering tendency. Also used for the first time, although destined for wider service, was the ZF Servotronic II power-steering system with electronically controlled speed-sensitive assistance. Brake pad materials were improved but the braking system was otherwise untouched.

There was still one more iteration of the XK8 story to come. In the third quarter of 2002 the car was predictably re-engined with the latest 4.2-litre AJ-V8 engines – with the Jaguar designation AJ34 – naturally aspirated and supercharged, delivering 300bhp and 400bhp (DIN) respectively. Among the changes now applied to the engine were variable valve timing on the exhaust as well as the inlet sides, a revised cylinder block, bedplate and camshaft drive chain design for even lower noise levels, a full-authority 'drive-by-wire' accelerator linkage, and in the supercharged version, Eaton's latest Roots-type supercharger with helical instead of 'straight-cut' lobes, the rotors now coated for higher efficiency.

The move to this new, longer-stroke engine derivative was predictable because a few months earlier, it had been announced in the S-type (but not in the big XJ saloon, for reasons which became clear later). Installation of the 4.2-litre V8 beneath the XK8 bonnet was a simple substitution but as in the S-type the standard automatic transmission now became the 6-speed ZF 6HP26. The additional power and torque, and the better gearing made a useful difference in terms of acceleration. The 0–60mph time for the coupé was now down to 5.2sec, the heavier convertible needing 0.1sec more. Maximum speed was still, officially, 155mph but in suitable test-track circumstances the XKR could probably reach this figure inside one minute.

To match this highest-ever level of performance, the XKR was now equipped as standard with a Brembo braking system, developed around even larger ventilated discs (355 x 32mm at the front, 330 x 28mm at the rear) with 4-pot calipers. In addition to the ABS, emergency brake assist (EBA) also now became standard, ensuring that any full-emergency stop would be just that, unless and until the driver completely released the brake pedal. To complement its active safety features, the XK8 had, in 2001, already been equipped with what Jaguar called ARTS (Adaptive Restraint Technology System) in which ultrasonic sensors detected the presence and position of both occupants. The signals to the safety systems computer then controlled whether the two-stage front airbags deployed fully or partly – if a passenger

happened to be leaning forward when an impact occurred, full airbag deployment could cause injury, while no passenger meant no airbag deployment on that side. One wonders, when being briefed on the complexity of ARTS, how earlier generations of Jaguar engineers would have reacted to the kind of safety concern which led to the system being developed.

The XK series proved a success from the outset and continues to be, but as we have seen, it is a larger and heavier car than the E-type, and even though the

Above and right: A further step was taken in 2000 with the announcement of the F-type Concept, which makes an interesting comparison with the XK180. Following the emergence of this car, it seemed for a time that

Jaguar had secured the backing of senior Ford management to proceed with a definitive F-type design, but the management changed and once again, everything was put on indefinite hold. (Jaguar)

pressures of modern regulations – and of larger customers – conspire to make it so, the thread of thought still runs through Jaguar engineering that it should be possible to use the latest technologies to evolve a new sports car which would be closer to the 40-year-old classic – a car in which high performance and agility would be achieved through lightness and small size rather than by high engine output and the latest electronic aids.

In September 1998 a tentative answer to this challenge emerged in the form of the XK180

prototype, exhibited at that year's Paris Motor Show. To some extent, this car was a celebration of the exercise run at Jabbeke 50 years previously, when a prototype XK120 proved itself capable of 120mph. There was little doubt that run under the same rules, so to speak, the XK180 would have shown itself capable of 180mph. It was based on a shortened XKR floorpan, powered by an over-boosted version of the 4-litre engine delivering 450bhp, and clad in a lightweight body shell hand-formed by Loades Design, a sister company of Jaguar's long-standing suppliers Abbey Panels. Jaguar never quoted a weight for the XK180 but with its smaller dimensions and aluminium body it would obviously have been significantly lighter than the XKR.

Because the prototype was to be a full 'runner', a production XKR had the same 5in section of platform and body removed from the cockpit area, the rest of the body remaining untouched, to act as a chassis development tool. The definitive XK180 body was 174in long, over a foot shorter than the XKR thanks to reduced front and rear overhangs. Clearance had to be provided within the body design for extremely large and wide wheels and tyres – 255/35ZR20 at the front and 285/30ZR20 (on 10in rims) at the rear.

The XK180 was impressive, but it was not a sufficiently large step in the right direction, having been conceived at a time when show-stopping concept sports cars were expected to have supercar power output and performance (even though some of them would have been hard put to it to be demonstrated in motion). But the feeling within Jaguar was that anything like a true F-type needed to be still smaller and lighter. Apart from anything else, the XK8 was already well established and any new production car – and this was still the ultimate aim – would need to be a clear class lighter, smaller and cheaper.

At the beginning of 2000, at the Detroit Motor Show, Jaguar unveiled its next move in this direction. The one-off prototype was called the F-type Concept, so the idea behind it could not have been more obvious. The aluminium-bodied roadster was resolutely modern, yet retained many Jaguar styling cues and a distinctly Jaguar look. Sadly, it was the last

design to which the company's former Director of Design, Geoff Lawson, contributed before he collapsed and died, in his fifties, while at work.

The F-type Concept was significantly smaller than the XK180, sitting on a wheelbase of only 94.5in (2.5in less) with an overall length of 162in (a full foot less). It was also 4in narrower. Beneath its bonnet, in order to fit the shortened engine bay, there sat a 240bhp AJ-V6 engine whose output could, as Jaguar pointed out, have been increased through supercharging. A year later, tantalisingly, Jaguar issued a press release headed 'Jaguar F-type Roadster is go!' The decision was officially announced by Ford's Premier Automotive Group (PAG) Chairman, Wolfgang Reitzle, at the Los Angeles Motor Show. He pointed to the 'overwhelmingly positive reaction across the globe to last year's concept' and promised, according to the press release, that 'it will take us around three years to bring the F-type roadster programme to market.' The press release was weak on specifics, its illustrations consisting of styling renderings of what looked like the F-type Concept with more radical treatment especially of the lighting arrangements, backed up by a selection of pictures from the archive.

One of the overwhelmingly positive reactions came from Ford's then-Chairman, Jac Nasser, who said in an on-the-record interview that Ford and Jaguar 'would be mad not to build it [the F-type]'. Alas, within a short time both Nasser and Reitzle had departed and the new management was reported to have returned the F-type project to the back burner. There were good reasons for this, including Jaguar's existing workload and the question of where the F-type would be built, since the demand seemed

Left: The XK8 Convertible was unveiled in New York in 1996, and for 1997 60 per cent of total XK8 production was earmarked for the US market. (Jaguar)

Right: The flagship XKR, seen here in 2003 form, is packed with technology, and powered by a supercharged version of the 4.0-litre AJ-V8 engine providing prestigious torque and power. (Jaguar)

likely to approach 30,000 units a year and, depending on specification and pricing policy, could easily have been more.

Will there ever be an F-type? The jury is still out. As the F-type Concept made clear, Jaguar's V6 engines are well suited to a more compact sports car and the supercharging technology exists, even if for the time being it is confined to the AJ-V8. The aluminium manufacturing technology now exists, as Chapter 17 makes clear. Other advances in tech-

nology now make it easier to conceive a car with comfortable seating for two, with excellent performance and handling. At the same time one might assume that the XK8, over seven years old at the time of writing, must itself be fairly close to replacement even though its spiritual forefather the E-type managed to last twice as long. On the sports car side, the Jaguar product planners face a number of options, and – writing in early 2004 – it would be foolish to predict which way they will jump.

16 A new V8, V6 and the S-type

ord took over at Browns Lane in 1990. Jaguar had enjoyed a decade of independent existence under the leadership of Sir John Egan, but it could not last for ever. The company was the wrong size for any option: too big to survive as a small-volume specialist serving ultra-niche markets, too small to compete effectively even with the German 'prestige' volume manufacturers, BMW and Mercedes. As 1990 approached it had one good modern product, the XJ40, and one very old and heavy one, the XJ-S. It had tried to give some better shape to its range with the XJ41 but all the effort spent on that project had gone to waste. Now Jaguar simply could not afford to develop even one all-new model to present a more convincing picture during the 1990s, and if anything it needed not one, but two. It appears (as yet there is nothing released to the archive) that Jaguar did embark on development of a new large saloon, the X90, in the late 1980s. Prototypes ran, powered by a variety of engines including the AJ26 V8, but the project was abandoned around 1990 and probably with good reason, given the likely cost.

The logic was inescapable. The name, the prestige and the existing assets – worth a great deal more than they had been in 1980 – had to be sold to the highest bidder. Ford won the auction. In some ways the price was high. Sir John Egan departed to run the British Airports Authority and future managing directors, beginning with Bill Hayden who was followed by Nick Scheele, were Ford-appointed (this was strictly true even of Mike Beasley, a Jaguar man of long standing, Production Director through many of the agonising Leyland days, who took the reins at the turn of the century and retired in 2003). On the ground, as pointed out in the previous chapter, the Radford factory was more or less condemned from the outset. Future engines – very different engines – would be designed and developed by Jaguar but with the aid of all Ford's modern facilities, and produced in a Ford works.

On the credit side, Ford acknowledged the need for a broader product range and allowed Jaguar to lay its plans accordingly. In essence, the first phase of the scheme was further to modernise the big saloon, the XJ6, in a series of stages reaching into the 21st century. This would be followed by a second phase which would see the launch of a somewhat smaller, lighter, more compact saloon which would be followed with an even smaller, lighter one. Along the way, and as quickly as possible, it also acknowledged the need to engineer a proper sports car to fly the company flag and re-establish its credentials. This more than anything would be the best riposte to the cynics who, in 1990, foretold the utter submergence of the Jaguar tradition within the Ford empire.

A whole new series of project numbers came into being to replace the XJs, which by this time had run into three figures. The basic system was simple except that the numbers did not run in the chronological order in which the cars eventually appeared. As we have already seen, X100 was allotted to the new sports car which emerged as the XK8 in 1996. Next, X200 covered the 'mid-size saloon', the S-type, which appeared in 1998. The X300 designation was applied to the 'big saloon' which was the first of the X-number projects actually to appear, in 1994. Finally came the X400, the X-type, eventually announced in 2001. Of these four projects – or rather, project series, since they began to spawn sub-numbers like X308, X330 and X350 – the X100 was examined in Chapter 15. This chapter looks at the surprisingly complicated evolution of the X300 and X200; while the next chapter brings the whole Jaguar product process up to date with the X100 and the latest developments including Jaguar's first 'in house' estate car and its first diesel-engined models to reach production.

In 1994, after a modest run (by Jaguar standards) of eight years the XJ40 was replaced by the X300, in effect the fifth major model variation to carry the XJ designation. Although a new car in most important respects, the X300 continued for the time being to use the slant-6 engine, now thoroughly updated into AJ16 form (Chapter 13). The V12 also continued, for a short while at least. (Jaguar)

One thing which was obvious as the product plan was being laid out was that it involved numbers way beyond the scope of the Browns Lane factory. That would continue final assembly of the XJ6 (X300) and of the new sports car (X100) but new facilities would be needed for the two smaller saloons, which would eventually boost Jaguar production to far higher levels. Naturally, there was a period of posturing as Ford and the British Government circled each other, the company threatening to take 'new Jaguar' production abroad, to the USA or possibly even to Eastern Europe, if as much 'support' as was allowed within the terms of the European Community rules on government subsidy was not forthcoming. In the end, a dual solution was found. The S-type (X200) was to be built in the Castle Bromwich factory, with several of its huge old aircraft-assembly buildings –

structurally still remarkably sound – totally refurbished and equipped to the latest standards. As described in more detail in the final chapter, the X-type (X400) manufacturing facility went into Ford's Halewood plant on Merseyside, as Ford Escort production was run down and the Escort's replacement, the Focus, was built elsewhere.

X300: development by stages

Successful though the XJ40 had proved, the new Jaguar management wanted to replace it as quickly as possible with a car which would be substantially improved in several important respects. The X300 which appeared as the 'New XJ6' in September 1994 was not, despite some protests to the contrary, an all-new car but a heavily evolved XJ40. On a careful reading of Jaguar's own 1994 press release one discovers that 'Every aspect of the vehicle from the sculptured new body shell to the AJ16 engine, and from the refined suspension systems to the luxurious interiors, has been *either* completely redesigned *or extensively developed*.' And again: 'Every *external* body panel has been changed from the previous XJ models.' The italics are the author's. The real object of the exercise comes in the following sentence where it is claimed that 'Jaguar engineers have made the new XJ series quieter, smoother, more comfortable, faster yet more economical, safer, more secure and more reliable.' Indeed it was; but the sub-structure, the platform which is the real determinant of whether a car is all-new, remained almost the same – hence the X300 and the XJ40 having identical wheelbase and front and rear tracks.

What Jaguar's press release could not say in quite the same terms, perhaps, was that product quality had been taken by the scruff of its neck. It is reliably reported that after his first tour of the Browns Lane plant, Bill Hayden admitted he had no idea anyone built cars like that any more. It wasn't a compliment, but neither did it reflect upon the workforce. Hayden, coming from the Ford world in which production lines and factories were updated almost as often as the cars they built, could not comprehend how anyone could manufacture a quality product in such conditions and with such equipment. And he was right; by the continuously improving standards of their rivals, they weren't. All they could do was their

best. Small wonder no less than £110 million of the £200 million spent on the X300 in the three years to 1994 went on better production equipment: £45 million in the Castle Bromwich press shop and body assembly area alone, £6 million on equipment to manufacture the 'closures' – the doors, bonnet and boot lid – plus £5 million in the paint shop and £8.5 million on a new final assembly line for Browns Lane. This was investment on a scale which the independent Jaguar could never have contemplated.

Even though the X300 might be described as an extremely heavy facelift, drawing in part on plans already prepared – more in hope than any real expectation – prior to the Ford takeover under the old project designations XJ90 (AJ6) and XJ91 (V12), its outer body was entirely new and the first Jaguar shell to be created entirely using computer aided design (CAD) with the 'master model' electronically stored and used for every possible purpose, including the cutting of press tools. The new body, although built on essentially the same platform as we have noted, was just over an inch longer than the old one – incidentally breaking the '5-metre barrier' in the process – but was 2½in (more precisely, 66mm) lower, for a useful saving in frontal area and reduced aerodynamic drag. Despite this, it was claimed that with the help of new seat designs, headroom was virtually identical to that of the old car. Seen from outside, one evident difference was that 16in wheels had been standardised (except for 17in wheels on the quickest, supercharged version). Another parameter that had changed with the body style was that the fuel tank had shrunk and was now 17.8 gallons (81 litres) instead of 19 gallons (86.4 litres).

Beneath the bonnet, as discussed in Chapter 13, came the AJ16 engine, a thorough revision of the AJ6; still the same basic design, with the same dimensions and 3.2-litre and 4.0-litre capacities, but with at least 100 new or seriously modified components including a new cylinder head, revised block, revised cam profiles, new high-compression pistons, 'direct' coil-on-plug ignition and the rest. The 3.2-litre engine thus gained 8 per cent in peak power and 6 per cent in torque, to achieve 219PS (DIN) and 315Nm; for the 4-litre, the improvements were 10 per cent and 4 per cent, to 240PS and 392Nm. Performance naturally benefited with the 4-litre in automatic form – even fewer customers were now opting for the manual gearbox alternative, yet it continued to be offered – reaching 60mph in 7.8sec and going on to a maximum speed of 144mph 'where permitted' as

most car manufacturers now felt obliged to say. The combined official fuel consumption figures showed the AJ16-engined car enjoyed around a 3 per cent improvement on its AJ6-engined predecessor – not much, but worth having.

Anyone who felt such performance was insufficient could now choose instead to buy the XJR 4.0 with a supercharged version of the larger AJ16, with pressure induction via an Eaton M90 Roots-type blower. In this form the car had the advantage of 326PS and 512Nm of torque, making an interesting comparison with the 318PS and 478Nm of the 6-litre V12, which was carried over into the X300, thus avoiding what might otherwise have been the embarrassment of the (XJ40) V12 having been available for barely a year before its demise. With either of these more powerful engines, naturally, 60mph was reached from rest in under 7sec and maximum speed was governed to 155mph (250km/h). When it came to fuel consumption, though, the XJR returned an official 23.4mpg in automatic form, while the V12 could do no better than 18.4mpg. Even without the problems it was having in meeting the latest emission standards, the

For the 1996 model year, the X300 range was further extended with the introduction of a new long-wheelbase derivative, produced on-line rather than being an outsourced adaptation. In its LWB form this car was briefly tagged as the Daimler Century, in celebration of the old company's centenary as a vehicle manufacturer. (Jaguar)

V12 was beginning to have difficulty making its case, even against its own in-house competition.

In other important chassis respects, the X300 AJ6 differed little from the XJ40. Its suspension remained the same in all but detail, most of the work on improving refinement having gone into the mountings of suspension to subframe and subframe to body. A nice piece of marketing detail, though, was the development of three different suspension set-ups according to XJ6 version, with carefully chosen and matched spring and damper rates and anti-roll bar stiffnesses. The XJR was also provided with a rear anti-roll bar which tended to reduce understeer and produce a more 'sporting' type of handling, although one had to be a fairly brave and determined driver really to feel the difference. Ventilated rear disc brakes became standard across the range, and the ZF power steering rack now featured a spring-loaded 'zero detent' to give the impression of more positive self-centring.

X330: X300 stretch

Several months later, a long-wheelbase version of the X300 appeared, known internally as X330. This was a rather different beast from the short-lived and specially assembled LWB derivative of the previous (XJ40) series. As the press release succinctly put it, the new LWB body shell was 'Fully tooled and designed for assembly on the main production line, alongside standard wheelbase models'. There would be no more pulling of bodies from the line to be sent away for major surgery. In principle, the lengthening

process remained the same, however, with a 125mm (4.9in) stretch inserted into wheelbase and body length, aft of the B-pillar, with a longer rear door. The consequent weight increase was quoted as a modest-seeming 22kg (48.5lb). Far from being a specialised product, this LWB body became standard for the flagship Daimler Six and Double Six saloons, and an option across the range except for the XJ6 Sport and XJR versions.

The New XJ6 range thus established, with choice of standard and long wheelbase and AJ16 or V12 engines, did not have long to run. Indeed, from the official release date of the LWB cars (28 June 1995) to the emergence of the very last V12 engine from the now-doomed Radford factory (17 February 1997) was a matter of 20 months only. But the X300 had served its main purpose, that of applying far

more modern equipment and procedures to the urgent task of bringing Jaguar's inherent manufacturing quality – as opposed to mere quality control – into the fourth quarter of the 20th century, and indeed to prepare it for the 21st. By then, however, the XJ6 had moved on another generation, for in 1997 it metamorphosed into the XJ8 which, on analysis, turned out to be a second 'phased-improvement' design with the internal designation X308. The '8' indicated the most important part of this latest evolution, the abandoning of the in-line 6-cylinder engine in favour of the V8 which had made its first appearance, a year earlier, in the XK8 sports car, the X100.

It was always clear that the new engine had not been developed for this application alone. In its announcement of the V8 in 1996 Jaguar had admitted a capacity of 50,000 units per year from the Bridgend 'factory within a factory', a number which neatly covered the requirements of the XK8 plus a re-engined big saloon. It was equally clear that the 4-litre V8, almost exactly the same capacity as the larger of the AJ16s and of comparable output, would directly replace the in-line engine when the time was right. The real news on the engine front was that a V8 family had been created, with a shorter-stroke but otherwise almost identical 3.2-litre to replace the similarly sized AJ16, and a new supercharged version to replace the XJR power unit.

That, however, is jumping ahead in the story. A glance at the main chassis dimensions – standard wheelbase 113in (the X330's longer 118in wheelbase alternative was likewise continued), front and rear tracks at 59in – is enough to confirm that the XJ40 platform had been carried over once again, with front-end changes to accommodate the V8 engine. Thus the car was by no means all-new, but a development cycle of only 28 months meant X308 work had not begun until after the X300 launch, and underlined the time-saving power of modern computer design and engineering systems properly applied. In fact, around 30 per cent of the structure was new or changed; in addition, the proportion of high-strength steel in the body was more than doubled. Because the majority of the previous body was retained (the X308 was just under an inch longer and exactly the same width and

height as the X300) it was possible to make a like-for-like comparison to demonstrate that the new powertrain, and various other changes had resulted in a weight saving of around 200lb – and not before time, some might have said.

The much shorter engine had allowed the installation of a second bulkhead in front of the original one, with the main electrical control modules behind it, better protected from heat and moisture. The double-skin effect also provided an extra barrier against heat and vibration entering the cabin. Another major measure was a strengthening of the B-pillar to meet the latest side impact safety standards, while in the floorpan, a stiffener was added around the mount for the centre propeller shaft bearing, for improved refinement. These changes made the revised body slightly stiffer but the most obvious visual change was to new-technology complex-surface headlights with smooth 'lenses'.

A completely hidden innovation was a switch to a multiplexed electrical system in place of a conventional wiring harness. This move, first seen in the XK8 sports car, was the culmination of a series of efforts by Jaguar to improve the reliability of its electrics, beginning with the 'low current earth-line switching' system introduced in the 1986 XJ40. This system, as it turned out, was slightly too good an idea in that its operating currents were so low that false and interfering signals could be created by adjacent wiring, components, or even external sources. Even so, it provided a step in the direction of lighter wiring looms and more reliable electrical connections despite being only a halfway house to full multiplexing which, with the launch of the XJ8, would become the Jaguar standard. The effect of the new system could be seen in the reduction in the number of electrical system relays, from 60 to 27, and the number of connectors needed (the crucial ones now completely sealed and equipped with gold-plated mating surfaces for the greatest possible reliability). Such attention to detail was vital if Jaguar was to match its German rivals in achieving high customer satisfaction.

As for the chassis, the new XJ6 naturally received the revised front suspension first engineered for the XK8, with its forged-steel wishbones mounted to the new cross-beam (in effect, a sub-frame) made necessary by the new engine with its different mounting points. The rear suspension was 'retuned', the ZF Servotronic power steering system standardised, the front brake discs increased in

Left: Within a comparatively short time, the X300 had changed its power unit to the 4-litre V8 first seen in the

XK8. Thus for a time at least, the XJ6 was dead, although it was scheduled to return. (Jaguar)

size, automatic stability control (ASC) made standard – easily done with the arrival of multiplexing, enabling the braking system controller to communicate with the engine management system via a controller area network (CAN) information exchange – and Pirelli P4000 or P6000 tyres fitted as standard, the XJ8 4.0 wheel and tyre size now rising to 235/50ZR17.

The focus of attention, however, was quite clearly on the V8 engines and the improved performance they provided. Valid comparisons with the 6-cylinder X300 versions were possible because in all three cases there was a direct equivalent. The 4-litre engine was by then a known quantity by virtue of its use in the XK8. The new 3.2-litre V8 had been created by shortening the stroke of the 4-litre from 86 down to 70mm, for an actual capacity of 3,248cc. The cylinder block remained the same, so the change called for a new, shorter-throw crankshaft and 8mm longer connecting rods. The shorter stroke would have meant a lower compression ratio if the original pistons had been retained, so the 3.2 pistons were domed to restore the compression to 10.5:1 (against 10.75:1 in the 4-litre). The variable inlet valve timing was deleted and the cam profiles revised. Little else was changed apart from the necessary re-tuning of the engine management system. The supercharged 4-litre V8, like its 6-cylinder predecessor, used a Roots-type blower, again sourced from Eaton but now the M112 in place of the M90, with higher delivery volume enabling its driving speed to be reduced, making it quieter. The supercharger naturally called for a substantial reworking of the induction system but otherwise, remarkably little was changed. The standard crankshaft proved amply strong and stiff enough without needing an expensive switch from cast-iron to steel; dished pistons dropped the compression ratio to 9:1 and a new, higher-strength cylinder-head gasket was fitted.

All three V8 engine versions provided higher output than their 6-cylinder predecessors and the differences are worth listing:

It is clear from this comparison that all versions of the V8 provided more power than their AJ16 equivalents but much less of a torque improvement. To exploit the power, more gear ratios and quick shifting were needed and the answer came in the form of standard 5-speed automatic transmission. 'Due to limited customer demand', as the preamble to the Jaguar press release text explained, 'no manual transmission option is available.' Perhaps it was easier to say of the XJ8 saloon than of the XK8 sports car.

The transmission for the two naturally aspirated engines was the ZF 5HP24, first seen in the XK8, but the ZF unit lacked the torque capacity to cope with the massive output of the supercharged engine. Accordingly, Jaguar did something that would have been completely unthinkable in Sir William Lyons's day: they sourced a bigger, stronger transmission from Mercedes-Benz. This unit, the W5A580, was strong but light, with an aluminium casing, enabling Jaguar to point out that the combined weight of the super-charged V8 and its 5-speed transmission was less than that of the supercharged AJ16 and its 4-speed transmission. An important factor in Jaguar's choice was that the Mercedes transmission was also all-electronic, and offered a similar range of operating modes as the ZF, and could thus be more easily interfaced with the Jaguar powertrain management system.

If one accepts Jaguar's performance claims as valid, then the combination of V8 engine and 5-speed automatic transmission worked. There is, incidentally, every reason why they should be regarded as valid; the days of the 'Bob Berry Special' were long gone and any anxiety was now that press test cars, and quoted performance figures, should be 'representative' of standard production. An inflated set of figures could result in a queue of angry customers brandishing lawsuits and asking why their own cars could not match them. Thus it is worth comparing not only the V8 and 6-cylinder engine outputs, but also the performance figures that resulted – bearing in mind, as already pointed out, that version-for-version, the XJ8 was around 200lb lighter.

Engine size/version	3.2		4.0		4.0 supercharged	
	Power PS(kW)	Torque Nm	Power PS(kW)	Torque Nm	Power PS(kW)	Torque Nm
AJ16 6-cylinder	219(161)	315	249(183)	392	326(240)	512
AJ-V8	240(179)	316	290(216)	393	370(276)	525
V8/AJ16, %	109.6	100.3	116.5	100.3	113.5	102.5

Source: Jaguar press releases

Engine size/version	3.2 auto		4.0 auto		4.0 supercharged auto	
	0–60mph sec	maximum mph(kmh)	0–60mph sec	maximum mph(kmh)	0–60mph sec	maximum mph(kmh)
AJ16 6-cylinder	8.9	139(223)	7.8	144(232)	6.6	155(250)
AJ-V8	8.1	140(225)	6.9	150(240)	5.3	155(250)

Source: Jaguar press releases

It is evident from these figures that acceleration was markedly improved, while maximum speed was already in an area where few owners should, surely, have cared except perhaps in Germany. The 155mph maximum of the XJR-V8 was of course artificially governed in line with the policy also adopted by BMW and Mercedes for their most powerful models. Without it, and given suitable gearing, the supercharged car with 44PS more at its disposal than its predecessor would clearly – for what it mattered – have been capable of approaching 170mph.

The 1997 launch of the XJ8 left the 'big saloon' range in good shape to remain highly competitive for a few years, and thoughts turned to the smaller saloon, the X200 which was to be built at Castle Bromwich. Early in 1998 it was announced that the new car, already the subject of much speculation, would be launched at the British Motor Show of that year. A month later, during the press launch of the XKR, it was announced that the new car would be the S-type, recalling the rather strange hybrid of the mid-1960s (Chapter 6). When the S-type actually appeared, it proved to be something of a product planning and engineering puzzle.

Here we had a car which had long been typecast – by Jaguar itself and by all commentators – as at least 'half a class' smaller than the XJ series. What we actually had was a car which had a longer wheelbase (114.5in compared with 113in) and well over an inch wider in front and rear track, and whose overall dimensions made it both wider 71.6in against 70.8in) and substantially taller (56.9in against 51.7in) than the XJ. Only in two respects could it be said to belong to a smaller class: it was around 7in shorter (191.4in compared with 198.7in for the XJ8) and it offered a 3-litre V6 engine, Jaguar's first, if one discounts the unfortunate XJ220, as an alternative to the 4-litre V8. There was just as much room in its cabin – with greater wheelbase, body width and height it would have been astonishing if there had not been. It was only slightly lacking in rear luggage space – 13.1cu ft instead of 14.4cu ft. The 4-litre V8 S-type weighed within a few pounds of the similarly powered XJ8. So this was the compact sports saloon for which we had been waiting?

In a sense it was, although for a time it was quite difficult to see why – taking late 2000 prices – anyone in Britain would buy a 4-litre XJ8 at £40,950 rather than a 4-litre V8 S-type at £35,350, unless they particularly admired the XJ8 shape which, admittedly, many customers did. But one should really have asked how the S-type could be made 14 per cent cheaper (at least, that was the presumption, since it was listed for sale at 14 per cent less). It might also have occurred, although it does so more easily with the benefit of hindsight, that the S-type planners would have known that the XJ was scheduled, eventually, to grow bigger.

The question of production cost is easy enough to answer. The S-type was in some important respects not uniquely Jaguar. Its platform was shared with the Lincoln LS, a new luxury-class car engineered by Ford for the top end of its US domestic market. To this extent the choice of wheelbase and track may not have been entirely Jaguar's (but naturally, we are now well into an area where relevant material has yet to reach the archive!). However, as Jaguar itself put it: 'The result of this collaborative programme … is a common underframe and crash structure.' The visible body was all Jaguar, leaning heavily on all the lessons learned, and the techniques developed during the X100 and X300 programmes. It was also able to exploit the abilities of the new machinery installed in the Castle Bromwich site, 'restored' in a programme which itself represented the biggest investment in UK urban redevelopment for many years. Possibly the best example of what was now possible was the pressing of the entire S-type body side, a panel 4m long running from the A-pillar and including the entire door frame, to the back end of the rear wing. Once the investment had been made, the savings – in the form of fewer operations needed during body assembly, and inherently greater accuracy of manufacture – began to flow.

Once more however the main point of interest lay in the powertrain. The 32-valve V8 was carried over with some important modifications. Among these were a change from two-position to fully-variable inlet valve timing, full-authority 'drive-by-wire' accelerator linkage, air-assisted fuel injectors for better mixture preparation, and a new double-walled exhaust manifold – lighter, and with smaller thermal capacity to speed catalytic converter 'light-off' after a cold start – replacing the previous single-walled type. The 24-valve, 4-cam V6 was not, as might so easily have been assumed, 'three quarters' of the V8 but rather a Jaguar-overseen evolution of the Ford Duratec V6 already used, in different sizes, in the Mondeo in Europe and the Taurus in the USA, with more applications planned. The Duratec had the correct 60° angle between banks to provide reasonable refinement without resort to balancer shafts (as a 90° V6 would have done) and provided the Jaguar with its foundation. Ford also provided the production facility at its huge engine plant in Cleveland, Ohio which was already building the Duratec in large numbers. The Jaguar engine, though, was built in a 'factory within a factory', as with the V8 at Bridgend.

The V6 was in some respects an interesting hybrid. Although it used the Duratec cylinder block with suitable modifications – not least to make it suitable for in-line rather than transverse installation – Jaguar designed new cylinder heads with their geometry closely based on the successful configuration of the V8, so that viewed end-on, the combustion chambers and valve gear appeared virtually identical. In principle, two of the biggest differences between the V6 and the V8 – apart from the number of cylinders and the angle between cylinder banks – was that the smaller engine used cast-in-place iron cylinder liners rather than the original V8's Nicasil plating, and a steel rather than a cast-iron crankshaft. With its bore of 89mm and stroke of 79.5mm the V6 was moderately over-square and had an actual capacity of 2,967cc. With its short stroke and very stiff crankshaft it was capable to running to high speed, and it achieved its peak power of 240PS at an eyebrow-raising 6,800rpm. However, a clever variable-geometry inlet manifold system – much easier to engineer for a V6 than a V8 – plus careful design of the exhaust system, spread the torque curve over a wide speed range and prevented the engine from feeling in any way 'peaky'. This was important because unlike the V8, the V6 could not very well be offered with automatic transmission only. The target market of sports saloon enthusiasts was going to include too many who would insist on manual, and once again Jaguar turned to Getrag for a 5-speed box, the Type 221. The ZF automatic remained standard for the V8 and also accounted for the majority of V6 sales.

With its all-new platform, the S-type provided the chance to design an all-new suspension, and here the engineers introduced one feature which represented a complete break with Jaguar tradition – a conventional double-wishbone rear suspension with fully articulated drive shafts replaced the 'E-type principle' first devised by Bob Knight. Double wishbones remained at the front, although here there was a clever mounting arrangement of twin cross-beams rather than a single member, splitting between them the responsibility for accepting the lower wishbone mountings and the front engine mounts.

The launch of the S-type in 1998 brings the story of Jaguar's conventional larger cars up to date – almost. In 2002, the S-type was facelifted, taking the internal designation X202, and given an extended engine range. The 4-litre V8 was enlarged to 4.2-litre capacity by lengthening the stroke from 86mm to 90.3mm, for a capacity of 4,196cc, a nominal 4.2-litres (and where might that idea have come from?). At the same time a new, smaller version of the V6 was created, with the bore diameter reduced to 81.65mm and a capacity of 2,497cc with a power output of 201bhp (DIN). Most exciting of all, the S-type now also offered a supercharged version of the 4.2-litre V8, delivering a full 400bhp (DIN). This, the most powerful Jaguar saloon ever produced, was capable of reaching 60mph in 5.3sec with the aid of the new 6-speed ZF 6HP26 automatic transmission, standard on the V8s and optional across the range.

The S-type innovations of 2002 did not stop there, including for example, a largely redesigned front suspension and a substantially revised rear

Left: The S-type – seen here with its 1960s namesake in the background – was an all-new design and supposedly a 'smaller' Jaguar, built in a completely refurbished plant at Castle Bromwich. The problem was that it seemed hardly any smaller than the (X300) XJ8, and few observers drew the correct conclusion. Further confusion was sown because the S-type also used the V8 engine, although with the alternative of a new V6. (Jaguar)

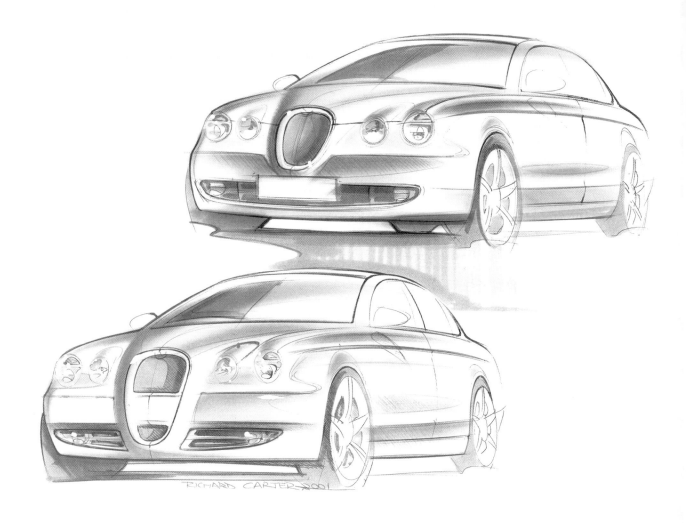

suspension, plus changes to the steering and to the braking systems (including a feature which would once have raised many an eyebrow, an automatic parking brake). But there is no space here for a comprehensive technical description and no need either, because at the time of writing, these cars are still current.

For a few months, observers wondered why the 4.2-litre V8 had been introduced in the S-type but not in the XJ8. The answer was not long in coming: an all-new XJ8 with a radically different body structure wasin the pipeline. That is a story for the final chapter, the bringing of the Jaguar story fully up to date …

Above: Jaguar designer Ian Callum came up with these drawings showing his ideas for the 2004 S-type facelift … (Jaguar)

Right: … and is worth comparing with the finished product as seen here. The Jaguar image is retained, but the appearance is significantly changed (Jaguar)

17 Right **up to date**

Jaguar entered the 21st century with a rush of activity which destroyed any lingering image of a rather staid company with a list of things it would never do. From an engineering perspective, its new moves included 4-wheel drive and then front-drive, an all-aluminium bodied volume production car, an estate car, and not one but two diesel engines. In combination these would surely have been enough to cause the engineering team of a generation previously severe indigestion, but within the aegis of Ford's Premier Automotive Group (PAG) which also included Volvo, Land Rover, Aston Martin and Lincoln, the plan was for Jaguar to expand its production and sales beyond anything previously achieved. The process had begun with the introduction of the S-type, with whose help Jaguar sales exceeded 90,000 in the year 2000, and this was supposed to be only the start. The downside, in so far as there was one, was that the product would have to appeal to a wider audience – hence the estate car and the diesels. First, however, the project for a genuinely smaller car, the X400, designated X-type for public consumption, had to be brought to fruition.

Unlike the S-type which had puzzled observers because it was scarcely any smaller than the XJ8, the X-type was indeed a class down in size. Compared with the S-type it was nearly 8in shorter in wheelbase and in overall length (and thus well over a foot shorter than the XJ8), over an inch narrower and 2in lower. Entirely predictably, it was powered by the S-type's AJ-V6 engine, in 2.5-litre and 3-litre sizes. What astonished the specialist press invited to a technical seminar on the car late in 2000 was first, that the engine was installed transversely and second, that the X-type used 4-wheel drive. This as much as the Jaguar image was part of the strategy aimed at allowing the new car to compete with the BMW 3-series and the Mercedes C-class.

The engine was installed transversely because, as a number of existing designs had shown, that made it easier to engineer the 4-wheel drive transmission. With an in-line engine and gearbox and a basically rear-drive layout, there are considerable problems involved in taking the drive to the front wheels, requiring careful design of the centre differential to move the forward drive sufficiently sideways to clear the powertrain, plus the problem of installing the front differential and taking one drive shaft either through or around the sump. Jaguar was well aware of this, having carried through its own 4-wheel drive programme to the road-running stage in the XJS with the XJ79 project (Chapter 11). It is far easier to begin with a front-drive package, with either a transverse engine or an in-line engine ahead of the final drive (like Audi or Subaru) and take the additional driveline to the rear wheels by 'tapping into' the front final drive.

Jaguar chose the transverse-engine route, which not only eased the task of engineering the 4-wheel drive transmission but also left open the possibility of extending the car's market downwards by creating a simpler, lighter front-driven version – as was duly done, within the year. At the X-type launch, though, the emphasis was firmly on driving all the wheels. Jaguar made some play of what it called its 'Traction-4 system', but the X-type transmission was actually developed along well-established lines with a centre differential giving a nominal front-to-rear torque split of 40:60. A viscous coupling built into the centre differential meant that if a wheel (or both wheels) at one end of the car began to spin, torque was transferred away from that end and towards the other. The centre differential shared a casing with the front differential and formed a single unit with the engine for the sake of space-saving and stiffness. A five-speed Getrag manual gearbox – with cable-operated shift – was standard but the transverse engine installa-

Unlike the S-type, the X-type was genuinely smaller than its immediate predecessors, perhaps as befits a car built in the former Ford Escort production facility at Halewood on Merseyside. It promised a considerable expansion in Jaguar volumes, to an extent never before contemplated – and it broke new technical ground in many respects. (Jaguar)

tion forced Jaguar to go to a new supplier for the 5-speed automatic alternative, which came from JATCO in Japan.

Alongside the transverse engine and 4-wheel drive, the other technical feature to raise eyebrows was the suspension. For the first time ever in a Jaguar, the X-type used MacPherson struts at the front, with a completely new multi-link arrangement at the rear. Purists shrink away from struts because when the car rolls, the roll centre can shoot far and fast away from its static position, leading to inconsistent handling. That is the classic objection, but a great deal has been learned about the taming of MacPherson in the last 40-odd years, especially by Ford who first used the arrangement in a volume car. The Jaguar chassis team under Mike Cross certainly had no qualms about installing it, and positively relished the advantages it conferred in the way of spreading the suspension loads for a more evenly stressed body, and isolating the

Although the X-type carried over the V6 engine already seen in the S-type, in this new model it was mounted transversely, mated with a 4WD transmission, another first for Jaguar. (Jaguar)

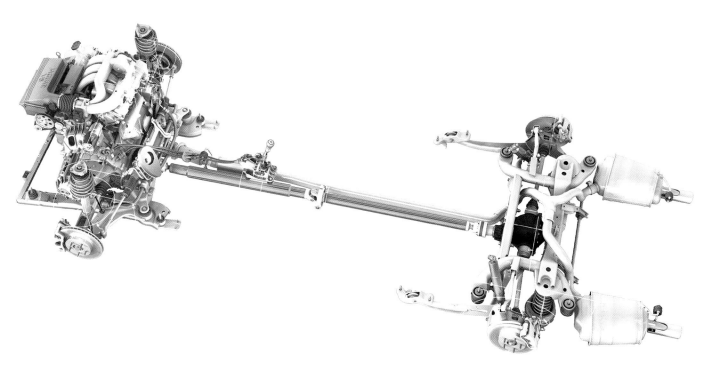

mounting points against the passage of noise and vibration. At the rear, the multi-link arrangement included a blade-type trailing link – more or less a vertical plate, hence very stiff vertically but deliberately weak horizontally so that the other links would transmit the cornering forces where they were supposed to go. It was an arrangement the technically informed had seen before – in the Ford Focus.

The Jaguar body engineers were extremely proud of their efforts with the X-type, claiming quite exceptional torsional stiffness which they said was 30 per cent better than that of the previous class leader. This was achieved through close attention to the detail of every joint and section rather than with specific features, unless you count the reduction in the actual number of joints through the use not only of a one-piece body side panel pressing (as in the S-type) but also a matching one-piece inner pressing. Needless to say, the best possible use was also made of the new production machinery which had been installed in the Halewood factory, and Jaguars began emerging where once Ford Escorts had been rolling out of the door.

A few months after the launch of the 4-wheel-drive X-type, another member of the family was announced: an entry-level front-driven derivative which, to the uninformed, may have seemed almost like a Jaguar-badged Ford Mondeo – for in truth, the two cars were of remarkably similar size and the Mondeo was itself a quality product. This was not just a Jaguar skin, however, but the entire vehicle re-engineered, with essentially the same chassis redeveloped by Mike Cross and his team for optimum front-drive behaviour. Under the bonnet, the engine had shrunk to a nominal 2-litre capacity – but it was still the AJ-V6 from the S-type and the 4-wheel-drive X-type. When reducing the capacity from 3-litre to 2.5-litre, it was the cylinder bore which had been shortened: to reduce it any further would have been something of a nonsense, so this time the 2.5-litre bore was retained while the stroke was reduced to 66.8mm, yielding an actual capacity of 2,099cc and requiring a new crankshaft. This was still steel, and with its shorter throws was even more formidably stiff, inevitably causing some to ponder on the possible combination of the 3-litre bore (89mm) with the 2-litre stroke, which would in fact produce a formidably over-square, potentially high-revving engine with a capacity of 2,493cc. In its '2-litre' form the AJ-V6 still delivered 157bhp (DIN) and 200Nm of torque, and since without the weight of the

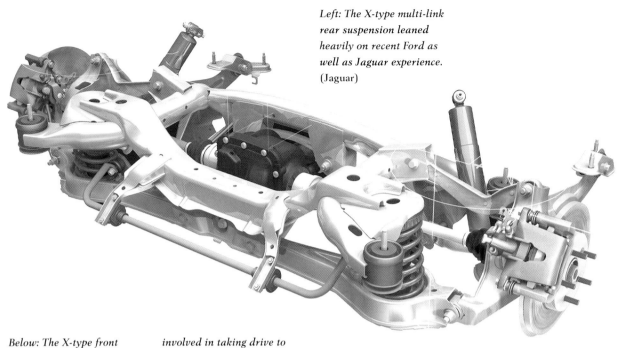

Left: The X-type multi-link rear suspension leaned heavily on recent Ford as well as Jaguar experience. (Jaguar)

Below: The X-type front suspension posed new challenges for the Jaguar engineering team. Except for the XJ220 concept car, they had never before confronted the problems involved in taking drive to the front wheels. Their solutions were neat if conventional, although MacPherson struts were another Jaguar engineering first. (Jaguar)

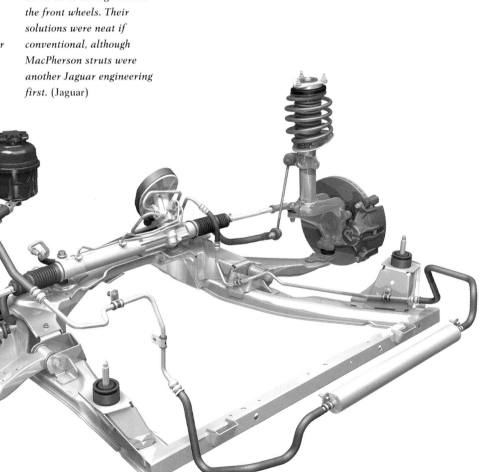

4-wheel drive system and all the other savings which followed in its wake the car was around 100kg (220lb) lighter, its performance was competitive, the standard manual-gearbox version reaching 60mph in 8.9sec and going on to a maximum of 130mph. The Getrag manual gearbox, and the alternative JATCO automatic, were retained.

The X-type, the X400, had in the first few months of its existence kicked over an astonishing number of Jaguar traces. Transverse engine, 4-wheel drive, front-wheel drive, MacPherson strut front suspension, multi-link rear ... but there was more to come. In 2003 came news of the X-type playing its part in two more pieces of Jaguar ground-breaking with the announcement first of a diesel-engined version, then of an estate car model.

The diesel had become essential if Jaguar was to claim its proper share of the European market. Its sports car customers may have shuddered at the very idea, but even they would surely have noticed that of Jaguar's deadliest rivals, Mercedes had been among the pioneers of passenger car diesel engines and had carried the technology forward ever since, while BMW had been offering high-quality diesels since the mid-1980s. Indeed, as noted in an earlier chapter, when Jaguar came closest to launching a diesel version of the XJ6 during the 1990s, the engine in question was BMW's 2.5-litre, 6-cylinder indirect-injection turbodiesel. Jaguar only abandoned the idea when it became clear that this engine, excellent though it was, was about to become obsolete as BMW introduced its new 3-litre common-rail diesel, a truly formidable power unit.

The X-type diesel was not as formidable, having begun life as the 2-litre (86 x 86mm, 1,998cc) Ford TDCi turbodiesel for the Mondeo. For the class in which the X-type was competing it was still a good engine, if rather late in its arrival to help Ford claim a share of the burgeoning European 'D-segment' diesel market. Given the constraints of time, economics and engineering manpower, Jaguar was certainly not going to develop its own diesel. It took the 'state-of-the-art' Ford 4-cylinder unit with 16-valve twin-camshaft cylinder head, common-rail fuel system and variable-geometry turbocharger with intercooler, but rather as with the petrol V6, although not quite to the same extent, it was given the chance to optimise the engine to its own requirements, especially when it came to noise level and operating refinement. Jaguar also consulted Ricardo, probably the world leaders in advanced diesel technology, about some

In 2003, Jaguar produced a diesel-powered car, the 2-litre X-type, for the first time, although studies for various diesel projects had been underway for many years.

The chosen engine was Ford's advanced 2-litre, 16-valve common-rail turbodiesel, providing the X-type with adequate power and excellent flexibility. (Jaguar)

aspects of its specification, such as its need for low external noise. As a result, the X404, as the engine was designated, gained its own air intake system and intercooler installation, a different type of fuel injector and revised engine management taking cylinder-by-cylinder signals from a 'combustion noise sensor' (CNS) similar in principle to a knock sensor in a spark-ignition engine. Because the CNS signals continuously trim the fuel delivery to each cylinder, there is no need for careful matching of the set of four injectors during engine assembly.

In terms of power, the X404 engine hardly matched up to existing Jaguar standards, delivering just 128bhp (DIN) at its peak. As increasing numbers of drivers have found, though, the power was not as important as the torque, and here the engine excelled, producing 330Nm at only 1,800rpm – more than the 3-litre V6 petrol engine. It also carried over Ford's 'overboost' facility which allowed a temporary

increase to 350Nm when the accelerator pedal was floored for overtaking or maximum acceleration. This massive torque output enabled the X-type 2.0D to reach 60mph from rest in 9.5sec – performance that would have been unthinkable in a diesel car a few years ago – while the maximum speed of 125mph was only 5mph short of that offered by the 2-litre V6 petrol version. Fuel economy, needless to say, was far superior with a combined EC test figure of 50.3mpg. The 2.0D was launched with a revised Getrag 5-speed manual gearbox only, not just because economy-conscious diesel buyers would be more likely to prefer manual, but also because the X404's prodigious torque output would have been too much for the JATCO automatic offered with the petrol engined versions of the X-type.

The estate car version of the X-type followed close on that of the 2.0D, the new shape appearing first at the 2003 Frankfurt Motor Show. There had been 'one-off' Jaguar estate cars before, not produced 'in house' but by specialist converters either to demonstrate their skills or to fulfil individual commissions from rich customers. One notable example was the Lynx Eventer, based on the XJS but with the roof and 'glasshouse' extended aft to a rear hatch incorporating the tail panel. With the advent of more severe and all-embracing safety regulations such conversions became more questionable but Jaguar had to acknowledge (as had Audi, BMW, Mercedes and Saab) that demand for estate cars in the upper D-segment was growing and had to be satisfied in order to claim a proper share of the market. Accordingly,

Left: Even more new ground was broken, so far as Jaguar tradition was concerned, with the announcement in 2003 of an estate car version of the X-type, seen here. (Jaguar)

Above: As in all recent Jaguar projects, care was taken to preserve the spirit of the 'Jaguar Tradition' even when creating new shapes like the X-type Estate. (Jaguar)

the Jaguar design team took the X-type body and restyled it from the B-pillars aft, thus requiring new rear doors, a new roof, a rearward-extended 'glasshouse', a rear hatch (with a separately opening rear window) and complete rear structure meeting all rear-impact safety requirements. To turn it into a proper estate, the back seat had also to be redesigned to fold flat (without having to remove the headrests) to extend the load platform. In carrying out the redesign the body team had to guard against the known perils of estate car conversions, especially the tendency for new noises to emerge from the revised structure. The X-type estate rear structure was therefore made as stiff as possible, while at the same time providing more stowage space than most of its rivals. Version for version, the estate weighed only 143lb more than the saloon despite its greater enclosed volume and larger glass area. One neat touch was the incorporation of a high-level stop lamp and the rear washer nozzle into the small but effective spoiler at the roof's trailing edge. Since it retained the entire existing X-type platform, the estate was able to accommodate both the front-drive and 4-wheel drive transmissions, the former for the 2-litre petrol V6 and

4-cylinder diesel, the latter for the 2.5 and 3.0-litre petrol engines.

When introducing the diesel engine for the X-type, Jaguar served notice that one diesel was not enough. It stated its intention, from 2004, of offering versions of the S-type powered by a completely new 2.7-litre V6 twin-turbo diesel engine, developed by Ford in partnership with PSA Peugeot-Citroën and due to enter production in Ford's Dagenham factory, now a 'world centre' for light diesel engine manufacture following the closing of its last car production line. When this new version was revealed early in 2004 it incorporated all the advanced technology of the X404 diesel plus several new and ingenious features, and provided the S-type with the entirely adequate power output of 206bhp

Above: The latest Jaguar diesel project is a version of the S-type, which is powered by a new 2.7-litre, 24-valve V6 common-rail diesel jointly developed by Ford and PSA, providing the Jaguar with nearly 200bhp and enormous torque output. (Jaguar)

Right: The arrival of the new XJ heralded the arrival of aluminium body technology, and a big weight saving which allowed the re-introduction of an XJ6, now powered by the V6 engine which was already familiar in the S-type. Because the new XJ was physically larger than the S-type, a proper hierarchy of Jaguar models was re-established, with the X-type, S-type and XJ in ascending order. (Jaguar)

(DIN), together with a of formidable 435Nm torque and outstanding 6-cylinder refinement.

While the X-type was entering the realm of the diesel engine and the estate car, new ground was also being broken at Jaguar in creating the latest series of the big XJ saloon – the seventh series to be introduced, counting back to the original XJ6 of 1968. The new car, internally the X350, was announced in a seminar at the very end of 2002, although it did not go on sale until the spring of 2003. By far its most significant feature was its all-aluminium body which, since its engines, transmission casings, and much of its suspension were already of the same material, made it virtually an all-aluminium car if one discounts glass, rubber, electrical system and trim materials.

Aluminium had long attracted car designers and engineers on account of its light weight, but was slow to make the breakthrough into body construction for two reasons: its price, and the difficulty of body manufacture, since the material is extremely difficult (although not impossible) to spot-weld. But Jaguar's team did its sums and calculated that an all-aluminium body could be made 40 per cent lighter than a steel equivalent. Evidently, a 40 per cent lighter body-in-white is not the same thing as a 40 per cent lighter car, since the untrimmed, unpainted body shell represents perhaps 30 per cent of the complete vehicle. However, a saving of 12 per cent (30 per cent of 40 per cent) is well worth having, and the seventh-series XJ weighs around 200lb lighter than the steel-bodied sixth-series car despite being a

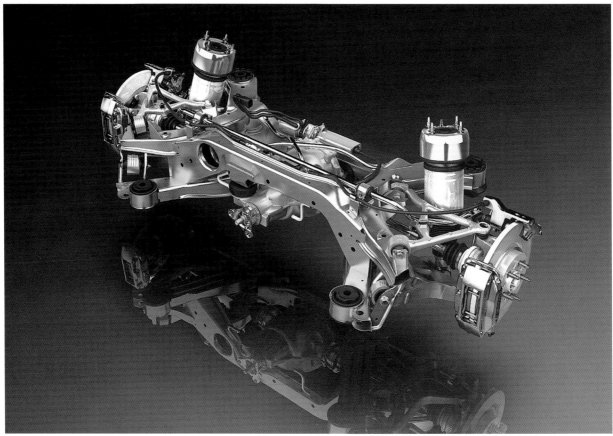

RIGHT UP TO DATE

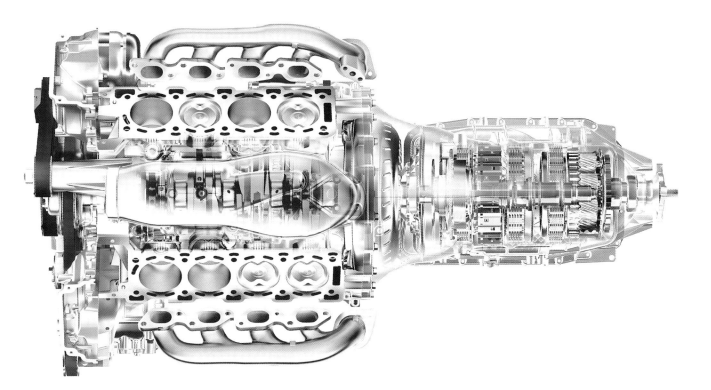

Top left: Because the XJ is rear-driven, Jaguar chassis engineers were able to return to a slightly more conventional approach when it came to front suspension design – but great care went into the detailing. (Jaguar)

Left: The XJ rear suspension shows evidence of a modern multi-link approach and the advantages of computer-aided design – all a far cry

from the independent rear suspension drawn up single-handedly by Bob Knight and applied to the E-type and Mark X. (Jaguar)

Above: With the arrival of the XJ, the top car got the top engine at last, in the form of the 4.2-litre V8, together with 3.5 and 3.0-litre versions of the V6. Transmissions, naturally, are automatic-only. (Jaguar)

good deal larger: over 6in longer in the wheelbase (although only an inch or so longer overall), over 2in wider, over 5in higher, and much roomier inside. The saving may seem small but it was enough to enable the XJ to offer the 240bhp 3-litre AJ-V6 engine from the S-type without needing to apologise for the performance (7.8sec to 60mph, 145mph maximum). The new car also inherited the 4.2-litre V8 from the latest-series S-type – explaining why the sixth-series car, with only a year or so to run, had not made the change. Of course, the 4.2 AJ-V8 was offered in naturally aspirated (300bhp) and supercharged

(400bhp) form, but there also appeared a new 'intermediate' V8, a nominal 3.5-litre unit with the same 86mm cylinder bore but with the stroke reduced to 76.5mm for an actual capacity of 3,555cc. This engine with its new crankshaft and longer connecting rods delivered 262bhp (DIN). A new ZF 6-speed automatic transmission, the 6HP26, was made standard. As for the chassis, the new platform meant an all-new suspension design, with double wishbones all round (no MacPherson struts here!). The other extremely significant change was a switch from mechanical (coil) to air-springs, opening up the future possibility of true variable-rate springing to complement the variable-rate CATS damping system.

For all the changes to the driveline and the more spacious body, it was naturally the aluminium construction which proved the centre of attention in the new XJ. After looking at all the techniques available, and used by other pioneers of large-scale aluminium construction such as Audi, Jaguar elected to adopt techniques rather closer to those of the aircraft industry, a combination of riveting and structural adhesive. Thus the XJ body is close to being an aluminium version of a conventional steel unitary structure, while rival teams have made much more extensive use of complex castings and extrusions.

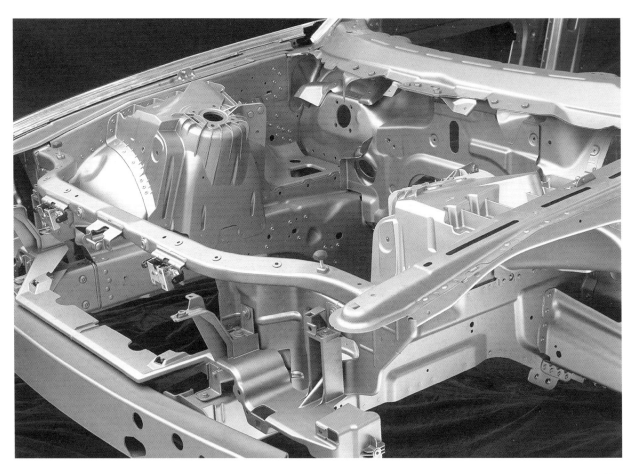

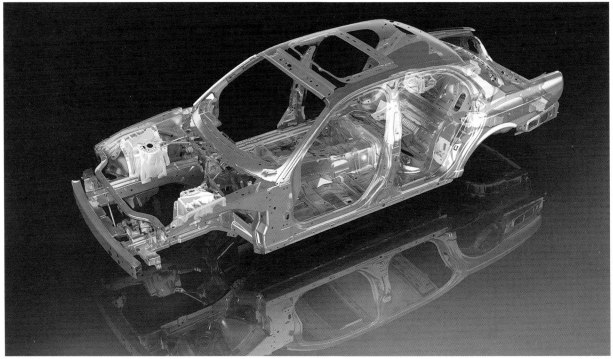

RIGHT UP TO DATE

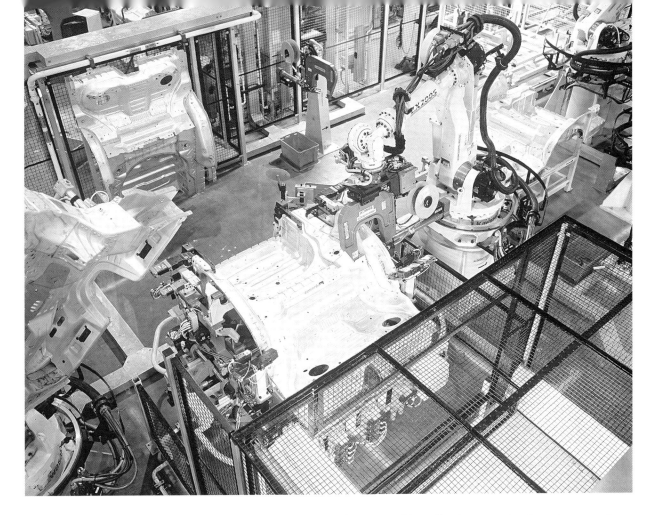

Top left: Jaguar engineers took the challenge of creating an all-aluminium body extremely seriously, combining pressings with castings, plus an original approach to mechanical assembly. The complete front-end structure is seen here. (Jaguar)

Left: Division of the XJ body structure between pressings and precision castings (in yellow) is evident in this view. (Jaguar)

Above: Jaguar's answer to the challenge of assembling an all-aluminium body was to avoid the possible problems associated with welding, and go instead for a combination of riveting and special bonding adhesive. The result is extremely strong joints, created almost entirely by robot. (Jaguar)

The Jaguar body uses a few such components but is mainly held together by single-sided Henrob rivets whose tails punch through adjacent panels and spread to form a mechanical join without actually piercing the back skin. Jaguar's engineers were pleased when tests confirmed their calculations that apart from the weight saving, the resulting body was 60 per cent stiffer. This welcome improvement was mainly thanks to the beads of adhesive which run along the seams (the adhesive cures in the paint ovens).

Like its predecessor, the new XJ body is manufactured at the Castle Bromwich plant. A press shop to form the aluminium panels has been installed in the last vacant building of the seven major structures on the site. Despite the different machine settings and material handling techniques involved, the whole process looks remarkably conventional. The same might well be said of the body assembly line, where the only obvious difference from the norm is the lack of sparks flying as the spot-welds go into steel bodies. The massed ranks of robots are much in evidence, but instead of welds they are either applying beads of adhesive, or punching rivets into place, taking them from 'bandoliers' carrying hundreds of rivets on flexible strips. Each body contains 3,180 rivets and 120m of adhesive bead. Jaguar has come a long way from its battles with Pressed Steel over the problems of hit-or-miss spot-welding.

Once again the factory is putting together riveted aluminium structures, just as it did between 1940 and 1945, only this time the end product is not Spitfires but bodies for luxury saloon cars. For Jaguar, it represents just one aspect of a technical advance across a broad front – with more still to come.

Appendix
XJ numbers

From the 1950s until the 1994, Jaguar identified its engineering programmes with XJ numbers. There is an assumption that XJ stands for Experimental Jaguar, but the truth is a little more complicated. As related in Chapter 2, the wartime research engines which reached the hardware stage were identified in a series XF, XG, XJ and ultimately XK (no XI for fear of Roman confusion, perhaps, but why no XH is not clear). There is almost as little logic behind the resurrection of the XJ designation for what became the four-cam racing V12 project. By some meta-morphosis – perhaps because it extended from the original racing engine into the radically different road-going engine of 1971 – the long-gestating V12 project became not just XJ, but XJ1, and from then on most Jaguar projects – engines or cars – were allocated an XJ project identity.

By this time, of course, some of the early post-war models, the large saloons pre-Mark X, the small Mark 2s and the XK120-XK150 sports cars (and the original E-type) had already emerged and no attempt was made to give them XJ numbers retrospectively; the system really began to take shape in the early 1960s. There was – probably deliberately – no attempt to differentiate between truly major projects and much more limited ones (such as XJ7 and XJ15; see below). It is also worth noting that during the 1980s especially, XJ numbers were not necessarily allocated in strict chronological order since the 'master logbook' of the time suggests the Programme Manager tended to pre-allocate small 'blocks' of numbers in anticipation of upcoming requirements; see the way in which each XJ6 saloon series spawned at least four XJ numbers – two wheelbases multiplied by two engines (6-cylinder and V12).

The list below is based on one prepared by Jaguar Chief Archivist Anders Clausager and is possibly the most complete yet published, several of the more obscure early numbers having emerged from the archive during research. For example, one useful additional list of then-current numbers came from a Bob Knight memorandum of May 1966, and the definitive (or at least intended) allocation of numbers (XJ27-36) of early-series XJS, XJ6 and XJ6 V12 versions comes from the minutes of a Model Programme Meeting dated 4 May 1971. I have also taken into account a fairly short list included in Philip Porter's *Jaguar Scrapbook* (Haynes, 1989), and a list compiled by Paul Skilleter in 1991 from factory sources. The latter worryingly indicates that some early numbers may have been re-allocated, but it should be borne in mind that the numbers were intended as current internal working references and not as a convenient framework for historians!

XJ1 Four-cam V12 racing engine for what became the XJ13
XJ2 (no trace)
XJ3 S-type
XJ4 '4/5-seater saloon' – eventually redesignated and launched as XJ6
XJ5 4.2-litre Mark X (In Skilleter's 1991 list: '2-door sports GT 102in-wheelbase' then in current production – i.e. the XJ-S)
XJ6 Originally allocated to the '12-cylinder and 8-cylinder engine range' (see Chapter 10) but eventually transferred to what had been the XJ4
XJ7 2.4-litre with SU instead of Stromberg carburettors
XJ8 E-type 2+2 (the original E-type was too early to have an XJ designation)
XJ9 (no trace)
XJ10 Mark X powered by V12 engine

XJ11 (no trace)

XJ12 Originally the 4.2-litre E-type (Series II with synchromesh gearbox); later often applied to the XJ6 Series 1 with V12 engine

XJ13 Mid V12-engined Le Mans car (in Bob Knight's 1966 memo, 'Open 2-seater – R.E.')

XJ14 (no trace)

XJ15 Mark 2 with 4-speed all-synchro gearbox and 'compact overdrive' to match with existing one-piece propeller shaft

XJ16 Restyled S-type project with 4.2-litre engine (the 420)

XJ17 '3-litre 4-seater' (Bob Knight 1966) (Porter allocates XJ17 to the Series II E-type)

XJ18 '3-litre production engine' (Bob Knight 1966 – possible early reference to the 'slant-6', or perhaps to a contemporary intention to launch the XJ6 with a 3-litre version of the XK engine)

XJ19 (no trace)

XJ20 (no trace)

XJ21 1968 E-type replacement (?)

XJ22 E-type Series 2, 2-seater versions

XJ23 E-type Series 2, 2+2

XJ24 (no trace)

XJ25 E-type V12 (Series 3) 2+2

XJ26 E-type V12 (Series 3) 2-seat roadster

XJ27 'XJ25 replacement' – XJS Coupé

XJ28 XJS convertible

XJ29 Long-wheelbase XJ6 Series 1

XJ30 Long-wheelbase XJ6 V12 Series 1

XJ31 Long-wheelbase XJ6 Series 2

XJ32 Long-wheelbase XJ6 V12 Series 2

XJ33 Standard wheelbase XJ6 Series 2

XJ34 Standard wheelbase XJ6 V12 Series 2

XJ35 XJ6 2-door Coupé (Series 2)

XJ36 XJ6 V12 2-door Coupé (Series 2)

XJ37 XJ6 2-door Coupé (Series 1) (Porter allocates XJ37 to the Series 2 XJ Coupé, possibly a proposed 3.4 version, but see XJ42 below). Possibly XJ37/38 were allocated retrospectively to cover prototype or pilot production Series 1 cars, although all 'proper' production XJCs were Series 2 (XJ35/36)

XJ38 XJ6 V12 2-door Coupé (Series 1)

XJ39 XJ6 Series 3 special bodies, including armoured

XJ40 New XJ6 (originally 'Series 4')

XJ41 New sports car project ('F-type' Coupé with AJ6 engine), terminated March 1990

XJ42 Apparently allocated twice: first to proposed

XJ6 Coupé Series 2 with 3.4-litre engine; then to cabriolet version of XJ41, terminated 1990

XJ43 Projected XJ6 4.2 LWB Vanden Plas

XJ44 Projected XJ30 with 6-cylinder VM diesel engine

XJ45 (Skilleter, 1991: 'Daimler X40 149' limousine', see Chapter 14 text references to projected XJ40 'stretch' proposals by Coleman-Milne and Jankel)

XJ46 (no trace)

XJ47 Projected 'flagship' V12 sports coupé – evolved into XJ99

XJ48 Projected cabriolet version of XJ47

XJ49 (no trace)

XJ50 XJ6 Series 3 V12

XJ51 XJ6 Series 3 3.4

XJ52 XJ6 Series 3 4.2

XJ53 XJ6 Series 3 4.2 Vanden Plas

XJ54 XJ6 Series 3 V12 Vanden Plas

XJ55 (no trace)

XJ56 (no trace)

XJ57 New series XJS Coupé with AJ6 engine

XJ58 Cabriolet version of XJ57

XJ59 Projected XJ6 Series 3 with BMW 6-cylinder IDI diesel engine

XJ60 XJ6 Series 3 'mules' with AJ6 engine (for XJ40 programme)

XJ61 (no trace)

XJ62 Projected limousine for Middle East markets

XJ63 Projected XJ57 with Getrag manual gearbox

XJ64 'Sports Car' – no other details

XJ65 Limousine to US Federal requirements

XJ66 (allocated to Dana axle development work)

XJ67 (allocated to seal development work)

XJ68 (allocated to limited-slip differential development work)

XJ69 'XJ40 4WD' – no other details, possibly linked to XJ79

XJ70 (no trace)

XJ71 XJS 'mules' for XJ41 development programme

XJ72-76 apparently not allocated

XJ77 XJS V12 Convertible

XJ78 XJS AJ6 Convertible

XJ79 XJS 4WD 'for development only', cancelled February 1989

XJ80 'Executive saloon' – (Mark 2 successor?) project cancelled

XJ81 Short-wheelbase V12 5.3 version of XJ40 (Skilleter, 1991: 'SWB Daimler X40 V12')

XJ82 Long (117in) wheelbase V12 5.3 version of XJ40

XJ83 Long-wheelbase AJ6 version of XJ40

XJ84 Long-wheelbase V12 6.4 version of XJ40 (Skilleter, 1991: 'Daimler X40 113-inch facelift V12')

XJ85 Proposed XJ40 2-door coupé V12

XJ86 As XJ85, AJ6 engine (Skilleter, 1991: 'XJS Coupe facelift AJ6 supercharged')

XJ87 XJS Coupé facelift, V12

XJ88 As XJ87, AJ6 engine

XJ89 XJS Cabriolet facelift

XJ90 XJ40 Facelift AJ6 (Skilleter, 1991: '4-door luxury saloon AJ27 family' – alternatively X90, a project for a large saloon of which prototypes were apparently run in the late 1980s with a variety of engines, see subsequent numbers – project cancelled c1990)

XJ91 XJ40 facelift V12 (Skilleter, 1991: 'X90 AJ26 V6')

XJ92 Skilleter, 1991: 'X90/Daimler X90 AJ26 V8'

XJ93 Skilleter, 1991: 'Daimler X90 AJ26 V12'

XJ94 'XJ90 Sports short (113in) wheelbase'

XJ95 Projected XJ40 2-door convertible, V12

XJ96 As XJ95, AJ6 engine

XJ97 XJS Convertible facelift, V12

XJ98 XJS Convertible facelift, AJ6

XJ99 'Sports flagship', formerly XJ47

XJ100 Saloon 115in wheelbase AJ6

XJ101 As XJ100, V12 engine

XJ102 Saloon 119in wheelbase V12

XJ103 Saloon 119in wheelbase AJ6

XJ104 XJ83 (long-wheelbase XJ40) facelift, AJ6

XJ105 XJ84 facelift, V12

XJ220 Sports (not an XJ sequence number, but reflecting claimed 220mph maximum speed – see text)

There was also a handful of XDM (Daimler) project numbers:

XDM2   2½-litre V8 saloon
XDM3   Limousine
XDM16   Sovereign 420
(and there may be others awaiting research!)

From the early 1990s, to reflect Jaguar's new management and the revision and extension of new model programmes, the old XJ numbering system was replaced by 'X-series' designations, those which can be discussed being as follows:

X100   XK8 sports car, introduced 1996
X200   S-type saloon, introduced 1998
-X202 S-type facelift, introduced 2002
X300   XJ6/XJ12, (the former XJ90/91), 1994-97
-X330 Long-wheelbase X300 1995-97
X308   XJ8 saloon, replacing XJ6/12, 1997-2002
X350   'Aluminium' XJ6/XJ8, replacing X308, introduced 2002
X400   X-type compact saloon, introduced 2001

Index